CHANEL

SERIES 6 PHOTOGRAPHED BY
BRUCE WEBER

SERIES 6 PHOTOGRAPHED BY BRUCE WEBER

+44 207 399 2030 PRADA.COM

MODERN
FUTURE
LOVED

SUDDENLY NEXT SUMMER

POINT DUME, CALIFORNIA
NOVEMBER 24-26 2016
BY ALASDAIR McLELLAN

SUDDENLY NEXT SUMMER

POINT DUME, CALIFORNIA
NOVEMBER 24-26 2016
BY ALASDAIR McLELLAN

miu miu

SUDDENLY NEXT SUMMER

POINT DUME, CALIFORNIA
NOVEMBER 24-26 2016
BY ALASDAIR McLELLAN

+44 207 399 2030 MIUMIU.COM

Richard Prince: I Changed My Name, 1988 © Richard Prince
Acrylic and screen print on canvas (142.5 cm x 198.7 cm)
Calvin Klein: Classic Denim Shirt (Calvin Klein Jeans Est. 1978)
Photographed at Rubell Family Collection, Miami

so I changed my name.

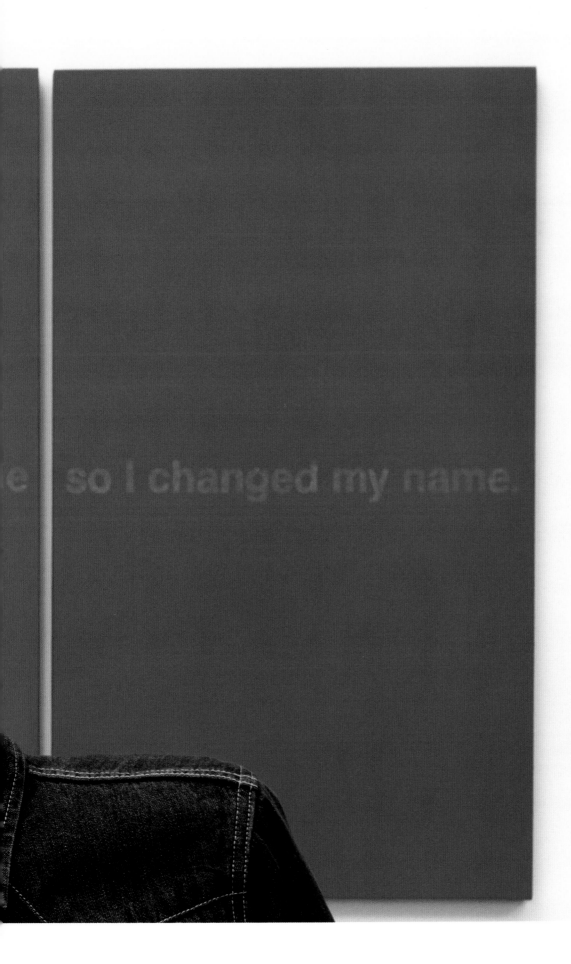

Sterling Ruby: FLAG (4791), 2014 © Sterling Ruby
Bleached and dyed canvas and elastic (443.23 cm x 871.22 cm)
Calvin Klein: Classic Cotton Briefs (Calvin Klein Underwear Est. 1981)
Photographed at Rubell Family Collection, Miami

Andy Warhol: Ambulance Disaster, 1963-64 © The Andy Warhol Foundation / ARS
Calvin Klein: Classic Denim Jeans (Archival Originals, 1980) and Classic Denim Jeans (Archival Originals, 1982)
Photographed at The Andy Warhol Museum, Pittsburgh

CALVIN KLEIN

MARCJACOBS.COM

KENZO
PARIS
KENZO FILMS #4

ALL is
30 BRUTON STREET LONDON W1
91-97 FULHAM ROAD LONDON SW3
STELLAMCCARTNEY.COM

LOVE
STELLA McCARTNEY

CÉLINE

byblos.it

GiGi
TOMMY HILFIGER
SP
A SPECIAL COLLECTION BY GIGI HADID #TOMMYXGIGI TOMMY.COM

2017
ny Hilfiger
HxGH

BALMAIN

LIU BOLIN PERFORMING FOR MONCLER

MOUNTAIN
CLIMBING
STORM
OVER THE
LAND
CARL SANDBURG
MONCLER
moncler.com

©2017 COACH®

COACH
1941

VERAWANG.COM

KENMARKEYEWEAR.COM #KENMARKEYEWEAR STYLE SHOWN: ZIA
VERAWANG

THEN THEY LAID
THEIR HANDS
UPON THEM AND
THEY RECEIVED
THE HOLY GHOST.
ACTS VIII 17

MOSCHINO.COM

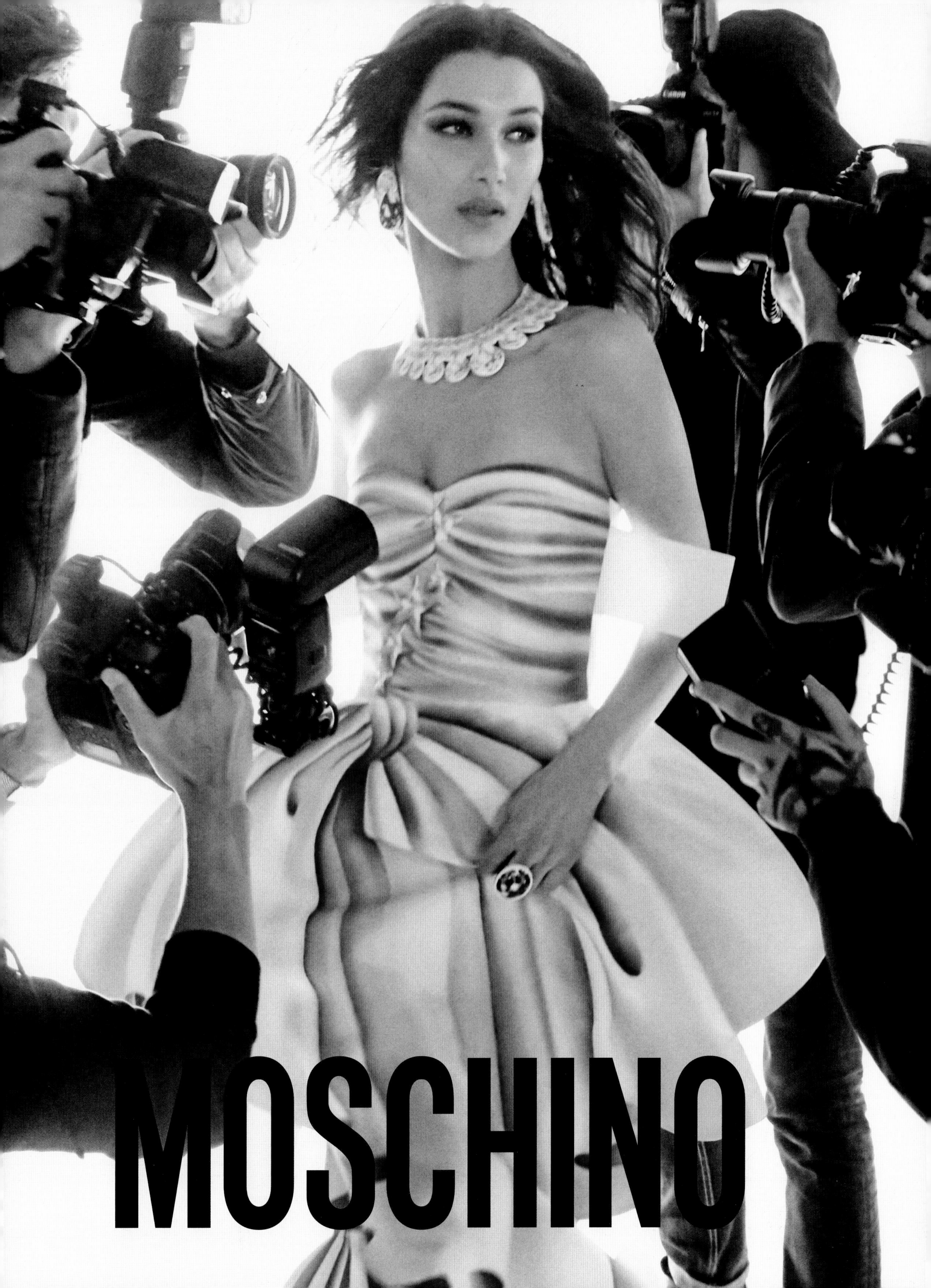
MOSCHINO

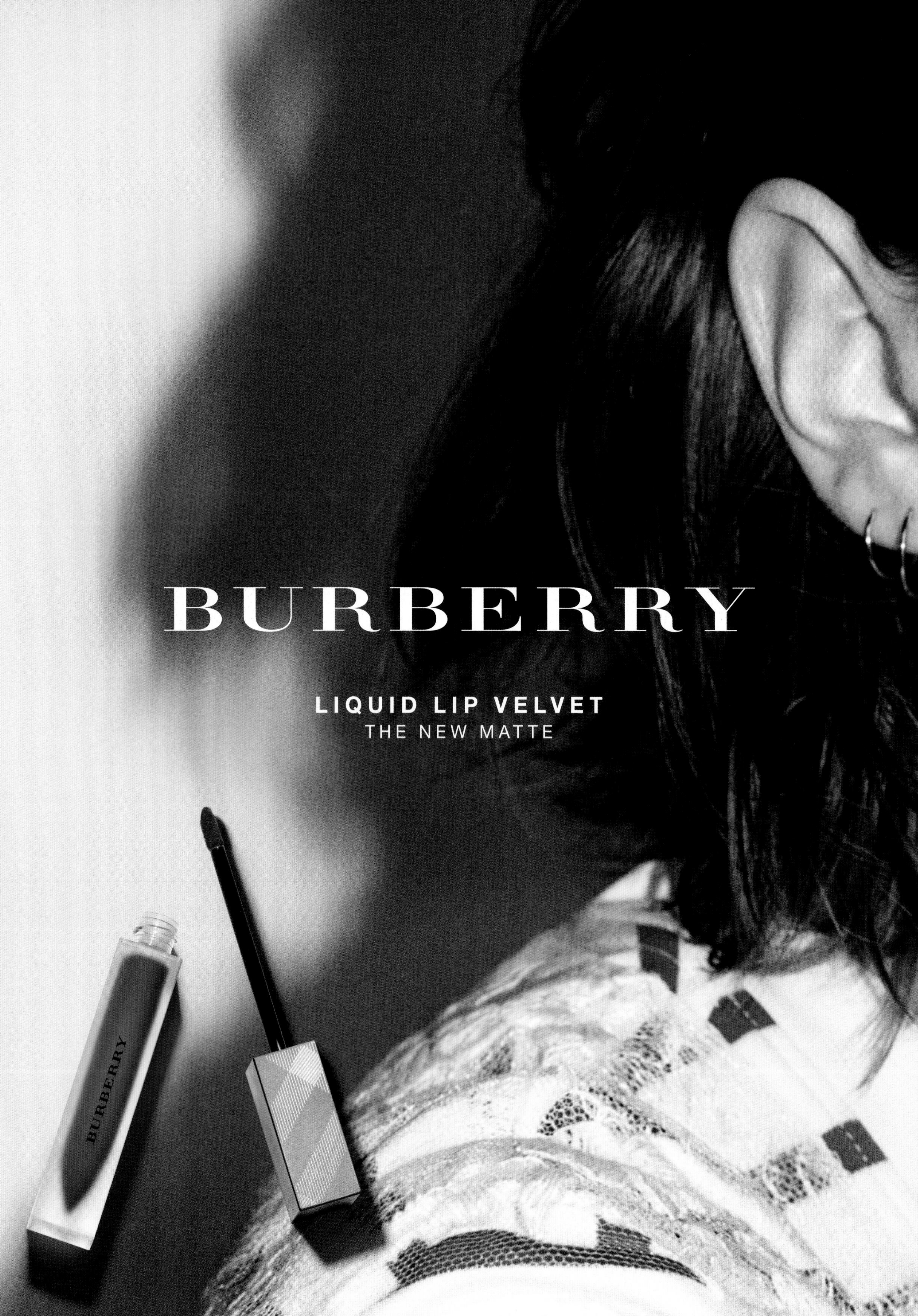
BURBERRY
LIQUID LIP VELVET
THE NEW MATTE
BURBERRY

KRIZIA

BALLY
IS

SUPER
BALLY.COM

ADRIANA LIMA BY ROE ETHRIDGE
SPORTMAX.COM
SPORTMAX

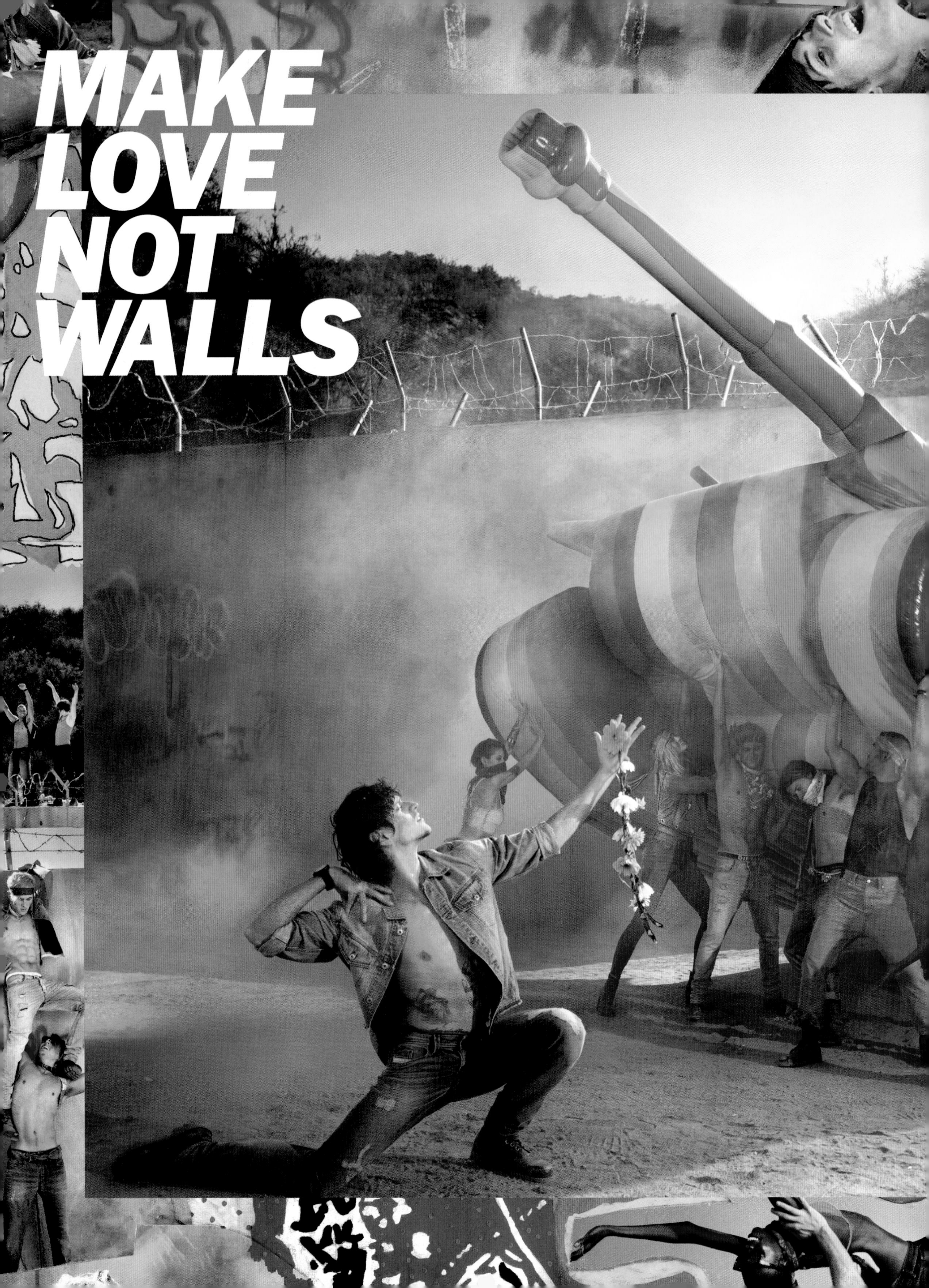
MAKE
LOVE
NOT
WALLS

DIESEL

California
Venice Rebels
1 9 81

Andreas
Kronthaler
Vivienne
Westwood

Juergen Teller AKVW SS17 UNISEX www.viviennewestwood.com Leonard Peltier is innocent

JOSEPH

joseph-fashion.com

FENDI

G
H

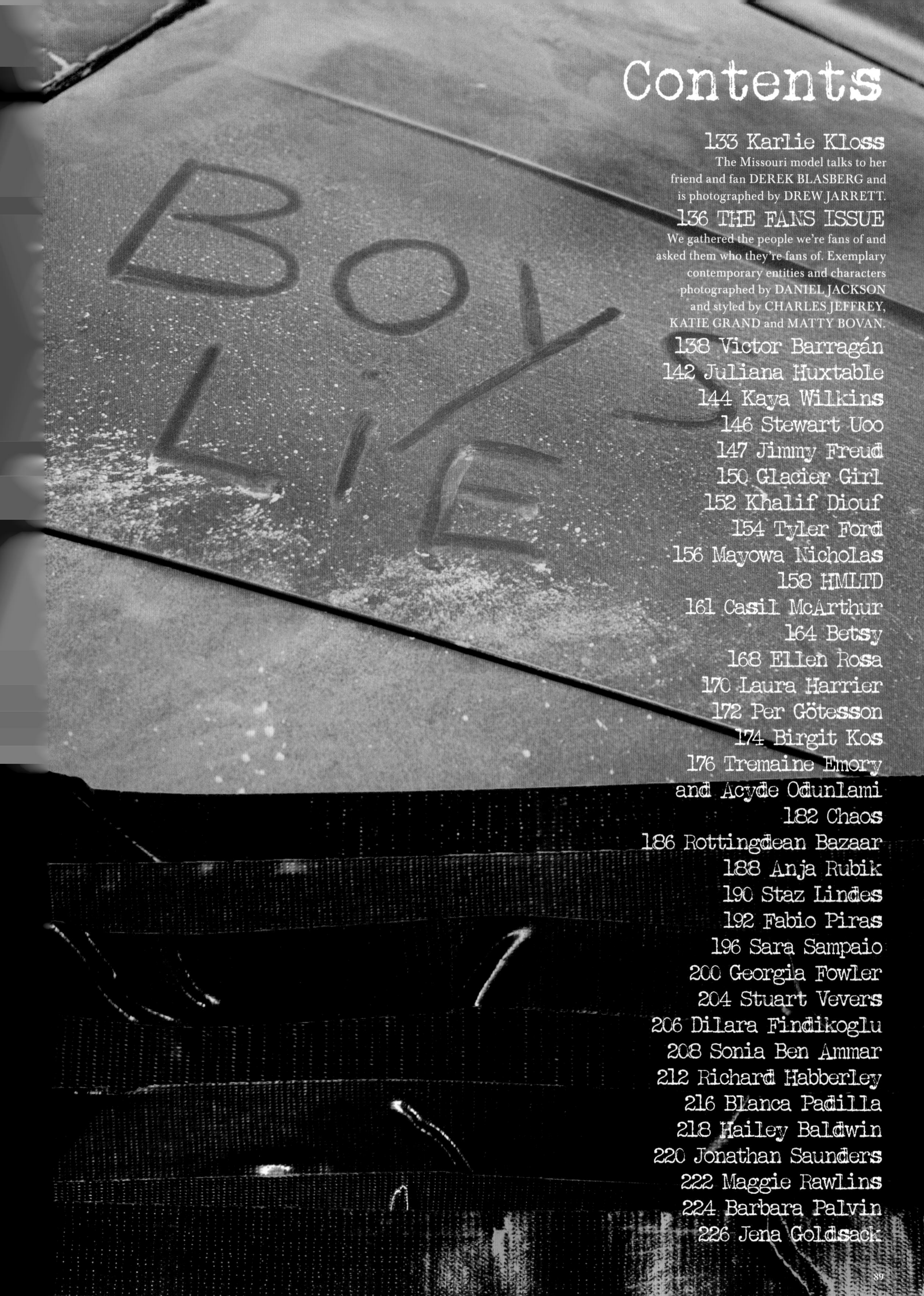

Contents

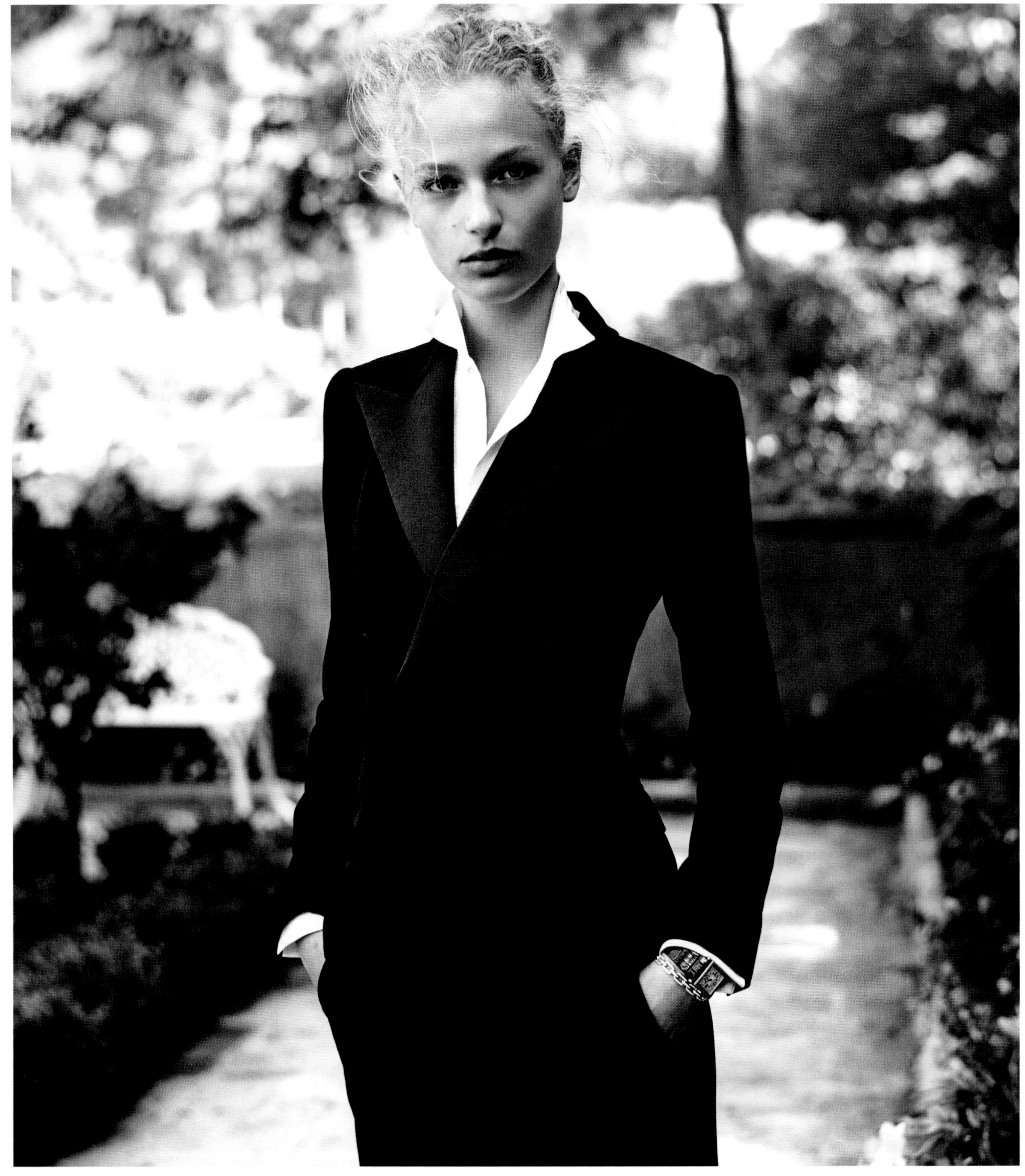

The TUXEDO, *2016*
Photographed by Steven Meisel
#RL*ICONICSTYLE*

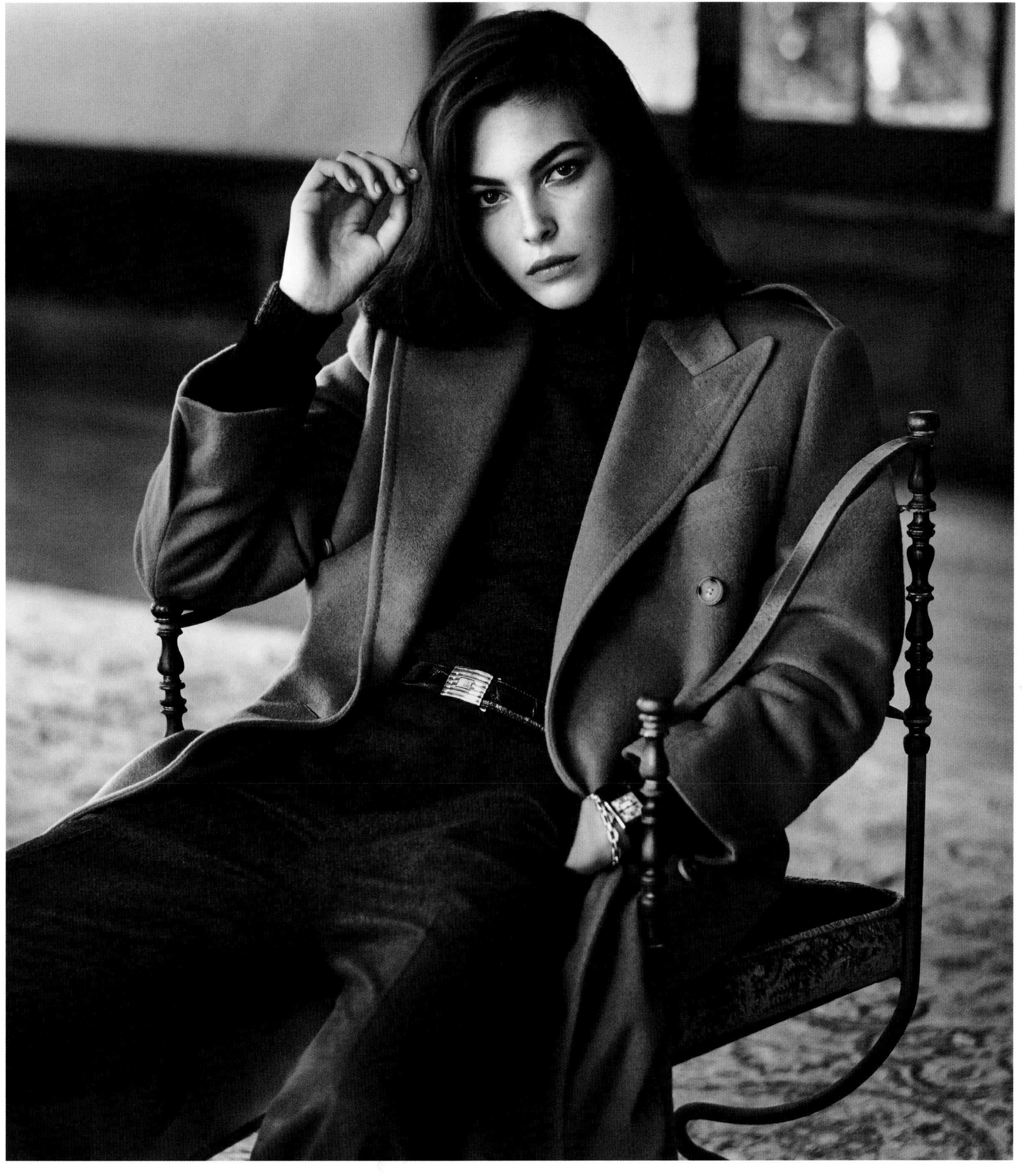

The SAILOR PANT, *2016*
Photographed by Steven Meisel
#RLICONICSTYLE

Contents

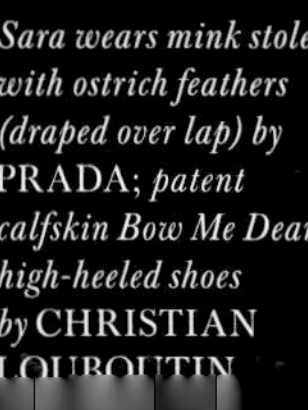

Sara wears mink stole with ostrich feathers (draped over lap) by PRADA; *patent calfskin Bow Me Dear high-heeled shoes by* CHRISTIAN LOUBOUTIN

Photographer DAVID SIMS Fashion Editor KATIE GRAND Hair GUIDO Make-Up DIANE KENDAL Manicure MEGUMI YAMAMOTO Set design STEFAN BECKMAN Model SARA SAMPAIO

Publicis EtNous
GALA
OBJECTS FOR LIFE
HERMÈS
PARIS

OBJECTS FOR LIFE

Editor in Chief
KATIE GRAND

Publisher
CATHERINE RUSSELL

Guest Creative Director
ROBIN DERRICK AT SPRING

Editorial

Editorial Director
MURRAY HEALY

Senior Contributing Editors
PAUL FLYNN, KENDALL JENNER

Senior Editor
HARRIET VERNEY

Contributing Editors
EDIE CAMPBELL, CARA DELEVINGNE

Editor of Unicorns
POPPY DELEVINGNE

Fashion

Fashion Director
PANOS YIAPANIS

Senior Fashion Director
STEVE MORRISS

Senior Contributing Fashion Editors
CHARLES JEFFREY, MATTY BOVAN

Fashion Editor
OLIVER VOLQUARDSEN

Junior Fashion Editor
PRINCIPAL YIP

Fashion Assistant
OGUN GORTAN

Creative

Art Director
MARTIN J TICKNER

Senior Designer
ROBBIE MAILER-HOWAT

Designer
LEWIS CHAM

Junior Designer
MONICA URQUIJO

Publishing

Advertising Director (Print and Digital)
ALLEGRA FAGGIONATO

Publishing Executives
CLAUDIA CARRERE, LAURA NEWRZELLA

Italian Agent
FABIO MONTOBBIO

Consultants

Production Editor
MATT FIVEASH

Casting Director
ANITA BITTON

Entertainment Editor
GREG KRELENSTEIN AT STARWORKS

PR Director
MANDI LENNARD

Bra Editor
ANGELA KURDASH

Online

Editor in Chief
KATIE GRAND

Creative Director
ROBBIE MAILER-HOWAT

Senior Editor
HARRIET VERNEY

Junior Online Editor
MONICA URQUIJO

Casting Director
ANITA BITTON

Thanks to: Ashley Javier, Aaron Newbill, Abi Newman, Akki, Alasdair McLellan, Alexander Fury, Alexis Roche, Anthony Turner, Anya Yiapanis, Bela Rofe, Calvin Wilson, Camilla Lowther, Cara Delevingne, Carin Backoff, Caterina Ospina Buitrago, Charles Jeffrey, Charlie Porter, Chris Alty, Chris Gay, Christopher Bailey, Christopher Michael, Ciara O'Shea, Complete Ltd, Cindy Crawford, Daniel Jackson, Daniel Marks, Danielle Cottrell, David Casavant, Donatella Versace, David Hughes, David Sims, Derek Blasberg, Diane Kendal, Drew Jarrett, Donatella Versace, Elli Weir, George Speros, Giles Deacon, Giorgina Jolly, Graeme Montgomery, Guido Palau, Hiromi Ueda, Hugo Scott, Ian Loughran, Ivan Bart, Jack Bradley, Jean Wang, Jessica Gaertner, Joey Jalleo, John Galliano, Jonathan Heaf, Jonathan Saunders, Jon Sever, Justine Foord, Kaia Gerber, Karolina Marczak, Kendall Jenner, Kristen Abel, Lauren Hadley, Louie Chaban, Lucy Bridge, Luke Hersheson, Lynette Garland, Madeleine Østlie, Marc Jacobs, Mark Carrasquillo, Matty Bovan, Nana Boatity, Nicholas Newbold, Niki Bagdonas, Oliver Hicks, Olivia McCall, Paula Ekenger, Poppy Delevingne, Richard Habberley, Ronnie Newhouse, Sally Dawson, Sarah Dawes, Simone Ireland, Sølve Sundsbø, Sophia Lee, Syd Hayes, Tatiana Krotovskaya, Thea Bichard, Theo Wenner, Tim Walker, TJ Sidhu, Vanessa Hsieh, Victoria Young, Zoe Springer, and extra special thanks to everyone who applied for #Loveme17
Special Thanks to Matt Roach
Extraordinarily Very Special Thanks to Ashleah Gonzales (Dragon Slayer)

LOVE MAGAZINE is a member of the Independent Press Standards Organisation (which regulates the UK's magazine and newspaper industry). We abide by the Editors' Code of Practice [www.ipso.co.uk/editors-code-of-practice] and are committed to upholding the highest standards of journalism. If you think that we have not met those standards and want to make a complaint please see our Editorial Complaints Policy on the Contact Us page of our website or contact us at complaints@condenast.co.uk or by post to Complaints, Editorial Business Department, The Condé Nast Publications Ltd, Vogue House, Hanover Square, London W1S 1JU. If we are unable to resolve your complaint, or if you would like more information about IPSO or the Editors' Code, contact IPSO on 0300 123 2220 or visit www.ipso.co.uk.

LOVE is published biannually by The Condé Nast Publications Ltd, Vogue House, Hanover Square, London W1S 1JU (020 7499 9080; fax 020 7493 1345). LOVE is distributed by Condé Nast & National Magazine Distributors Ltd (Comag), Tavistock Road, West Drayton, Middlesex, UB7 7QE (01895 433600; fax 01895 433605). To subscribe, call 0844 848 5202 (Mon-Fri, 8am-9pm) or visit magazineboutique.co.uk. Colour origination by Tag Publishing. Printed in the UK by Wyndeham Roche.

Associate Publisher US: SHANNON TOLAR TCHKOTOUA
US Advertisement Director: KERYN HOWARTH
Advertisement Director (France): HELENA KAWALEC
Advertisement Manager (France): NATALIE WALTHER

Marketing Director: JEAN FAULKNER
Deputy Marketing and Research Director: GARY READ
Associate Director, Digital Marketing: SUSIE BROWN
International Communications Director of Condé Nast International and Director of Press & PR of Condé Nast Britain: NICKY EATON
Deputy Publicity Director: HARRIET ROBERTSON
Circulation Director: RICHARD KINGERLEE
Newstrade Circulation Manager: ELLIOTT SPAULDING
Subscriptions Director: PATRICK FOILLERET
Production Director: SARAH JENSON
Commercial Production Manager: XENIA DILNOT
Production Controllers: MARIE RHYS-EVANS, HELEN CROUCH
Commercial Senior Production Controller: LOUISE LAWSON
Commercial and Paper Production Controller: MARTIN MacMILLAN
Syndication Enquiries: syndication@condenast.co.uk
Director of Editorial Administration & Rights: HARRIET WILSON
Editorial Business & Rights Executive: PHOEBE GAYDON
Finance Director: PAM RAYNOR
Financial Control Director: PENNY SCOTT-BAYFIELD
HR/Personnel Director: HAZEL McINTYRE
Deputy Managing Director: ALBERT READ

NICHOLAS COLERIDGE:
Managing Director, Condé Nast Britain
President, Condé Nast International

JONATHAN NEWHOUSE:
Chairman and Chief Executive,
Condé Nast International

www.thelovemagazine.co.uk

©T&CO. 2017 0800 160 1837 | TIFFANY.COM
TIFFANY T COLLECTION

ALBERTAFERRETTI.COM
ALBERTA FERRETTI

Editor's Letter

JONATHAN SAUNDERS, ROKSANDA ILINCIC, KATIE GRAND, CHRISTOPHER KANE AND RICHARD NICOLL AT THE LOVE CHRISTMAS PARTY, 2015
Photographer DAVE BENETT

This issue started with some weird idea in the back of my head that took a while to get to the front of my brain. Kendall had shot, very beautifully, Kaia Gerber for our last issue. I was pleasantly surprised by how well the pictures turned out, and for about a month at least I thought about the power of Kendall as a photographer: nothing like Kendall has ever come along before. By proving herself behind the camera she had well and truly shaken off the idea that she was 'just a name with a (rather generous) social media following'.

From time to time I think about how much I would like to find a new cover star, a new face, someone unknown. But the truth of the matter is the person viewing the cover on Instagram or (more rarely) in the magazine shop doesn't really care, to go back to my editorial roots with 'The Death of the Cover Star'. And then it all slotted in to place.

We had done a media search with Marc Jacobs for a project called #castmemarc where we met amazing people – the most famous one being someone who unfortunately slipped through the net, Hari Nef. I thought about doing a similar project but putting the casting call out to people who had an impressive and passionate voice and a dynamic attitude. And if we did this with Kendall shooting, people would sit up and take notice!

Kendall and I met in a SoHo hotel room during New York Fashion Week in September – she had eggs, me sparkling water – and we hatched a plan. We would launch a project together looking for people who felt they had something to say. They could be unknown or famous, they could be on Instagram or not – just as long as they had some kind of message or talent they needed to get out there.

One hundred and ten thousand applicants later, and after much frantic direct-messaging between myself, Kendall, Ashleah (Kendall's very patient, hilarious and leggy agent) and Harriet Verney, we got the applicants down to around 100 people, who we asked to send us a video. Various 'celebs' also contacted us along the way, some through email, some on Instagram and even some on Twitter. We had quite a laugh at some of the ones who wanted to be involved and their demands which weren't quite adhering to the spirit of the project.

Needless to say we ended up with three videographers as their videos were so impressive and an assortment of known and very unknown faces (at the time of going to press our cover star Mia has 164 followers).

What was to happen in the desert on the chilly mornings of 18th and 19th November 2016 wasn't going to change just the lives of the people we photographed but also mine and those of the writers on the project, Paul Flynn and Jonathan Heaf. It's hard to describe life-changing shoots. Hindsight helps, but when we left in the car with Gwendoline Christie after the last shot we knew something very special had happened. With tears in our eyes and bottles of prosecco in our arms, we knew it had been a shoot that actually meant something. Even Panos, the ultimate moody goth who was there styling the shoot, celebrated with us at the Sunset Tower Hotel and marvelled at how great everyone had been.

I've kept in touch with nearly all of the people we shot on those two days. Belle is working for LOVE on digital and on a project for Miu Miu; Danny (fingers crossed) will start at Saint Martins or study fashion design somewhere fabulous; Isold is making films for the LOVE website and is so phenomenally talented I hope she goes on to make amazing Woody Allen-type feature films; Mia has signed to be a model with Kendall's agent The Society and will appear in Miu Miu's pre-fall presentation; and beautiful Christina will hopefully not be quite so shy next time she's in front of the camera. When Paul Flynn listened back to his recordings of the kids' stories, he cried. And at the end of putting this issue together, a tear comes to my eye as it's been so bloody special.

Talking of special and tears, I wanted to include Lauren Hutton as she's such an incredible legend. When we were working at Bottega Veneta this season I happened to say to her, 'You were with Malcolm McLaren, weren't you?' Her eyes welled up and she said he was the love of her life. She really is amazing and I wanted to dress her in archive Westwood to remember Malcolm.

Finally, as we were putting this issue together we heard the sad news that Richard Nicoll had died. As someone who played an integral role in our generation of designers, he was very close to our friends at LOVE and we had a lot of fun together. We'll miss him, and this issue is dedicated to his memory.
– Katie Grand

PS As we go to press on this issue news reaches us that Nicholas Coleridge, my favourite person in publishing, is stepping down from his current roles at Condé Nast. I have loved every minute of working for him and am still stunned and thrilled that he launched LOVE with us eight years ago. It's been the most amazing journey and a dream come true. I will miss his sly glances, his occasional use of the word 'wanky' and his absolute love and passion for magazines.

Photographer KENDALL JENNER
Creative Director KATIE GRAND
Fashion Editor PANOS YIAPANIS
Sienna Miller styled by OLIVER VOLQUARDSEN
Hair ASHLEY JAVIER
Make-up CIARA O'SHEA

Arianna wears white cotton poplin and lace dress with broderie anglaise trim by BURBERRY FEBRUARY 2017 COLLECTION.
Belle wears white cotton poplin and lace dress with broderie anglaise trim by BURBERRY FEBRUARY 2017 COLLECTION; *ring Belle's own.*
Destiny wears honey Sandringham long heritage trench coat by BURBERRY.
Hari wears black sweatshirt by GIVENCHY BY RICCARDO TISCI.
Joyjah wears embroidered velvet dress by MARC JACOBS.
Kaia wears tailored jacket by BURBERRY MENSWEAR; *vintage eyelet belt from* PANOS YIAPANIS'S ARCHIVE.
Mia wears custom-made wool argyle jumper with ruffles by PANOS YIAPANIS'S STUDIO.
Sienna wears white cotton poplin and lace dress with broderie anglaise trim by BURBERRY FEBRUARY 2017 COLLECTION;
A Great Unknown ivory cape attributed to Callot Soeurs c1949 from WILLIAM VINTAGE.

CHRISTY TURLINGTON BURNS
HARLEM, NEW YORK
NOVEMBER 2ND 2016

BLESNYA
PLACE VENDOME, PARIS
OCTOBER 20TH 2016

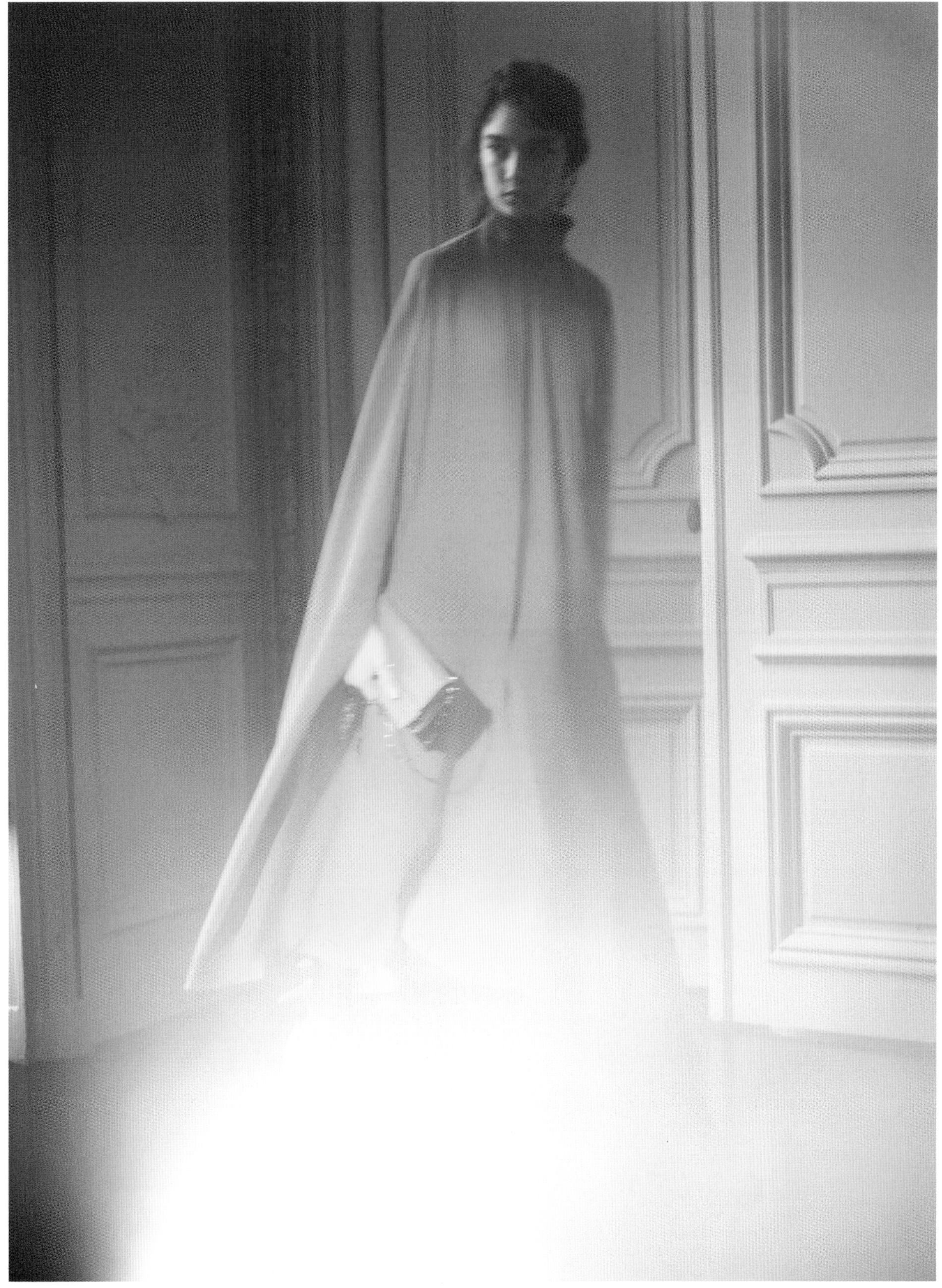

THE SHOW FINALE
HOTEL SALOMON DE ROTHSCHILD, PARIS
OCTOBER 2ND 2016

People we'd like to thank...

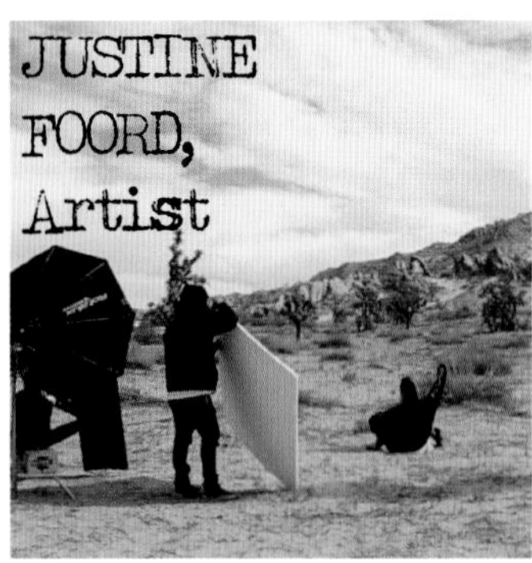

Worked her retouching magic on Kendall Jenner's photography.

Have you met your hero?
'Yes – Paolo Roversi. I can proudly say I have met the wonderful Italian gentleman.'

What's your favourite band?
'Radiohead.'

What's your favourite book?
'*The Alchemist* by Paulo Coelho – it had a very big impact on my life.'

What's your favourite smell?
'Café Rose by Tom Ford.'

Who's your biggest fan?
'My mummy.'

He and his team took care of production for the #LOVEME17 shoot.

Who are you the biggest fan of?
'My husband – he's smart hot, and generous and makes me want to be the best I can be.'

Have you met your hero?
'A hero has to remain someone I can fantasise about. But I did bump into Jack Nicholson once checking in at the Delano Miami when I was 21 and on holiday.'

Favourite band?
'Am loving George Michael and *Listen Without Prejudice.*'

Favourite smell?
'My newborn twins Lola and Cosmo.'

Favourite movie?
'I'm a sucker for sci-fi: *Logan's Run, Dune, Terminator...* Love *Dark City* and can't wait for *Alien: Covenant.*'

Who's your biggest fan?
'My husband – he's always there and so supportive.'

Styled the young icons-in-waiting in LA.

Who are you the biggest fan of?
'Soi Dogs, HRC in the Wild.'

What's your favourite song?
'"Wild Horses" by Susan Boyle.'

What's your favourite smell?
'Halfeti roses.'

What's your favourite film?
'*Damien: Omen II.*'

Interviewed our young hopefuls.

Who are you the biggest fan of?
'Jackie Collins.'

Have you met your hero?
'Yes, twice. The last time was in her house in Beverly Hills. She had a copy of *Candy* magazine on her coffee table, everything was made of marble and she rented next door out to Al Pacino. She showed me her swimming pool and said, "Do you like it, darling?", explaining that she'd tried to buy the Hockney painting in the Seventies, heard the price of it and decided to get a replica of the pool made in her courtyard instead. Jackie was everything you want from a human being and a bit more.'

Favourite song?
'"Your Silent Face" by New Order.'

Favourite smell?
'Cheap cigar smoke, Paco Rabanne and gold jewellery.'

Favourite book?
'*The Orton Diaries.*'

Favourite movie?
'*Letter to Brezhnev.*'

Who's your biggest fan?
'The *Grazia* reader who did her A Level English language coursework on my TV page.'

Represents Kendall Jenner.

Who are you the biggest fan of?
'Kevin Durant – till he went to Golden State... KD, WHY YOU WANNA BREAK MY HEART?!'

Have you met your hero?
'Sadly, no. KEV!'

What's your favourite song?
'"I'll try anything once" by Julian Casablancas/The Strokes.'

What's your favourite book?
'*This Is How You Lose Her* by Junot Diaz.'

What's your favourite film?
'*Mermaids.*'

Who is your biggest fan?
'My friend Gerber.'

CHRISTOPHER BAILEY, Chief Creative and Chief Executive Officer, Burberry

Gave us exclusive access to the Burberry February 2017 Collection. You saw it here first!

What inspired the Burberry February 2017 collection?
'Henry Moore has long been an inspiration of mine, and with our February collection we wanted to capture the way he played with form, texture and sculptural detail in a way that we haven't before. As well as referencing his iconic sculptures, the collection was also influenced by the creative process behind them, which in so many ways is as inspiring as the works themselves.'

The Vice-President of Culture and Communications at Standard Hotels arranged for our #LOVEME17 talents from around the world to stay at the wonderful Standard Downtown Hotel in LA.

Who are you the biggest fan of?
'My parents, because without them I am nothing.'

Have you met your hero?
'I have – but it was beyond a disappointment, so I'd rather not elaborate.'

What's your favourite song?
'"Everything She Wants" by Wham!'

What's your favourite smell?
'Gardenia.'

What's your favourite book?
'*A Mind of Its Own: A Cultural History of The Penis* by David Friedman – FASCINATING.'

Took care of everyone so that they could make it to the shoot.

Who are you the biggest fan of?
'Princess Margaret and Roald Dahl.'

Favourite band?
'Goldie Lookin Chain, ESG, Whigfield.'

Favourite smell?
'Tuberose and petrol.'

Favourite colour?
'Black and gold.'

Who's your biggest fan?
'Someone on Instagram called @nosejob keeps liking my photos – got the hint.'

SHOP AT DSQUARED2.COM

People we'd like to thank...

NAME: Kendall Jenner **AGE:** 21 ♡

WHO ARE YOU THE BIGGEST FAN OF ?
Winona Ryder

SINCE WHEN ? helloooo, birth.

WHAT FIRST ATTRACTED YOU TO.......
her unique Style and look

WHAT IS YOUR FAVOURITE THING ABOUT THEM ?
All her hot boyfriends.

YOUR FAVOURITE FAN ITEM..
dad hats

HOW HAVE THEY INFLUENCED YOUR LIFE ?

HAVE YOU MET YOUR HERO ?
Sadley not

FAVOURITE SONG ?
give me one reason
tracy Chapman

FAVOURITE BOOK ?
what we talk about when we talk about love
Raymond Carver

FAVOURITE SMELL ?
Vanilla

WHO IS YOUR BIGGEST FAN:
My mom

FAVOURITE BAND ?
tame impala

FAVOURITE FILM ?
the notebook

FAVOURITE COLOUR ?
pink

BELLE SMITH, Creative

Photographed by Kendall Jenner for #LOVEME17 and shot a behind-the-scenes film on set for LOVE online.

Who are you the biggest fan of?
'Probably Tim Burton – I am clinically obsessed. I'm also obsessed with Karl Lagerfeld, Winona Ryder, Charlie Chaplin, Dr Seuss, Steve Jobs, Heath Ledger, Katie Grand, Alessandro Michele. Half are dead… what a shame.'

What's your favourite band?
'I've recently got into the grind of Radiohead – all their stuff just makes me feel like I'm living in a Nineties movie. I'm also a sucker for The 1975… so catchy.'

What's your favourite film?
'So many, but a constant love is *Edward Scissorhands.* Like so many of Tim's films, it's so rich with the mixture of the light and the dark, the comedic and the twisted, it evokes some of the most strangely bottomless as well as beautifully pitting emotions that exist.'

Who's your biggest fan?
'My nana. She recently texted me a photo of her wallpaper that was a close-up of my face. Hilarious.'

ÍSOLD HALLDÓRUDÓTTIR, Filmmaker

Our successful #LOVEME17 applicant who made a film about the shoot.

Who are you the biggest fan of?
'I've always admired Yoko Ono's mind.'

Have you met your hero?
'Yes: my mother. To call her my hero would be an understatement. She is the sun.

Favourite song?
"This Is Love" by PJ Harvey. Been singing along loud and proud since I was 5 years old.

Favourite smell?
'Coconut oil.'

Favourite book?
'*Hugmyndir: Andvirði hundrað milljónir* by Halldór Halldórsson. The author writes about his ideas, thoughts and poems, and as it is genius it's also hilarious.'

Favourite movie?
'It's a tie between *Dirty Dancing* and *Rock'n'Roll High School.*'

JONATHAN HEAF, Writer

Interviewed our young hopefuls.

Who are you the biggest fan of?
'AA Gill.'

Have you met your hero?
'I have. He insulted my shoes, an act which I consider the greatest compliment.'

Favourite band?
'Oasis in all their mid-Nineties pomp.'

Favourite book?
'*Lolita* by Nabokov or *Tender Is the Night* by Fitzgerald.'

Favourite smell?
'Boris's inner ear after a nap. (He's a lurcher.)'

Favourite movie?
'Anything with Jack Nicholson in, but *Chinatown* especially.'

Who's your biggest fan?
'Why else do you think I got the dog?'

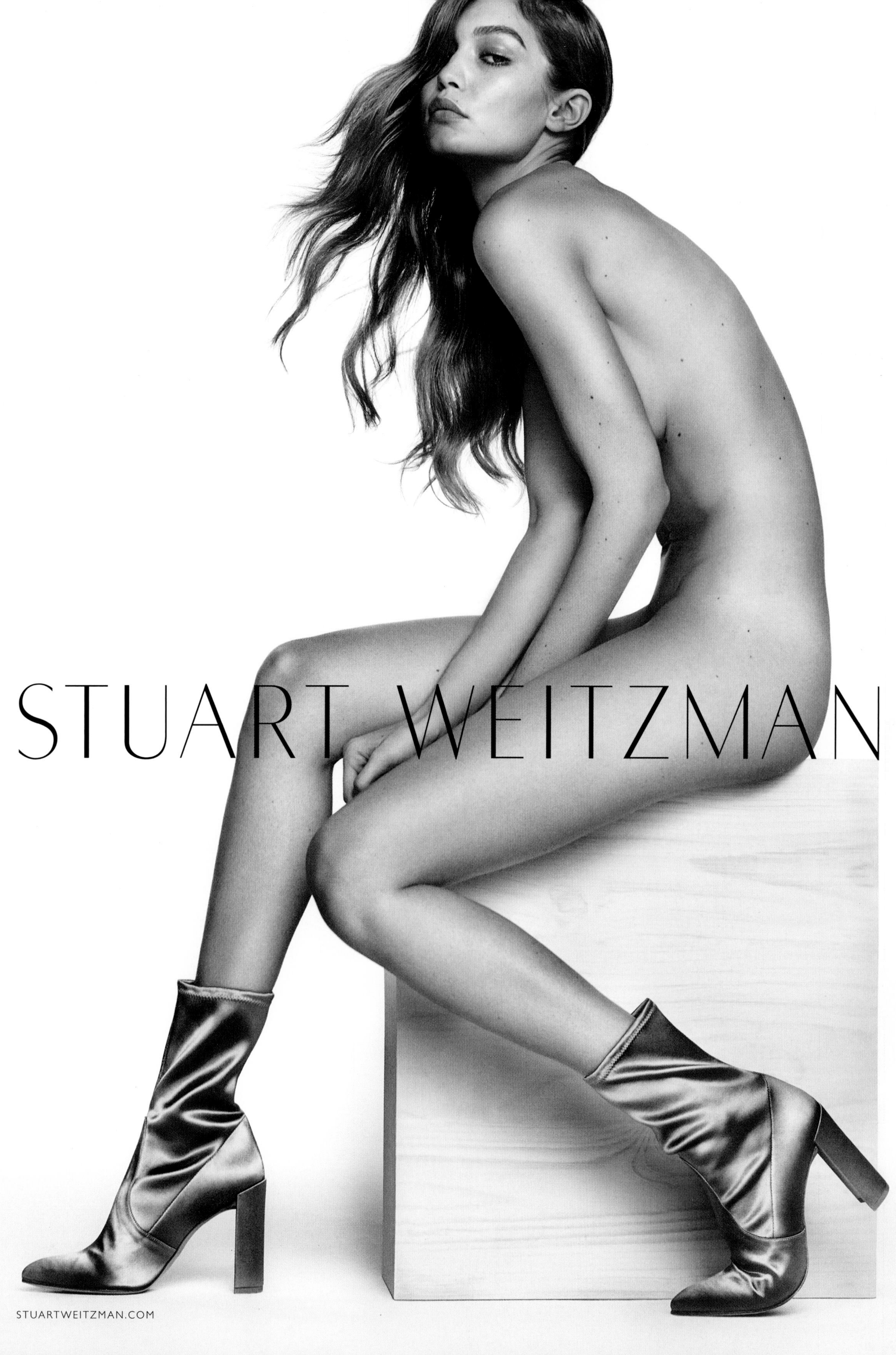
STUART WEITZMAN
STUARTWEITZMAN.COM

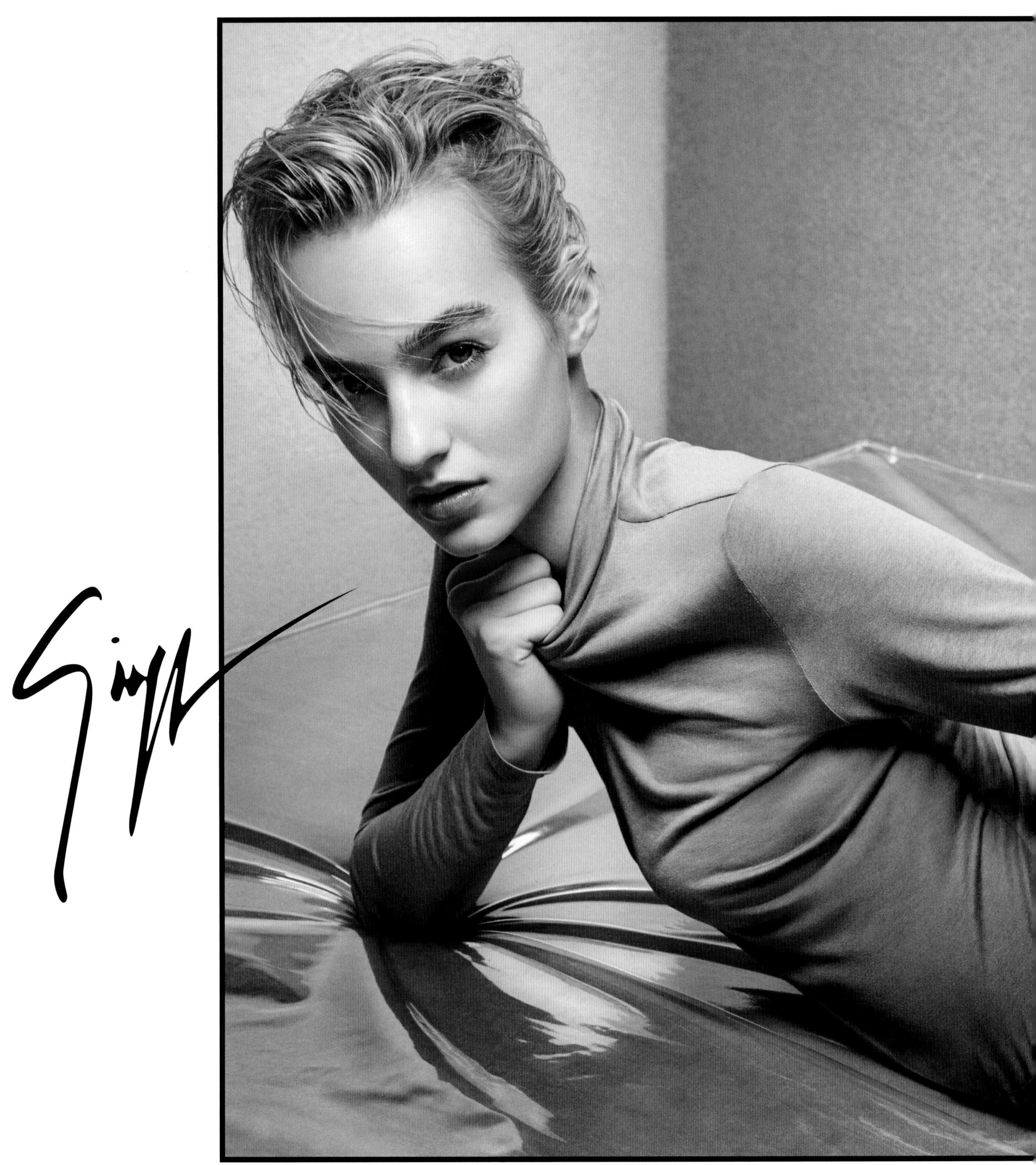

RN
SGDN
Kiki photographed
by Craig McDean
www.sacai.jp

sacai

TOPSHOP.COM

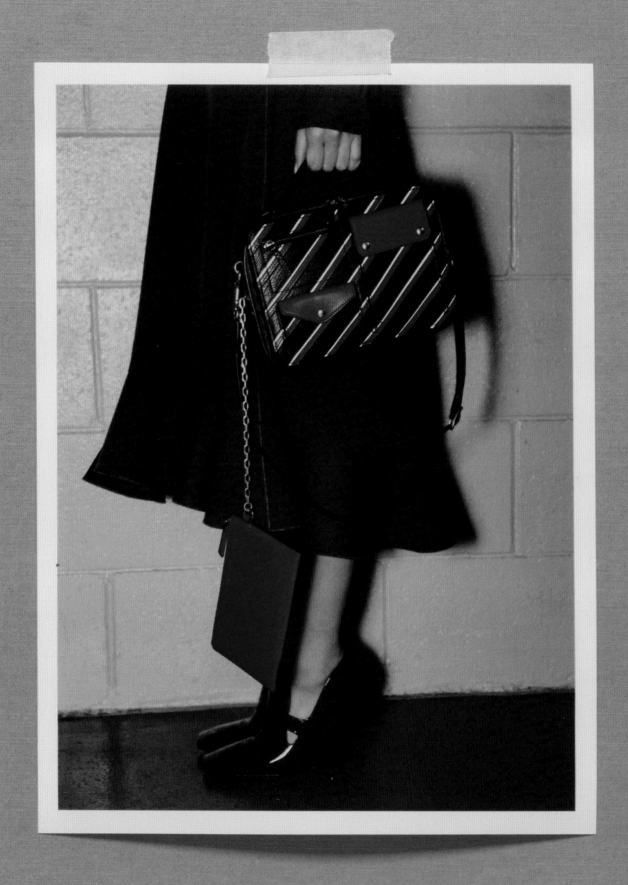

b o n e

forte_

forte

marni.com

MARNI

marni.com
MARNI

Karlie wears red ruffle top by GUESS; *black embellished polka-dot tulle skirt by* ROCHAS; *vintage silk chiffon evening gloves from* COSPROP; *silver diamanté fringe earrings by* KENNETH JAY LANE; *vintage silver floral brooch from* STAZIA LOREN

NAME: Karlie Kloss

Photographer DREW JARRETT
Fashion Editor STEVE MORRISS

AGE: 24 :)

WHO ARE YOU THE BIGGEST FAN OF ? BEYONCÉ

FAVOURITE BAND ?
Bruce Springsteen & the E-Street Band ♡

FAVOURITE FILM ?
Pretty Woman/Anything with Julia Roberts!

FAVOURITE COLOUR ?
Purple

Hair CECILIA ROMERO Make-up LISA HOUGHTON Set design PHILIPP HAEMMERLE Production SOCIETY MGMT Retouching KAPSURE Thanks to SUNSET STUDIOS

KARLIE KLOSS / Model

Derek Blasberg chats to his friend and fellow native of St Louis about the nature of fandom in the age of instant-access celebrity

Interview DEREK BLASBERG

DEREK: *The most obvious question here is: who is your biggest fan? And the most obvious answer is: me, Derek Blasberg.*
KARLIE: 'Definitely it's you. You've been the most loyal president of my fan club since I began!'

Is this a good time to point out that it's been an unpaid position?
'Oh, shush! You just get paid in good karma, love and cookies.'

When you were a kid, what were you a fan of?
'Sports teams and New York City ballerinas. I knew of all the ballerinas and principal dancers in ABT.'

What was your favourite team?
'The Cardinals, of course! C'mon, we both grew up in St Louis, where being proud of the Cardinals was a requirement of living there. That's fandom on a whole other level. When I was little, I knew every person in the starting line-up.'

Back in high school in Missouri, I found that so much of the socialisation was based on high-school sports, too.
'It's like a religion. In small towns, you care as much about the high-school sports team as much as you do the professional teams. Actually, I think people cared more about the high-school team than they did about the pros.'

Maybe that was a good life lesson. Maybe that's why you and I are so friendly and work so well with others, because from a young age we are encouraged to participate in group sports and teamwork. That's when we learned 'there's no I in team' and all that.
'For sure! The whole community were fans, and everybody pitched in, whether it was fundraisers, bake sales, chilli fests, whatever – it was to help support the team. I think that's definitely fandom on a very personal level.'

How was your high-school team?
'Better than yours!'

That's because you had a bigger student body, and just by the law of averages a bigger student body means a better team. But, ha! It's interesting that even now we are fighting over who had the best team.
'This is true. But it's like this pride and this joy that comes from supporting the teams and being part of the games and I don't know, I don't find that I've felt that same kind of loyalty in sports, even in New York.'

What are you a fan of now?
'I'm a fan of Derek Blasberg.

Correct answer! But what else are you a fan of?
'Now I'm a fan of individuals more so than I am of teams. Though I still have a soft spot for dancers, like Misty Copeland, who's a boundary-breaking ballerina in New York City. Derek, who are you a fan of?'

That's easy. Ricky Martin.
'This I know.'

Apart from athletes, who are you a fan of?
'Artists? I'm a fan of Alex Israel. I'm a fan of Beyoncé. I'm a fan of Melinda Gates. I like people who are creators, people who have blazed their own trail and stand out in their industries because they're being true to themselves and following their passion. I think individuality – a person who doesn't just follow what the crowd is doing – is admirable, too.'

When I ask who you'd be a fan of in the fashion industry, who comes to mind?
'Arthur Elgort. He was the very first person to give me a break as a model.'

Which job was that?
'I did a photoshoot with him for *Teen Vogue* when I was, like, a baby. He knew I was a ballerina so when I went to meet him in his studio he kept asking me to jump. It was a big deal to me because I knew he had photographed so many iconic dancers. Like, he photographed Baryshnikov. I think he could tell that I knew it was a big deal to him, so he saw something in me and supported me through the rest of my career. So maybe we were mutual fans of each other from then.'

Do you feel a certain pressure to entertain your fans? With Instagram and Snapchat and Facebook and Twitter… Tell me about the modern relationship with fandom.
'I think that for a long time fandom was about exclusivity and not fully giving yourself away. Not showing everything, not showing the behind-the-scenes – and that's for everyone and for all industries. It was about illusion and smoke and mirrors, right? But now we live in a world where what is so exciting is a direct relationship from creators of all kinds to their fans and to their fan base. I think that it's really exciting because the people who are truly unique and passionate create work that really stands out. You can have access to them through technology, through social media, through so many different ways. There is a much more honest, intimate relationship that people have with their fans. It's not necessarily a responsibility or something you have to do, but I think it creates a much stronger relationship with the creator.'

So being able to show more is a good thing?
'I think that the intimacy leads to, hopefully, a longer relationship and the idea that someone is really invested. They feel like they really know you, and I love that.'

Do you show the real you to your fans?
'Yes, and you have to. I think people know when you're not being genuine. And I think the idea of fandom is really feeling like you're a friend of someone.'

Does it come naturally to you?
'For a long time it was tricky, especially when I was living at home in St Louis and balancing this normal high-school life of football games and pep rallies with starting to build a career in the world of high fashion and being recognised. Honestly, it made me uncomfortable. Any time someone would come up to me and say, "Karlie, can I take a picture with you? I'm a fan," I would feel odd. Not because I felt like people were invading my privacy, more because I felt I didn't deserve that recognition or that I didn't earn it yet.'

Is it easier now?
'Now it is, because of how connected everyone is. It's easier to start developing a fan base. You don't have to be the most famous person in the world, you can just put yourself out there in an authentic way and people really connect.'

Is there anything that you wouldn't share with your fans?
'I probably don't share everything in my life, but I definitely care about using the following that I have and the influence that I have in a way to draw attention to things that matter to me. Whether it is trying to help teach girls different things like coding or share cooking recipes, I recognise that it's a special opportunity to build a relationship. I care about the people that pay attention to me. I feel grateful they care, so I want to share what I feel comfortable sharing.'

Is that enough on fandom?
'I hope we didn't forget anything.'

Taylor Swift! Shouldn't you say you're her fan, too?
'Ha! Yes, I'm a big fan of Tay Tay, but I love her for who she is and what a wonderful friend she is. So I'm a fan, and a friend.'

BOUCHERON
PARIS
QUATRE
Grosgrain & Clou de Paris
Bracelets
FIRST JEWELLER OF THE PLACE VENDÔME
In 1893, Frédéric Boucheron is the first of the great contemporary jewellers to open a Boutique on the Place Vendôme

THE FANS ISSUE

A round-up of people we're fans of – exemplary contemporary characters and entities – and the people they're fans of, and their fans. Fan love refracted, reflected, recursive: fans of fans of fans of fans of fans of fans...

Photographer DANIEL JACKSON
Fashion Editors CHARLES JEFFREY, KATIE GRAND, MATTY BOVAN

Hair (London) LUKE HERSHESON
Hair (New York) AKKI Make-up HIROMI UEDA
Manicure (London) CHISATO YAMAMOTO
Manicure (New York) RICA ROMAIN
Digital technician KAREN GOSS
Production JESSICA DALY
Photographic assistance JAKE MERRILL
Fashion assistance OLIVER VOLQUARDSEN, PRINCIPAL YIP, OGUN GORTAN, DAVID CASSAVANT, JULIA VIRJLER, MEGAN H SORIA
Hair assistance (London) MITRA MIRLASHARI, NICHOLAS THOMAS LATHAM
Hair assistance (New York) TOMOKO KUWAMURA, REBEKAH CALO
Make-up assistance (London) SAMANTA FALCONE, CLAIRE URQUHART, LIBBY JAMES
Make-up assistance (New York) CHISA TAKAHASHI, YUUI
Manicure assistance (London) EMMA WRIGHT
Production assistance COLLEEN CULLEN
Thanks to SPRING STUDIOS and PIER 59 NEW YORK

LA FEMME
PRADA
MILANO

L'HOMME
PRADA
MILANO

PRADA
MILANO

PRADA
MILANO

DAL 1913

PRADA
MILANO

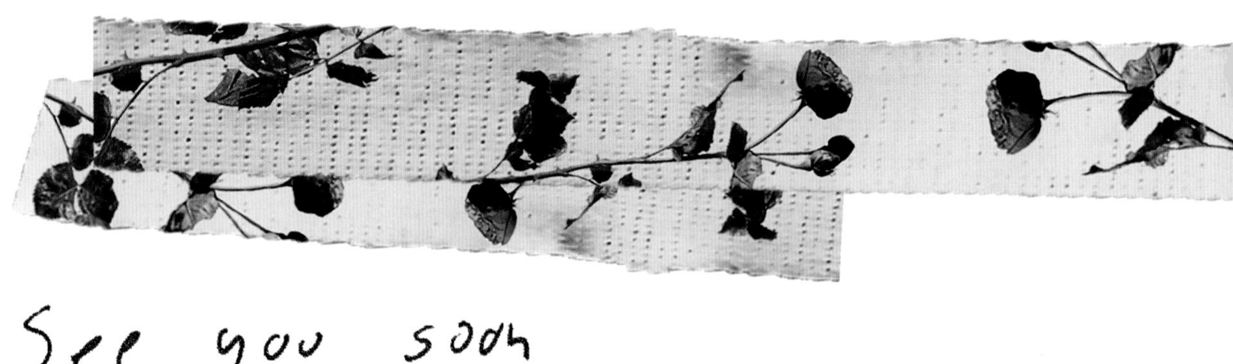

See you soon

VICTOR BARRAGÁN / Designer

The Mexican-born New York Fashion Week newcomer whose spectacular, sexualised fashion pushes well beyond dated gender binarisms speaks to Charles Jeffrey

Interview CHARLES JEFFREY

CHARLES: *Hi, how are you?*
VICTOR: 'I'm drunk.'

Good, that's the best way to start an interview. So, can you talk me through how you went from industrial design to fashion?
'I was studying industrial design because I couldn't get into fashion school. But at the same time I was making white T-shirts, something really simple, and I started to get a lot of work from them. So I focused on just making clothes. Then I tried to take some extra classes, and they were really bad, so next I thought maybe I should move to another city. So I went to Europe. I went to London, Paris, Brussels, Berlin. I didn't have too many belongings. When I moved to New York it was my first time in the city, so I arrived with the same attitude I had about Europe: "Let's just see." I really liked it, so I stayed.'

What is it about New York that makes you like it so much?
'I think London is really similar to New York in some ways, culturally perhaps. But when I was in London I didn't feel or think too much about my own culture; maybe that isn't good. It's been hard to be so far away from everything, but here is pretty similar to Mexico in some ways, a lot of people speak Spanish. That really helped a lot. New York is the main city for fashion, anyways.'

Starting a label is quite difficult – to fund a show, to fund production. Do you find New York offers those aspects of support? I've found it difficult, but luckily I've had help from funding bodies like Fashion East towards making a show. How did you get to that stage?
'It's really hard, everywhere.'

Do you have to work on the side?
'Not right now. I guess for now I can keep doing the simple stuff but, either way, it's really hard to be in New York. It's so expensive. I have really good followers on my Instagram, some people who like to support me. So that has helped a lot.'

On the subject of Instagram, I can't help noticing that you have a fair bit of pornography in your feed. Would you say that porn is important to your work?
'I think it is important in some ways. I like that website BiLatinMen.com – this guy [who runs it] pays so much money to get people to fuck each other. For me, it's important to show the gay Latin community like it's more open, but they're hiding in some way. So that helped a lot just for my personal research, I guess.'

You draw on Latin culture quite heavily – that way of looking at Latin men in a straight way but subverting it is a massive theme in your work.
'Yeah, it's kind of turning around those taboos of being gay in Mexico, and being a person of colour in America. So playing with that really inspires me a lot. If you want to look feminine or you want to look masculine, that's fine – as long as you're having fun in some way, it doesn't even matter. I want to have diversity.'

Do you have any super-fans who are completely obsessed with your work?
'Some people use photos to pretend to be me – use my face, my pictures. That's pretty weird. I don't feel like it's creepy – I just think like, "Eh…?" I also get a lot of nudes.'

You get sent nudes?
'Yeah, because they see the pornography.'

Do you send any back?
'If I like the guy, yeah.'

If you could send a nude to anybody, who would you send it to?
'I used to love Leo DiCaprio when I was really young, just because I used to watch him all the time – but maybe not really sexually… In a different way.'

So, you'd send it to a young Leonardo DiCaprio?
'*Noooooo*. I don't know – Bruce Willis, maybe?'

Bruce Willis?
'*The Fifth Element* – the outfits… Amazing. So that version of Bruce Willis.'

Victor (left) wears denim trench coat by BALMAIN; *tapestry and leopard-print bodice by* MAISON MARGIELA; *wide denim jeans by* BARRAGÁN. *Michael wears cotton and chainmail jeans, embroidered black cotton T-shirt and metal collar all by* BARRAGÁN; *Sweeping Wave sinamay, lace overlay and crin edge hat with handblocked flower by* PHILIP TREACY; *Shelter large-veiled boater hat by* STEPHEN JONES; *small boater hat in parasisal with patent band and crescent veiling by* PHILIP TREACY; *black oversized tulle feather and fringe Extravaganza veil by* PIERS ATKINSON; *underwear (just seen) by* CALVIN KLEIN UNDERWEAR

NAME: Victor Barragan AGE: 29
Fashion Designer NYC

WHO ARE YOU THE BIGGEST FAN OF ?
SELENA QUINTANILLA

SINCE WHEN ?
AFTER I SAW THE MOVIE

WHAT FIRST ATTRACTED YOU TO.......
MUSIC and Outfits

WHAT IS YOUR FAVOURITE THING ABOUT THEM ?
HOT AF

YOUR FAVOURITE FAN ITEM..
SPARKLIN BRA "Bustie"

HOW HAVE THEY INFLUENCED YOUR LIFE ?
Inspiration

HAVE YOU MET YOUR HERO ? NO

IF YES ELABORATE.....

FAVOURITE SONG ?
Better off Alone - Alice Deejay

FAVOURITE BAND ?
Sonic Youth

FAVOURITE BOOk ?
a 100 Recepies of $4 USD or less

FAVOURITE FILM ?
5th Element

FAVOURITE SMELL ?
Cigarrette before burn

FAVOURITE COLOUR ?
Mustard

WHO IS YOUR BIGGEST FAN:
IDK

Michael wears embroidered black cotton T-shirt, cotton and chainmail jeans and metal collar all by BARRAGÁN; *underwear (just seen) by* CALVIN KLEIN UNDEWEAR; *(from left) 'Sweeping Wave' sinamay, lace overlay and crin edge hat with handblocked flower by* PHILIP TREACY; *Shelter large-veiled boater hat by* STEPHEN JONES; *small boater hat in parasisal with patent band and crescent veiling by* PHILIP TREACY; *black oversized tulle feather and fringe Extravaganza veil by* PIERS ATKINSONI

NAME: JULIANA HUXTABLE **AGE:** 28

ARTIST/DJ NEW YORK, NY

WHO ARE YOU THE BIGGEST FAN OF ?

K8 HARDY

SINCE WHEN ?

I SAW A VIDEO OF HER IN THE BROOKLYN

WHAT FIRST ATTRACTED YOU TO.......

HER HUMOR, WIT, STYLE + DIY AESTHETIC

YOUR FAVOURITE FAN ITEM..

SPICE GIRLS ~~ADDRE~~ CONTACT/ADDRESS BOOK

HAVE YOU MET YOUR HERO ? YES

IF YES ELABORATE.....

WE'RE FRIENDS

SONG I LIKE

~~**FAVOURITE SONG**~~ **?**

~~[illegible]~~ ASIAN DOLL - BARBIE EVERYWHERE

~~**FAVOURITE BAND ?**~~

I LIKE TEEN: SLEATER-KINNEY

FAVOURITE BOOk ?

LEFT OF DARKNESS, URSULA K LE GUIN

FAVOURITE FILM ? STARE, GEORGES BATAILLE

SANTA SANGRE + BATTERY REICH

FAVOURITE SMELL ?

COOL WATER WOMAN + FLOWER BOMB + COCONUT LIME

FAVOURITE COLOUR ?

GUNMETAL

WHO IS YOUR BIGGEST FAN:

A BLOGGER I KNOW ON TUMBLR

♡ Y'ALL

JULIANA HUXTABLE
/ DJ / Artist

Juliana wears multicoloured crystal beaded dress and copper and zinc necklace both by BALMAIN; *hoop earrings Juliana's own*

NAME: KAYA AGE: 26 MUSICIAN NEW YORK

WHO ARE YOU THE BIGGEST FAN OF ?
My little brother Elias
SINCE WHEN ?
Since he had a tiny little pea head
WHAT FIRST ATTRACTED YOU TO.....
His tiny little pea head
WHAT IS YOUR FAVOURITE THING ABOUT THEM ?
He's not a grown up yet
YOUR FAVOURITE FAN ITEM..
Miya Folicks 'God is a woman' shirt
HOW HAVE THEY INFLUENCED YOUR LIFE ?
By making good music!
HAVE YOU MET YOUR HERO ?
Yes, I met Prince at a nightclub once but he wouldn't shake my hand
WHO IS YOUR BIGGEST FAN:
Vornado
FAVOURITE SONG ?
Life is too short for certainty, right now it's Nina Simone's Baltimore

KAYA WILKINS / Singer

The winsome Norwegian–born singer–songwriter who's turning her attention to acting

Writer MONICA URQUIJO

Kaya Wilkins is a musician from Nesoddtangen, a village on the outskirts of Oslo, who is now based in New York. Her fragile intensity seems almost at odds with her brooding, bleak songs, the inspiration for which she traces back to an early encounter with Bob Dylan. 'I went to my friend's house once,' she says, 'and their dad would always put on Dylan, and I was like, "I need to learn how to do that."' Wilkins claims her first love though was Otis Redding. 'The first time I heard him I was like, "Oh shit, this is love." But I was a small child, so when other kids started finding their musical niche, I was still kind of all over the place. My brother is this black-metal dude, my other brother is a punk dude, and I was really into soul music 'cause my mum's really into it. So I was never a girl who had the token Bowie poster. I was very schizophrenic in my tastes.' The 26-year-old trained as a dancer in high school, which is still apparent in her poise as she quietly commands the room. 'My dancing teacher was giving out stuffed animals at the end of the three years of teaching everyone and she gave me a cow, because I wasn't afraid of being ugly.' She laughs. 'Ugly in a movement way. I was like OK, cool – whatever the fuck that means!'

Kaya moved to New York to be a model, but found her interest in it waned as she began writing music and lyrics. Now she records as Okay Kaya, an achievement she could barely have dreamed of back when she was writing alone in her apartment as an antidote to the cold, dark New York nights. 'I never really thought the songs would leave my bedroom. But, yeah, I guess I started writing a lot after I'd been living in New York. I was kinda like, "Wait – I have too much spare time on my hands." I was pretty lonely and I didn't really know anyone.' This sense of dislocation is palpable in Kaya's songs: their dark power points towards a feeling of alienation, not quite fitting in, trying to process the world. 'I just do it to keep me sane.'

When she first put her music on Soundcloud she attracted only 11 followers. However, one of them went on to become her agent and her music career began. The size of the venues she played – art shows, basements – began to grow and last year she played the Øya Festival, billed alongside PJ Harvey and Massive Attack. The bigger gigs have failed to resolve her severe stage fright. 'I was playing this show and [the audience] was really loud, and my music is really quiet. I could hear, "Stacey, what are you drinking?" from the audience. I thought, "Ah, this is what busking is like."' Yet for a girl who suffers from performance anxiety, she is remarkably fearless. Her next project is acting in Joachim Trier's supernatural thriller *Thelma*, to be released later this year. She has no previous experience as an actor. 'I was like, "No way, I don't act!" Then [Trier] sent me the script and I fell in love with it.' It is this openness to the unpredictability of life that makes Kaya such a shot of energy. She says that when she plays in her native Norway, her friends tease her with heckles of 'Loner!'. She may indeed be a lone voice on stage, but sometimes it's the solitary notes that ring the loudest.

Kaya wears velvet suit jacket (just seen) by BRIONI; *football shirt (just seen) by* MARTINE ROSE; *black gold Antifer fully pavéd choker by* REPOSSI; *jet and silver jewelled asymmetric earring by* ALEXANDER McQUEEN

Stewart wears leopard jacquard suit jacket and trousers and white cotton ruffle shirt all by ALEXANDER McQUEEN; *vintage red gloves from* MODES AND MORE; *red and white tulle from* CLOTH HOUSE; *black crocodile leather platform boots by* MAISON MARGIELA

STEWART UOO / Artist

Interview page 148

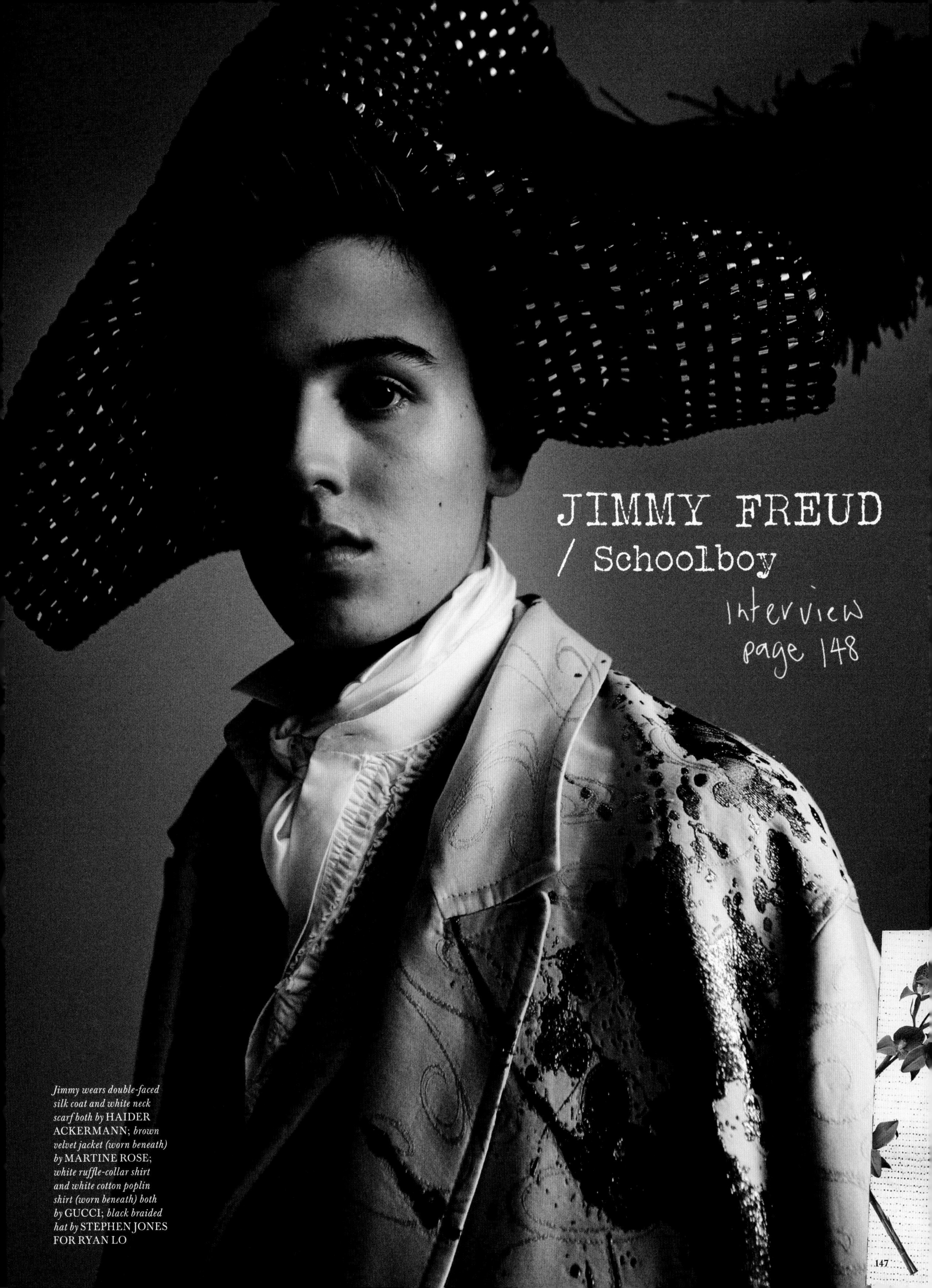

interview page 148

Jimmy wears double-faced silk coat and white neck scarf both by HAIDER ACKERMANN; *brown velvet jacket (worn beneath) by* MARTINE ROSE; *white ruffle-collar shirt and white cotton poplin shirt (worn beneath) both by* GUCCI; *black braided hat by* STEPHEN JONES FOR RYAN LO

STEWART

Best known for his mannequin sculptures, he interrogates the possibility of the obscure, the subversive and the underground in an age of instant digital ubiquity

Writer PAUL FLYNN

At 31, Stewart Uoo has found himself in the slipstream of a generation gap. 'I didn't grow up with a computer,' he notes. 'It used to be about people who grew up with or without television, or before or after this or that war. And now it feels like generations are separated before and after this or that app was developed.' This complicated purgatorial space is becoming more and more interesting to Stewart. 'I like when things become intersectional and complicated because people aren't able to take specific positions. They're nowhere and everywhere and trying to figure out where subversion is in that. It is not located any more. Subversion is functioning in a different way. How are you supposed to figure out what your positions are?'

Stewart is a smart man who is currently working on a series of soft sculptures exploring menswear as window dressing, exploring where haberdashery ends and an art statement might begin. He grew up the son of first-generation, working-class Korean immigrants in Napa Valley suburbia. He's currently learning the Korean language, adding new angst to his generational identity issues, because 'it turns out I'm not very good at languages, even supposedly my own'. At art school in Oakland he noticed a changing frame of subversion. In the emerging digital age, with automatic access to mass audiences, what did the punk ideal of glorious obscurity even mean any more?

'The attention economy is so bizarre,' he says. 'I mean, you're trying to be obscure, but obscurity doesn't make any sense any more. It's really crazy. I think about that too much, about how I am and am not supposed to feel. It's difficult.' By 24, he had made Brooklyn his home and was running the brilliant Ecstapussy parties, mostly at Nichola Formichetti's old three-storey studio space in Greene Street, Soho, with his friends Hayley and Marie. He is currently thinking about his place in New York's nightlife as well as its art world, as friends move further down the trainline out of town.

In life as in art, Stewart is part of a network split between the peculiar brands of heroism implicated at either end by Henry Rollins and Kris Jenner. 'And I don't dislike either of them, that's the thing,' he says. His central question is: how does a hyperpopulist viewpoint square with being anti-establishment? 'The mainstream can be so weird. I feel like there is a subversion going on now of people's moral compass and their relationship to selling out. Selling out is not a pejorative any more. It's almost not even a boundary.' A friend was recently talking to him about her Instagram account, 'How she's channelling Kim Kardashian and her siblings. She said, "People don't understand that my interests in them are not about their plasticity; it's not simply superficial."'

Like every artist before him, Stewart is working out what's real and what's fake in a world on a rapid spin cycle of change. Like everyone else, he had a weird 2016. He reckons he's going through the same phase Janet Jackson was when she made *The Velvet Rope*. 'That was a post-depression or reflective period where her work developed a new maturity, a moment where she was able to disentangle parts of her identity and figure out which ones were the ones she was devoted to or not.' There is a dramatic pause. 'That's where I am,' he says.

JIMMY

The genetically gifted dilettante with the intellectual heavyweight ancestry and fashion designer mum

Writer HARRIET VERNEY

Recently, 16-year-old Jimmy Freud and his friends have made a ground-breaking, life-changing new discovery. It may not be quite on a par with his great-great-grandfather Sigmund's *Psychopathology of Everyday Life*, but it's still very, very important. Jimmy has discovered The Pub. 'Yes,' says the six-foot schoolboy, delighted at this major advancement for the psychology of mankind. 'For the last few months my friends and I have been going to "The Pub". It's great. I never knew I could get into pubs. You meet a drunkard every time you go there. It's really fun.'

Jimmy's best subjects at school are English and science, specifically the GCSE physics he's studying. 'It concerns the wider universe,' he says. 'I like science fiction becoming something that exists, I find that really cool.' He has also found a new love for a Malian folk-singer called Ali Farka Touré and has a little sideline in photography.

In an Adam Ant get-up on set, Jimmy is metamorphosing from cherubic chubby-cheeked boy to chiselled man-boy literally as we speak. He is frighteningly clever, adorably charming, and thankfully hasn't yet reached the stage where grunting is the only form of communication. He doesn't even mention football once, and would much rather talk of his other newfound obsession, Joni Mitchell. He has a stupidly, ridiculously handsome schoolboy face: sculpted jawline, hair that restlessly flops from side to side and falls across his face, with cremnitz-white skin and two giant conker-coloured eyes which, when they aren't looking bashfully at the floor, resemble those of a wide-eyed puppy that is about to do something naughty (or in his case, has just discovered The Pub).

Alas, with underage pub visits comes the difficult task of finding a good fake ID. I ask to see Jimmy's and he proudly produces a green provisional licence for me to inspect. Only problem is, when he opens his wallet the licence is sat next to his Zip Oyster card for under-18s, which happens to be neon green. Bit of a giveaway, Jimmy? 'Oops,' he says. And when I turn his quite passable fake ID over, it reads in quite legible font 'this is not a real ID'. Oh dear. I mention this to his mum, the knitwear designer Bella Freud, after our interview. 'Shit,' she says. 'I got him that.'

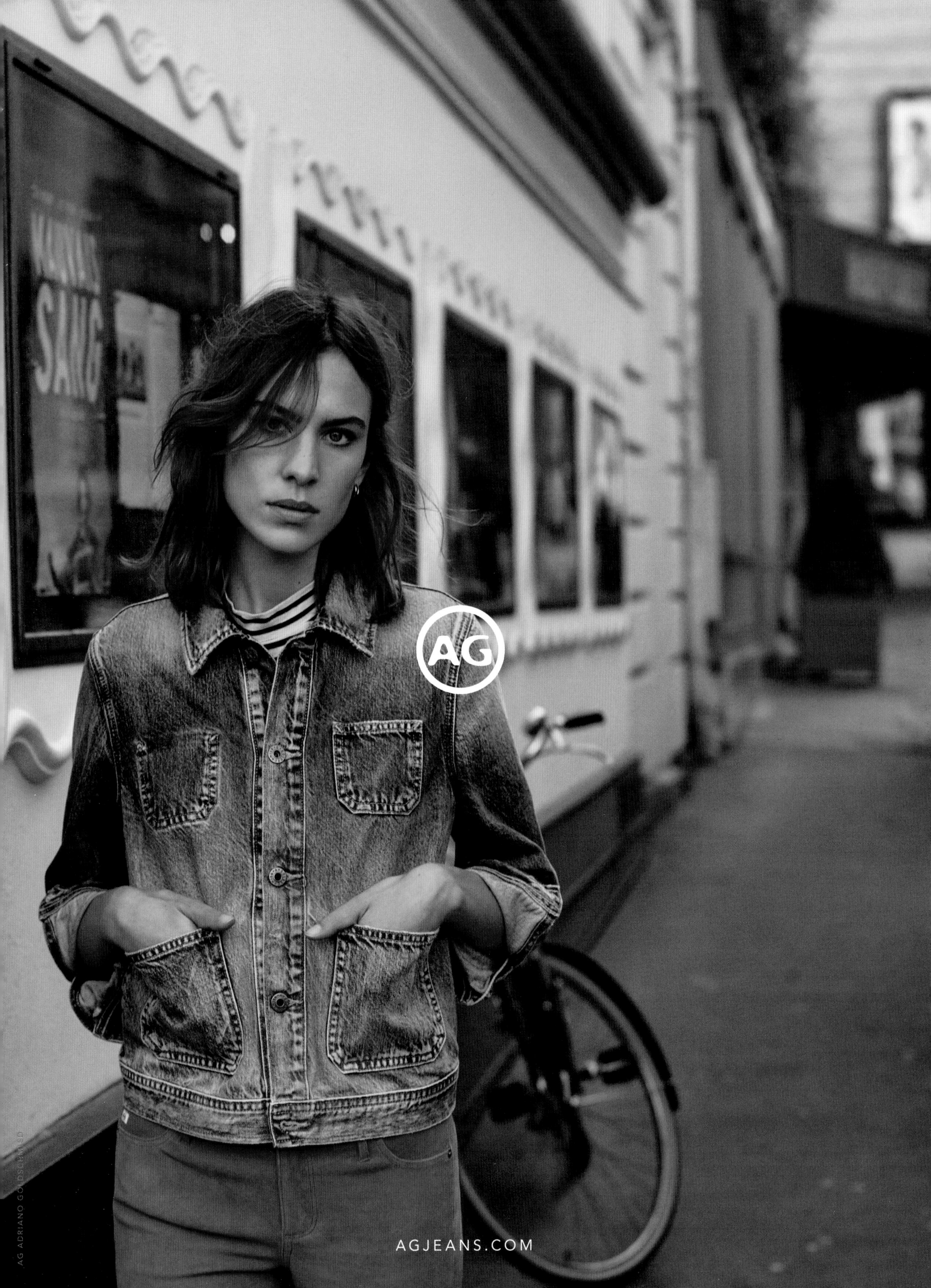
SANG
AG
AGJEANS.COM
AG ADRIANO GOLDSCHMIED

Interview CHARLES JEFFREY

GLACIER GIRL

/ Activist / Artist

Saving the glaciers, one Instagram post at a time. Elizabeth Farrell, aka Glacier Girl, believes her generation must lead the way when it comes to making a change

Elizabeth has devoted herself to 'raising awareness about climate change, adapting the aesthetic of "eco friendly" to appeal to the iGeneration and the unaccountable generations to come' – or so it says on her Instagram bio. She does all this through her Remember the Glaciers multimedia project, pushing a green message using everything from customised sweatshirts to environmentally conscious shoots on Tumblr.

CHARLES: *What are you trying to do with your work?*
ELIZABETH: 'Raise awareness about climate change through visual techniques, using visual media to make it more relatable to young people.'

What inspired you to start doing this?
'At the start I was pissed off that we weren't taught about climate change at school until I was like 18. I started doing an art project on it, and then I found Naomi Klein's book *This Changes Everything: Capitalism versus the Climate.* That was the start of the outline of all of my work since.'

Which other people are you fans of?
'A lot of climate activists I'm not that into – I started this because I didn't like what else was out there. But there are a lot of people who have done really amazing stuff. I like [Honduran environmentalist] Berta Cáceres – she knew she was going to get assassinated because of the work she was doing, but she continued to do it anyway. She did a lot of protests and Blockadia stuff [global network of campaigns against fossil fuels], which was really cool.'

Your medium is photography and you create your own images. Do you find that this has a more direct effect on young people and gets your message across?
'Yeah, definitely. I think imagery is like a universal language and people can take their own ideas from it and then create their stuff from that, and I think that's more powerful than words. But also I'm not very good with words – as you can tell from this interview!'

Same here, I can't fucking talk half the time.
'That's why my work is mostly visual. But it's also important that people have something physical to see, because climate change is so invisible.'

So what's your favourite glacier and why?
'I've actually only ever been to one glacier, which is probably my favourite for that reason: the Sólheim glacier in Iceland. It was actually quite sad because we were walking for ages and there was no glacier for a mile or two – that's how far it had melted. But when we finally got to it, it was amazing.'

Do you like Fox's Glacier Mints?
'Yeah, I do.'

Cool!

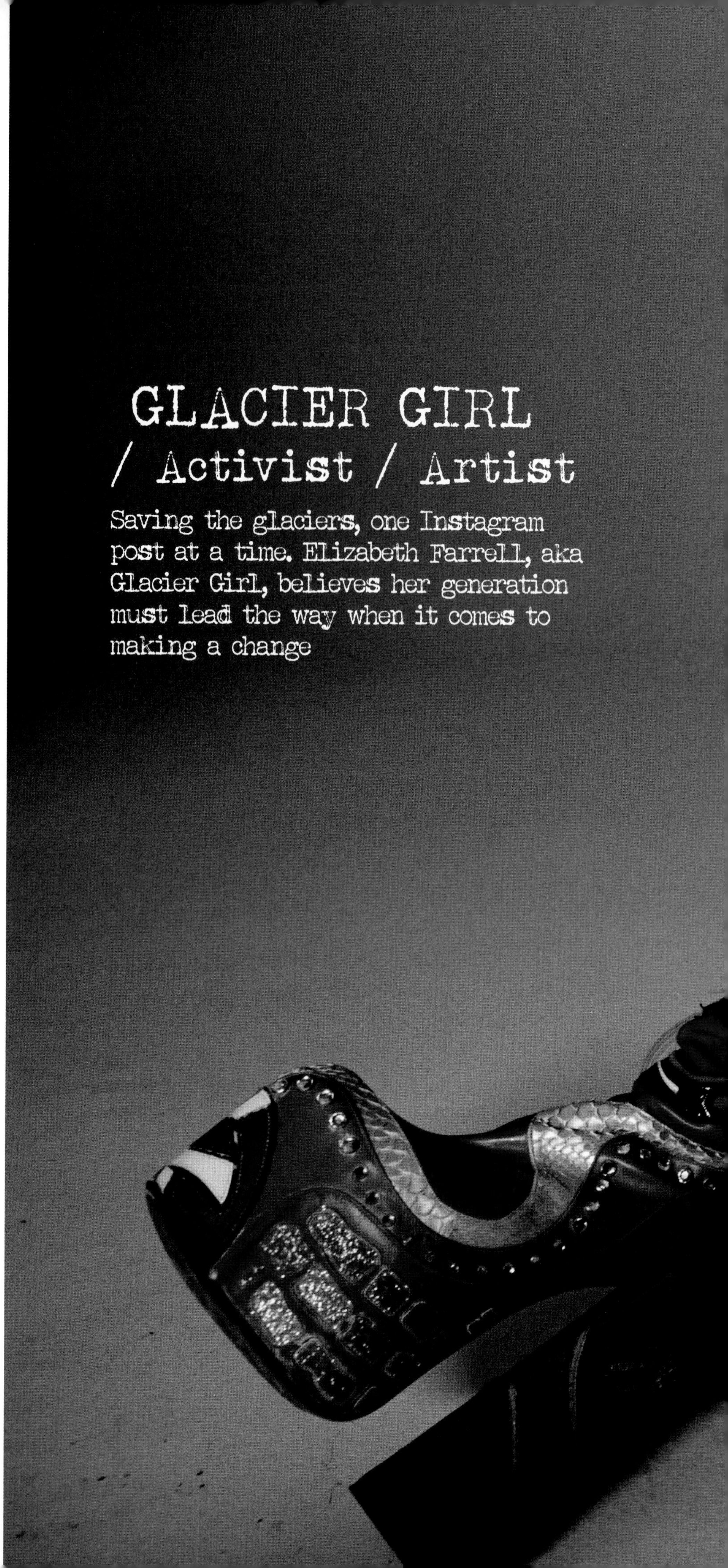

Elizabeth wears cotton and silk puff-sleeved military jacket by DSQUARED; *red mesh dress (just seen by* BALLY; *pink sequin skirt by* MANISH ARORA; *python appliqué platform boots by* MARC JACOBS; *fishnet tights by* WOLFORD

FAVOURITE SONG ?

Incubus 'Drive'.

FAVOURITE BAND ?

Kings of Convenience

FAVOURITE BOOK ?

I'm reading Giovanni's Room by James Baldwin

FAVOURITE FILM ?

Fantastoc Planet

KHALIF DIOUF / Singer / Producer

You might know him as Lelf. But a tough time in his love life has seen him change his style, his output and his name

Writer PAUL FLYNN

Since the release of his debut album *Riot Boi* in 2015, Khalif Diouf, the artist formerly known as Le1f, has been a busy boi. Busy mostly getting his heart broken and re-evaluating everything he wants to do with his musical life. 'It's Le1f no more,' he says certainly. Conjoined at the media hip into a threefold queer hip hop assault with Mykki Blanco and Zebra Katz, Khalif looked to be on the edge of a major global breakthrough two years ago. 'It never really was my intention to be a rapper,' he says now. It certainly wasn't his intention to be part of any movement. 'We were all friends before, but it was never meant to be a thing. Just because we did rap and we were gay people, that made it such a thing to talk about. I want to move away from the expectations of that.'

This spring Khalif will launch again, shrouded in a more interior aspect of his musicology. He's going to be the new Adele. 'Kind of!' he says, exploding with laughter. Here's the story. Just after *Riot Boi* dropped, Khalif fell in love, hard. 'I had a tumultuous, very fast-up/fast-down relationship that ended up in a lot of betrayals and triangles and all sorts of fun things.' He can just about laugh about it now. At the time, clearly it was terrible. 'I still have respect for him, so it's not about airing it right now. But I met him and some other friends and over the course of 12 months I went from thinking they were the people that were going to be in my life forever to realising they were people I could never see again, ever.' Some journey, eh? 'If all this emotional turmoil is happening in my life, I need to turn this into something other than really dumb tweets. Maybe I should make a break-up EP and start singing.'

Khalif says he's always had an emo side. 'Incubus's 'Drive' is literally one of my top-five songs ever, always has been.' Now he has begun to let it out. He recently hit the artistic danger zone of 27 years of age. 'The Saturn's Return, whatever they call it. And it's not as if I'm famous enough to die, so I have to live through this bullshit and make a record about it. You know?' Getting used to his singing voice has been about learning whether he has the musical tool to tell his heartbreak tale truthfully. 'Yeah, barely. It's interesting to see what my voice can do and what it cannot, but then that's always been part of my process.' Yet from therein, great art came. Who wouldn't give the sound police Ian Curtis over Alicia Keys? 'Actually,' nods Khalif, smiling.

The other big progression from hip hop to alt.pop is Khalif's lyrical skills. As a rapper, he says, 'I practiced my Amanda Blank verses so that I could rap as fast as her.' He secretly harboured the loftier artistic ambitions which recent relationship traumas allowed him to access. 'It was always supposed to be something deeper and more personal to me,' he says. Allowing himself to write more bleakly and obliquely has let through something more honest. 'All the events that are documented in the lyrics. It just pushed my pen to be more esoteric, which I was always afraid of doing.'

The album is titled *Vista En Nu*. 'It's totally fixed my outlook on life. As a gay teenager with my free adolescent voice, it was painful to hear myself say some Björk-type shit. So I decided I was going to be a rapper so that I could make money making art.' The braggadocio of the genre didn't suit him, ultimately. 'The funk I was in before the relationship and in the relationship... This feels like an ego death album. It feels like the right place to be.'

Khalif wears black trench coat and cotton and chainmail trousers both by BARRAGÁN; *black whale-net tights (worn as sleeves) by* WOLFORD; *necklace by* CHARLES JEFFREY; *vintage belts (worn around wrists) all from* ROKIT

WHO ARE YOU THE BIGGEST FAN OF ? Björk Hey girl :)

Tyler wears metallic top and trousers both by DROME; *metal earrings by* ALEXANDER WANG

WHO ARE YOU THE BIGGEST FAN OF ? Sia

SINCE WHEN ? 2009

WHAT FIRST ATTRACTED YOU TO.......
Her album Some People Have Real Problems

WHAT IS YOUR FAVOURITE THING ABOUT THEM ?
Her art and her heart

YOUR FAVOURITE FAN ITEM..
a video she recorded for me

HOW HAVE THEY INFLUENCED YOUR LIFE ? Her music has gotten me through many rough years and her artistry constantly inspires me.

HAVE YOU MET YOUR HERO ? yes

IF YES ELABORATE..... The first time we met, I just happened to run into her outside of a restaurant.

TYLER FORD / Activist

The Glee Project participant who has created a life beyond the reductive binaries of gender

Writer PAUL FLYNN

For anyone confused by the rapidly changing boundaries of gender in the second decade of the 21st century so far, Tyler Ford would recommend reading Janet Mock's *Redefining Realness*. Tyler identifies as agender. 'Agender is genderless – I have no gender,' explains Tyler, who consequently uses the pronouns 'they', 'them' and 'their'. 'I don't feel tied to being any specific way, any specific thing, any specific type of person. I don't identify certain traits with certain genders. Some people would say, "Oh, Tyler is dressed very masculine today" or "feminine today" or "neutral today" and I'm like, but what does that mean? What does it mean that a skirt is feminine or that certain gestures are feminine or masculine, why is "strength" masculine? I cut everything down. I am who I am. I have all these different traits and they are not tied to gender.'

Freshly dropped out of Vanderbilt University in Nashville, Tyler was a part of the smart search-for-a-star initiative *The Glee Project*, in which one lucky auditionee would win a seven-episode narrative arc in Ryan Murphy's all-singing, all-dancing TV show. Tyler moved to LA afterwards and began a career that now involves LGBTQ awareness seminars and speeches at US universities, performance art and an increasingly arresting writing portfolio. They are keeping temporarily schtum about a book on the go that already has agency representation.

'It changed my entire life,' Tyler says of *The Glee Project*. 'Not just being on TV but being in that world and in that workspace and meeting the people I met on that show. I was out on TV as a trans person. I've sort of only known how to be open and be in public, it's just that now I have a bigger audience. It wasn't that difficult for me. I've always been the kind of person to go after what I want, and that combined with my work and who I know has just opened a lot of doors.'

In 2013, Tyler read the entirety of *The Rookie Yearbook*, the annual print anthology of the online magazine aimed at teenage girls, in a bookstore at home in Florida. Shortly afterwards, Tyler went to a signing at the same store by the book's editor-in-chief, Tavi Gevinson. 'I was like, listen, I don't have a copy of your book because I don't have enough money right now, but I read it cover to cover and I really want to write for you. I said, do you have any trans writers? And at the time they didn't and [Tavi] was like, email me with your writing samples. And the next week I was writing for them.' Tavi, Tyler says, has been a good, encouraging friend and mentor. 'It was very serendipitous. Because I wasn't a teenage girl, I hadn't read *Rookie* because it wasn't meant for me, but I've always worked with teenagers since I was a teenager. So I read the yearbook and thought, this is what I want to do.'

Tyler says their utopia is not an agendered world. 'No, my utopia is everyone gets to define their own gender and their own self, and other people don't get to define it for them or label it for them.' This is a new dawn, a new landscape for millennials to own. 'It scares a lot of people, for sure. It's not the only reason but a lot of the reason there is pushback against non-binary gender people is because people are really scared to look at themselves and be like, well, if they're agender what does that mean about me? What does that mean about my gender? Is my gender valid? Am I even a man or a woman? It's a lot to think about.' Tyler says the world can constantly feel stacked against you as a non-binary person. 'I wouldn't call myself a victim, but I am on the receiving end of a lot of hate and a lot of vitriol and a lot of violence. But I am always going to be myself, no matter what.'

MAYOWA NICHOLAS / Model

Since winning an Elite modelling competition in Nigeria two years ago, Mayowa has acquired a loyal following that occasionally borders on the obsessive. Her number one fan, however, 'is really nice', she says. 'I don't know her personally, but I'm sure she's nice'

Mayowa wears archive coat adorned with buttons, crystals and fabric patches by VIKTOR & ROLF COUTURE; *sequin collared dress by* OLYMPIA LE TAN; *yellow patent leather bathing cap by* MIU MIU; *metal and ribbon earrings by* DSQUARED

Mayowa wears hooded sweatshirt by VETEMENTS X CHAMPION; *pink gold, yellow gold and white gold Juste Un Clou rings, pink gold Panthère de Cartier ring with tsavorite garnets and onyx, and yellow gold Cactus ring with diamonds all by* CARTIER

NAME: MAYOWA NICHOLAS **AGE:** 18

WHO ARE YOU THE BIGGEST FAN OF ?

RIHANNA

SINCE WHEN ?

PON DE REPLAY

WHAT FIRST ATTRACTED YOU TO.......

HER MUSIC AND HER STYLE

WHAT IS YOUR FAVOURITE THING ABOUT THEM ?

HER OUTFITS. HER STREETSTYLE

HMLTD / Band

From left: Duke wears leather suit by HAIDER ACKERMANNN; *blouse by* ZADIG & VOLTAIRE; *earrings by* ELISABETTA FRANCHI; *belt by* MAISON MARGIELA; *bangle (attached to belt) by* DSQUARED; *necklace (in front pocket) by* MULBERRY. *Nico wears suit and handbag both by* VIVIENNE WESTWOOD; *helmet from* COSTUME STUDIO; *scarf (tied to bag) by* HAIDER ACKERMANN; *necklace by* ELISABETTA FRANCHI; *socks by* ITEM M6; *leather shoes (just seen) by* BRIONI. *Achilleas wears armour from* COSTUME STUDIO; *trainers by* PRADA; *nose-ring Achilleas's own. Henry wears catsuit by* PAM HOGG; *earring by* MATTY BOVAN X TATTY DEVINE; *platform boots by* BALENCIAGA. *Zac wears suit by* VIVIENNE WESTWOOD; *shirt by* GUCCI; *earring by* DSQUARED; *ring by* RODARTE; *vintage tie Zac's own. James wears Seastorm suit by* GUCCI; *leather collar with pendant by* MATTY BOVAN; *bondage belt with collar and harness from* COSTUME STUDIO

HMLTD

The international troupe formerly known as Happy Meal make music without borders for digital natives

Writer PAUL FLYNN

Three men in aubergine lipstick are sitting in their recording studio discussing the nature of art, music and the digital world. Welcome to HMLTD, a new band with 21st-century brand values, invested with some of the urgency of old punk and a whole new sound that can shift on a sixpence from subdued introversion to all-out anarchy. HMLTD look like pop stars should look: strange and sexual. With an average age of 20 they are possessed of a steely line in quiet confidence that can teeter toward the finest edges of precociousness. 'We didn't come here to talk about sex and drugs and rock'n'roll,' says singer Henry. HMLTD buy most of their clothes from the internet and the women's department of charity shops. 'I am not about to reveal my sources,' he quips when asked which ones.

If you are looking for impish tribalism in a new act, HMLTD satisfy on every count. Their incendiary live shows have taken enough chaotic and frequently semi-naked tangents to bear comparison with Fat White Family – though while FWF are demarked by their very particular, frantic testosterone impulse, there is something more ambiguous about HMLTD. There are no intra-band relationships. 'No, actually,' says Henry. 'It ends here.' 'Obviously we are attracted to one another, otherwise we wouldn't be able to create together,' says Duke, the strident Frenchman who acts as Henry's guitar-playing wingman. 'But if there was anything more than this it would probably implode.' They are currently spending 12 hours a day perfecting the material they will send into the world. A taster calling card, 'Is This What You Wanted?', dropped at the end of last year to growing online fervour, a song in several movements that skips from languor to livid at the pulse of a heartbeat.

HMLTD began life as the more provocatively titled Happy Meal 18 months ago. Their six-strong cast met at parties facilitated by their mutual friend Honey, one of what one suspects will be a litany of bit-part players in their myth-making story should they get to fulfil their dreams. 'We want to force a new cultural movement,' says Henry, bluntly, 'to change the state of culture as we know it.' He sees an open door for a British pop band invested with ideas, a strong sense of personal identity, a sideline in philosophy and an astute political mind. 'That ambition isn't in any way connected to our sense of pride,' he says. 'It's not facilitating our egos.'

The original name, they say, was not changed on account of interference from the McDonald's corporation. They didn't choose Happy Meal for derisory reasons ('we're not interested in irony') but rather for its implications of a culture of consumption that interests them, the changing nature of appetites in a digital age. 'There are two levels of personality now,' says Duke. 'The physical sphere, where we are right now as we speak, and the virtual sphere, where people have avatars. We're all lucky to be digital natives; that displacement of the personality is something we want to play a lot on with HMLTD. We embrace the fact that information gets out in microseconds. It's an inherent part of the 21st century. Consumption is different. The collage of media and art is new.'

For Henry, the old rock band is part of an anathema from the pre-digital age, one that the band intend to forcibly disrupt. 'That 20th-century idea of the city is being eroded,' he notes, 'and the possibilities that are being opened up by virtual spheres are changing. The communities that makes possible are really exciting.' The first time he saw a pop idea presented to his complete satisfaction, he says refreshingly, was Lady Gaga's 'Bad Romance': a song, idea and arresting visual presentation that hit him hard at 13. 'Fuck,' he says, still visibly astonished by the power of what pop can do to a young mind. 'The Haus of Gaga, the amount of curation that went into the staging, the performances, the outfits – it was a complete vision. She had totalitarian control over everything. It was so ambitious.'

With HMLTD, there is a written manifesto, like The Smiths and Manic Street Preachers before them. It accompanies them to rehearsal every day. Because they are made up of British, French and Greek members, they have a new target to rail against. They are interested in internationalism as the world retreats behind proscriptive borders. 'We're all politically engaged as individuals but our concern is to not be pedagogical,' he says of the UK's decision to abandon a peace process and leave the European Union. 'It can be quite tiring. We'd rather describe than tell.' For Duke, a Parisian in London measuring his dreams against music, there is a more sanguine aspect to Brexit. 'We will make it work. Because we have to.'

ISABELLA PESCHARDT • @Ibellapeschardt

SARAH SNYDER • @sarahfuckingsnyder

RUBINA DYAN • @rubinadyan

CHIARA SCELSI • @chiarascelsi

Juicy

Juicy
Couture
Juicy Couture
BLACK LABEL
los angeles

WHO ARE YOU THE BIGGEST FAN OF ? well, I Like this one Anime Character. Mink. He's from a visual Novel game called "BL"

SINCE WHEN ?

Since 2013 I think...

WHAT FIRST ATTRACTED YOU TO.......

Definitely his presence Dramatical Murder

WHAT IS YOUR FAVOURITE THING ABOUT THEM ?

His Cold Personality

YOUR FAVOURITE FAN ITEM..

A Few things, wall scroll, Plushie, figurines..

HOW HAVE THEY INFLUENCED YOUR LIFE ?

I guess he influenced my will to Cosplay

HAVE YOU MET YOUR HERO ?

I am/ my hero

IF YES ELABORATE.....

Cosplay!!!

FAVOURITE SONG ?

Rev 22-20

FAVOURITE BAND ?

Puscifer

CASIL McARTHUR / Model

The nature-loving barista from Colorado who has walked for Coach and Calvin Klein

Writer PAUL FLYNN

'At the Inkwell, we're very serious about making coffee,' says 17-year-old Casil McArthur. Casil splits his time between home in Estes Park, Colorado, where he is a barista, and modelling shifts in New York. Casil doesn't want to tell you how beautiful Estes Park is, in case it spoils it for locals. 'Because people will move there and I'm like, don't. Please don't move to Colorado. It's right next to the Rocky Mountain National Park and basically there are about 17 trees to a person. It's so nice.' He feels at home in nature. 'I prefer getting lost on a hike to being lost in a city full of people – that's really stressful to me.'

Casil has been shot by Collier Schorr, Craig McDean and, in one arresting editorial study for *W* magazine, by Steven Meisel, which made the pages of the local paper back home. 'I panicked about that,' he says, 'because Estes is a conservative town where if one person knows something, everybody knows. I want Estes to be my safe place.' Casil is a trans man. 'I'm afraid of hate crimes. That's never happened before but there are a lot of kids in the school that just aren't good people. At the same time, I can't be scared.'

He began modelling at 12, when his mum signed him to a local agency. 'I was modelling as a girl up until last year when I quit modelling because I had to take time away for myself.' In 2015, he re-signed to Soul, New York. 'I just told my agents I will not model unless I can model as a guy. That's it. Sorry.' He says the agency has been 'amazing' in nurturing and incubating their young charge's public identity. 'I could not ask for more. Now I'm this really outgoing person, but I struggle because I'm horribly socially awkward. I'm trying my best, though.'

Casil is, in fact, a disarmingly candid and fluent conversationalist. It was as a barista that he was first offered the warm hand of inclusion and friendship towards his transition. At the time he was working at the coffee counter of The Stanley, the Colorado hotel that *The Shining* was based on. 'My boss Jim was the most amazing person,' he says. 'My co-worker told me, in confidence, he said, "I hope you realise that Jim would literally fight for you if anybody ever tried to disrespect you for who you are."' Sometimes the kindness of strangers comes from the most unusual quarters. 'Jim is Catholic. He's religious. But he doesn't let that stop him. He's super-old and sadly he has a whole bunch of illnesses that good people don't deserve. But he looked after me.' For Casil, that one act of personal generosity was enough to make him want to strive ahead and spread a bit of goodness himself. 'Having a part-time job is good because on my name-tag I get to have my chosen name. So people in the town get to relearn who I am, as Casil.' So far, so good.

Casil was delighted when the trailblazing trans model Hari Nef got in touch with him on Instagram for a few reassuring words. 'She's amazing,' he says. He may yet follow her lead, putting the model into role-modelism. 'It's something I know I can carry well. I think people think this is a job that's easy to do and it isn't. Add being trans on top of that and it brings a whole bunch of other fuckery you don't want to deal with. Look, if I could have lived my life as a cis male I would have, but I couldn't. And the thing is, if I don't speak out for the trans community, who's going to? Who's going to be the person who teaches everybody else?'

Casil wears transparent and red plastic and cotton trench coat, transparent plastic top and cotton shorts all by COMME DES GARÇONS HOMME PLUS; *flannel shirt by* RALPH LAUREN; *vintage white ruffle top (just seen) from* NEW YORK VINTAGE; *socks by* FALKE; *black lace-up leather shoes by* DIOR HOMME

CASIL

No one owns you, your fears don't own you.
You own your self. Do whatever you can to be happy.

BETSY / Siren

Betsy wears diamanté bandeau top, skirt, fringed collar and multicoloured charm (attached to belt) all by MATTY BOVAN; *jewelled rainbow drop earrings and Afghan-hound fire-pearl necklace both by* MIMI WADE X VICKI SARGE; *metal bracelets by* BALMAIN; *black and gold leather flower arm cuff by* LOEWE; *jewel-edged belt by* DSQUARED

#TOUCH IT
www.replayjeans.com

BETSY

The Welsh belter of a singer-songwriter with a voice that can move mountains who abandoned Balenciaga to follow her first love

Writer MURRAY HEALY

'I don't hold back in general, darling,' declares Betsy, who is perched on a stool at the bar, as striking as a supermodel and clutching a big glass of white wine, her nails painted the same vivid shade of blood red as her lipstick. It is midday and she is recounting a recent interview she did with the BBC. 'We went out for cocktails. So by the time we started the interview I was like, *WOOOOO...*'

The full-disclosure policy that the singer-songwriter observes in her interviews is embraced even more enthusiastically in her songs. 'All of them are autobiographical,' she says, and most of them touch on tragedy. 'Lost and Found', for example, is about a boy Betsy fell in love with at 16. 'Rosie' is about a family friend who died in her teens. She's slightly hesitant when it comes to revealing the person who inspired last November's belter of a love-regret anthem, 'Wanted More'. 'Um... A Latin supermodel. That'd be the best way to describe him.' She was going out with him for a couple of years until 'it turned out he was married. So that song's about having a relationship and wondering why there's always a distance between you. "Oh, is it because you're married and you've got a child? Oh fuck, yeah – *that'll be why*!" I can't write unless there's something I have to get off my chest. This sounds so fucking pretentious, but I do actually have to feel the emotion of it when I'm telling the story.'

Consequently there's a torch-song intensity to the emotional range of her compositions, but Betsy always emerges sounding steely and determined and ultimately victorious. 'I see myself as quite a ballsy woman, you see,' she says. 'I wouldn't let anybody make me downtrodden. I suppose my songs are the most fragile bit of me, and music is the only place in my life where I get that out. It's like a therapy session.' Writing 'Fair', a tragic song about an unmendable love affair ('I know it ain't fair / To hold on to a love... That's no longer there') left her 'fucking bawling. I thought, well fuck me – this situation can't go on any more, clearly!'

Before she devoted her life full-time to music, Betsy had a flourishing career in fashion. She left her BA course at Saint Martins to assist head designer Alistair Carr at Balenciaga under Nicolas Ghesquière. 'It was a sensational job.' But music was her true love, and she'd take the Eurostar back to London to sing at open-mic nights. After failing to be talent-spotted, she knew she had to make a choice. 'That was difficult. 'Cause it's not a shit-hole, Balenciaga, is it? But I always wanted to be a musician more than a designer.' Then one year into her stint there, Nicolas and Alistair moved on from the brand. 'At that point I had the offer to go to... various places. It would have been absolutely sensational. But I just had to do the music.'

She moved back home to Wales, taught herself GarageBand, recorded a demo on a computer in her brother's bedroom, burnt some CDs, stuck a selfie snapped on PhotoBooth on the cover and sent them to a mailing list she'd compiled from a supposedly authoritative music industry directory. 'It went out to everyone and his dog – and nobody gave a shit.' Through a relative of a friend in London, though, her demo finally fell into the hands of the men who now manage her. They gave her a modest fee and told her to devote the next six weeks to creating more music. 'So I went to live in my brother's caravan. The shittiest caravan you've ever seen in your life.' The walls were caked in the orange gloop that condenses from frying fat. 'I spent three days scraping that off – never mind the rest of the shit I had to clean up. It was still horrible: no water, no heating. But I knuckled down and wrote what is the majority of what will be the album. And from those demos I got record deals with Columbia, Warner Bros and Warner/Chappell.' Her tracks have since been treated to an upgrade, which included a spell in the studio with a 19-piece string section to ramp up the melodrama. Betsy was beside herself with joy. 'There I was with the best cellist in the fucking world. And she's playing my song written in a fucking caravan! I mean, Jesus.'

Growing up on a farm in Nevern in Pembrokeshire, she was always surrounded by music. 'In Wales there's music everywhere, so I've always sung since I was tiny-tiny, just school stuff, and my dad and uncle were in a band, too.' One of her earliest memories is watching them singing and playing guitar around a fire on a camping holiday. 'They were quite hippy-dippy in those days. So I think that's where the obsession came from. My dad liked all kinds of shit: classical, Hendrix, Nina Simone, Eighties, whatever. Very broad. And that's how I am today.' You can hear the breadth of her taste in her music, from Aretha Franklin to Fleetwood Mac to Massive Attack.

Her interest in style emerged a few years later. When she was 10 she put together a homemade fashion magazine to impress her brother's godfather when he came to dinner. 'I remember thinking, "I'm gonna show him," 'cause he made underwear and baby clothes for Marks & Spencer.' In her teens she started paying attention to fashion magazines. But the biggest influence on her style, which she describes as 'trashy opulent', comes from the previous generations of women in her family. 'They're from the Valleys, a mining community, and they're very strong, feisty women. Hard women, but still incredibly glamorous.' She paints a picture of her nan at 95: 'in a pink velour tracksuit, pumps covered in diamanté, knuckledusters, giant nails, jet-black hair – she was still dyeing it – and loads of gold jewellery. She'd sit there in the kitchen in this tiny little Valleys house looking like an utter diva with this cig on, and she would not tap the ash off till she'd finished it. They were all glamorous women and it was all too much, and I think that's what drew me to fashion: that excess and drama and glamour. Which also drew me to music, 'cause you have it there as well.'

Shirley Bassey is another big inspiration. 'She looks a lot like my grandmother, she's from the same area and her story's very similar: overly glamorous and very tough.' There's an early performance of 'This Is My Life' that Betsy likes to watch on YouTube: 'It's in black and white and she's got all these violins behind her. I think of that every time before I go on stage. When she's singing it, she's meaning it.' Tina Turner is another favourite. 'When she did "Rolling on the River" with Beyoncé...' begins Betsy, recalling their 2008 Grammys performance. 'I mean, Beyoncé is absolutely sensational, doing a fucking out-of-this-world-class job. But nobody can deny that Tina is singing like her soul's on fire.' This is what it's all about for Betsy. 'When I write, do you see, that's the thing, that's why I have to feel it' – she thumps her clenched fist against her heart – 'feel it coming out of me like a flame.'

ELLEN ROSA / Model

This Brazilian beauty's biggest fan is definitely her mum. Even when Ellen posts a picture where she's 'not looking her best', she explains, her mum will, without fail, comment, 'Wow, that's beautiful!'

WHO ARE YOU THE BIGGEST FAN OF ?

My Mom

SINCE WHEN ?

This 17 years

WHAT FIRST ATTRACTED YOU TO.......

Her character, Her strength and Her sincerity

WHAT IS YOUR FAVOURITE THING ABOUT THEM ?

Her heart

HOW HAVE THEY INFLUENCED YOUR LIFE ?

Always fight for what you want

FAVOURITE SONG ?

Gunslinger from Avenged Sevenfold

FAVOURITE BAND ?

Papa Roach

FAVOURITE BOOk ?

A Rosa Da Meia Noite

FAVOURITE FILM ?

Barbie and Pirates of The Caribbean

FAVOURITE SMELL ?

Coffee

FAVOURITE COLOUR ?

Black

WHO IS YOUR BIGGEST FAN:

My mom and my sister

Ellen wears jersey gazar embellished coat by PRADA; *yellow earring by* SIMONE ROCHA

WHO ARE YOU THE BIGGEST FAN OF ? Neil DeGrasse Tyson

SINCE WHEN ? The first time I went to the museum of natural history as a kid

WHAT FIRST ATTRACTED YOU TO....... My obsession with space and the cosmos

WHAT IS YOUR FAVOURITE THING ABOUT THEM ? how he makes big ideas accessable to people from all walks of life

YOUR FAVOURITE FAN ITEM.. Cosmos!

HOW HAVE THEY INFLUENCED YOUR LIFE ? expanded my inner nerd

LAURA HARRIER / Actor

Starring as Spider-Man's love interest in her first major film role has launched her into the obsessive world of comic book fandom

Writer HARRIET VERNEY

Fans come in varying degrees of devotion. There's the obsessive, the weird, the flattering, the stalkers, the imitators and the downright odd. Then there are the hardcore Comic Con fans, and they are in a league of their own. This is exactly what 26-year-old model-turned-actress Laura Harrier discovered recently when she arrived at her first Comic Con convention in San Diego. Chicago-born Laura and her fellow cast members of Marvel's new film *Spider-Man: Homecoming* surprised an 8,000-strong crowd when they made an impromptu visit to the annual get-together of science fiction, comics and movie fans. Flying in straight from filming in Atlanta, Laura was thrown in at the deep end and taken straight to Marvel Camp. 'I go into this green room and there's every famous person I've ever seen,' she says. 'Tilda Swinton, Rachel McAdams, Chiwetel Ejiofor. I started crying.'

Laura plays Liz Allan, the love interest in the first of a new Spider-Man series, which doesn't remake the previous films but instead starts again from scratch with full creative control for Marvel. Laura says it's a relief she isn't playing your typical giggling high-school girl. 'To be a woman of colour playing the love interest in a movie like this – that's really exciting.'

Her co-stars were pretty exciting too. Brit actor Tom Holland plays Spider-Man: 'He is lovely, such a sweetheart.' Do they snog? 'I can't tell you. I've signed an NDA!' Another cast-mate was Disney pop star Zendaya. 'I love her; she was my bud. We'd be hanging out and strangers would just run up to her sobbing. I'd be like, "Oh right, you're like really famous." It's crazy!'

Born in Chicago, Laura's family moved to Evanstan when she was seven. 'It was a really cool place to grow up. It's very liberal and diverse: racially, socioeconomically, in all ways.' A role in a science-fiction film like *Spider-Man* seems fitting for Laura, who as a child was obsessed by space: instead of posters on her wall, she had a galaxy of glow-in-the-dark stars stuck to the ceiling above her bed. 'I went to the planetarium and my mind was blow. I was fascinated by how infinite the universe is.' She says Neil deGrasse Tyson (scientist, Nobel prize winner and director of TV show *Cosmos*) is someone she is a huge fan of. 'He's the first major black astrophysicist and he built his way up to being one of the top scientists in the world. He is one of those people who I would kinda freak out over if I met.'

A move to New York presented her with a chance to do some modelling, but after a short stint she realised it wasn't what she wanted to do at all. 'I loved film and always loved movies, but I didn't think that could be a viable career.' But not long after leaving acting school she landed a role in an HBO pilot, which just so happened to be directed by Steve McQueen. 'He was brilliant and it was eye-opening. It definitely led me to be doing what I'm doing now.' The pilot never made it to a series but McQueen made a big impression on the young actress. What was the best advice he ever gave her? 'Don't be boring. You can be anything you want, just don't be boring.'

Laura cites Robin Wright, Viola Davis and Meryl Streep as some of the women she looks up to for their acting careers. 'There are so many strong women who carry their careers and go beyond the ingénue or the pretty girl or whatever. Not enough, but so many.' Is there a dream role she has her heart set on? 'Yes. But I don't want to jinx that, though.' Something tells me, with the way things are going for Laura, she'll probably get it.

Laura wears green crayon-drawing blazer by PAUL SMITH

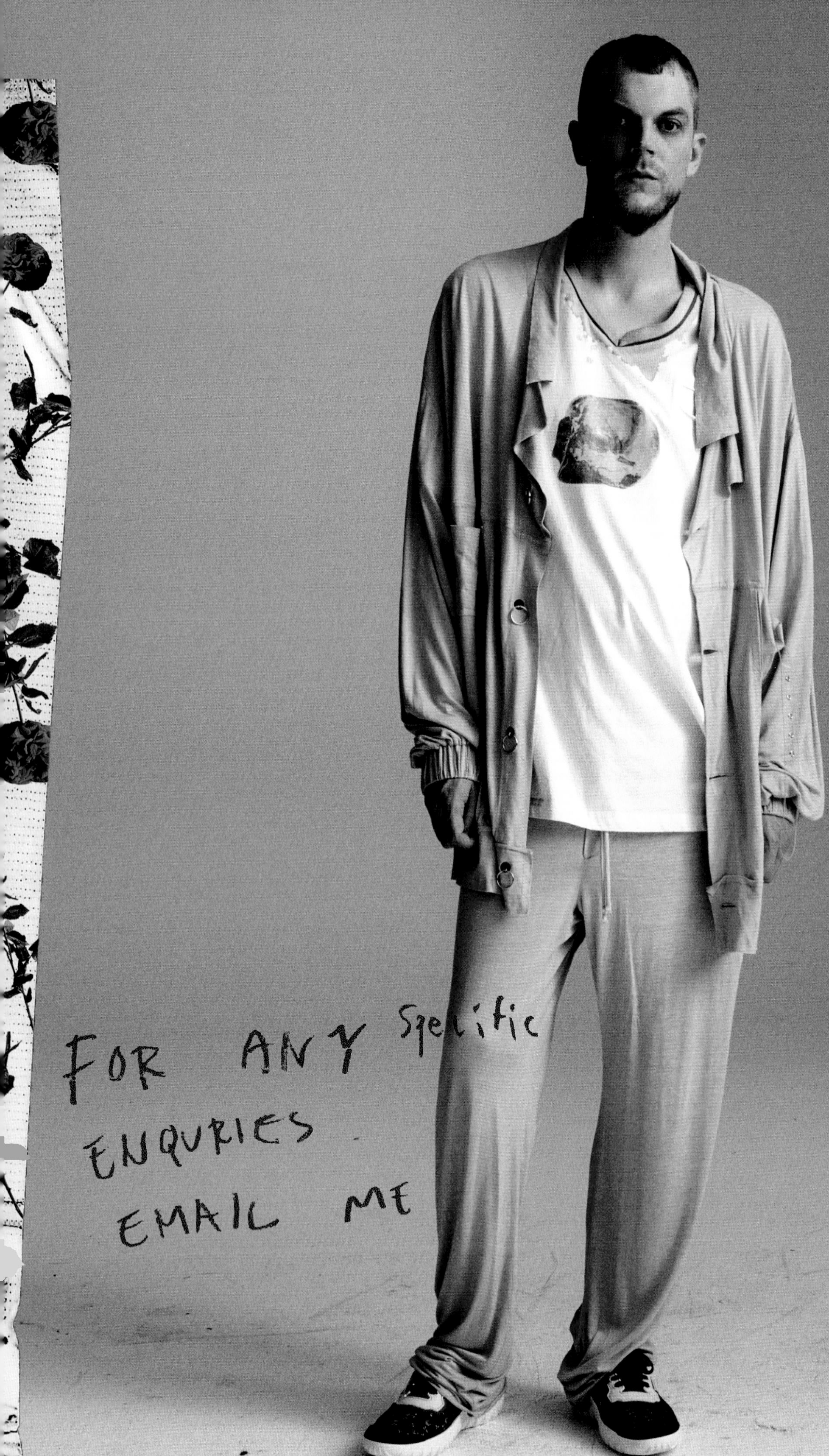
FOR ANY Specific
ENQURIES
EMAIL ME

Per wears green jersey pyjama tracksuit and Coffee T-shirt all by PER GÖTESSON; *clear plastic belt (worn in pocket) by* MIU MIU; *patterned trainers by* PRADA

PER GÖTESSON / Designer

The overnight success from Sweden whose clothes play with scale: his attitude might be easygoing but his autonomy is non-negotiable

Writer MURRAY HEALY

It was last May when Per Götesson got the call telling him he'd been selected for his Lonodn menswear week debut as part of the MAN show. The bad news was that there was barely a month to go for him to put together his first collection. Even trickier, he was still an MA student at the Royal College of Art, and the MAN show was taking place the day after his graduate presentation. 'I thought, OK, this is going to be really stressful,' says Per. Luckily the RCA then decided to stage a mammoth group show in an abandoned hotel in Hyde Park, requiring each student to submit only a single look. So he calmly repurposed his MA collection for his MAN debut, holding back one look for the RCA show. Then as soon as that was over he left his fellow graduates as they partied and headed straight back to the studio.

As he talks in his quiet, understated way about the 24 hours that propelled him into the international spotlight of London fashion, Per's tall, lean frame is sprawled almost horizontal on a huge sofa. 'I'm quite an easygoing person,' he says. His collection proved to be as relaxed and free of glitzy histrionics as he is: simple cotton and denim jackets and trousers and jersey tops, featuring raw edges and coffee stains, and hung with key chains. The word I'm trying to avoid here is 'wearable'. 'Most of it is very... *wardrobe*, I guess you could call it,' says Per. What stood out was its eccentric mix of oversized and tight cuts, the least 'wardrobe' piece being his extremely large jeans, each multipleated leg containing a curtain's worth of fabric. 'That was an experiment in attraction and materiality. But people bought those too! They are clothes to be worn and to work in. They are clothes I would wear to the studio. But that's maybe because they are for me.' Per designs his clothes for his own body, fitting the toiles on himself as he goes along, as well as for his own taste. 'For me it's all about attraction. It's important to feel attracted, even sexually, to your work. So of course it's about yourself. I'm not saying that I'm taking the way I dress and proposing for others to dress the same – it's more about fits and proportions that I like. I have this way of dressing, of how things fit and sit, and that is a big part of the process. It's not just about referencing something classical.'

Growing up in a small town in Sweden, he always had a 'weird relationship' with clothes. 'My first real boyfriend was very interested in fashion,' he says, but it was 'fashion' in the sense of 'you should wear this blazer to go to this sort of occasion', and this was not how Per thought about dressing. 'I never had any hierarchies about style or self-expression, so from five or six I did all these weird things. You know, like Tesco bags? I used to do them as a swimsuit. Maybe this is nothing special. But I was always experimenting.' He'd wear outfits all of one colour and paint his nails to match, and dye his hair, and draw what might be described as fashion looks, without knowing what those were. 'When I was six I'd draw girls in polo-necked dresses and Dr Martens boots and hair – what do you call it?' He gestures a centre parting. 'I remember drawing it and thinking, this is the best thing I've ever seen.' His older sister, who's six years older and was into Nirvana, was a big stylistic influence, as was German MTV. 'This was a small part of my life and you move on. I wouldn't say it has shaped my identity. I imagine in interviews its importance gets blown up. But I guess it still has significance.'

He did a degree in fashion at Beckmans College in Stockholm, where the emphasis was on developing technical skills. 'You can train to become a pattern-cutter for H&M. If you want to do your own thing, that's valued too – but you're on your own.' Per wanted to do his own thing, so he came to London to do his Masters. 'Here it's much more about the personality of the designer and it's seen as a business; it's an export, I guess.' The teaching methods at the RCA came as a surprise, though. 'My tutor was so dedicated and taught me so much. But for a Swedish person it's very hard because you're not used to people being rude to you. So you're shocked when they scream at you. Then you realise, oh they don't actually go home at night and think about this – it's just a tool. So then you feel betrayed. And then you're reflecting on this instead of acting, and then they get angry with you because you're being so Swedish and sensitive.' He doesn't go back to Sweden often. 'I've always been a person who feels quite comfortable being rootless. For me that's a freedom.'

Running his own label is definitely his best option, he reckons: 'I am very unmanageable, I think.' He had this confirmed while working as a design assistant for Cheap Monday under Ann-Sofie Beck after graduating in Stockholm. 'It was a really great experience. But you feel bad that you can't do your job and get fired, even though you know you are good and everything's going well.' Hang on – you got fired? 'Yeah. We had a great time but she said, "You need to go and do your MA." I understand now. Maybe I am always going to be unmanageable.'

Per currently works from a big studio in Seven Sisters that he shares with Mimi Wade and KTZ's Marjan Pejoski. He says he's lucky to have his current set-up with the support of the Fashion East-backed MAN initiative, which doesn't impose anyone who might seek to restrict him. He reckons that he might be able to work within a more hierarchical structure some day, but he would have to come to an understanding with his bosses first. 'If you want I can do it, but I will have to remain unmanageable. Otherwise I don't think it will make anybody happy.'

Birgit wears white cotton cape-dress by KRIZIA

Birgit wears printed sequin dress by OLYMPIA LE TAN; *blue patterned platform shoes by* PRADA; *black tights by* FALKE

BIRGIT KOS / Model

Dutch model Birgit, who currently stars underwater in the new Miu Miu campaign, really enjoys outdoor activities such as hiking and snowboarding. She is presently working on her wall-climbing skills at her local sports centre and ultimately hopes to scale mountains

TREMAINE EMORY / Creative

WHO ARE YOU THE BIGGEST FAN OF ? My Mom & Dad
SINCE WHEN ? when I Relised everyone Does not Have family they would be friends with even if they weren't Related
WHAT IS YOUR FAVOURITE THING ABOUT THEM ? They never stop growing as Human beings, parents or as a couple
YOUR FAVOURITE FAN ITEM.. my mothers Red velvet cake
HOW HAVE THEY INFLUENCED YOUR LIFE ? taught me to have an Open mind & Heart. Also to question everything... even what they taught me.
HAVE YOU MET YOUR HERO ? Met the Both July 29th, 1981
FAVOURITE SONG ? It's Always changeing but right now it's Future Free by frank Ocean
FAVOURITE BAND ? R.A.G.U
FAVOURITE BOOK ? The AUTOBiography of miles Davis
FAVOURITE FILM ? The Empire strikes Back
FAVOURITE SMELL ? Fresh popcorn & Butter when yo walk in a movie theater
FAVOURITE COLOUR ? FALL
WHO IS YOUR BIGGEST FAN: my little Brother Torrin Emory

Tremaine wears multilayered coat by JOSEPH; *red oversized fold-up parka (worn over shoulder) by* VETEMENTS X CANADA GOOSE; *light blue Black Bust oversized shirt by* RAF SIMONS; *tracksuit bottoms by* GOSHA RUBCHINSKIY X KAPPA; *leather loafers by* LOEWE

KENYA KINSKI

ERMANNO SCERVINO

TREMAINE BY ACYDE

Renaissance phenomenon Tremaine Emory talks to fellow polymath Acyde Odunlami about how being a fan can kickstart the creative process

Interview ACYDE ODUNLAMI

After moving from New York to London in 2010 to work at the Marc Jacobs store, Tremaine Emory began hosting nights at the secretive club Manero's in Dalston with his co-conspirator Acyde Odunlami. Tremaine has since gone on to work with some of the most exciting names in music. He was a contributor on Frank Ocean's *Boys Don't Cry* magazine, the large-format, limited-edition glossy which accompanied his album *Blonde* last August. He is frequently in contact with the A$AP Rocky Mob, and hosted a raucous Boiler Room night with them, Skepta and Stüssy. Then there are the connections with Kanye, whom Tremaine has been working alongside since September (details TBC thanks to a hefty NDA). In London he's probably best known for the brand that he runs with Acyde, No Vacancy Inn, creating everything from podcasts (soundcloud.com/novacancyinn) and pop-up shops to exhibitions and club nights – even a clothing line that sells in Dover Street Market. Here the two of them sit down over triple Tequilas with two limes to talk about Tremaine's work and influences and the inspirational aspects of revering your idols.

ACYDE: *I'm a big fan of yours for several reasons. Firstly, you never seem hungover even when you are, which is a trick I need to learn. And secondly, you are also truly a gentle giant. That's why so many people like you. When you were growing up, who were you a fan of? And now that you're older, has that changed?*
TREMAINE: 'I was a big fan of anything that encapsulated the idea of adventure. Like George Lucas, who created Star Wars and Indiana Jones, or the comic books I was reading, like Frank Miller's *Sin City*. My parents always had us go on adventures on the weekends. My first adventures were riding my bike from Jamaica, Queens back to my old neighbourhood of Flushing, getting into stuff and then riding back. Then my adventures were going from Jamaica, Queens to Manhattan and hanging out in the city.'

As you grew up, did the nature of your adventures change?
'I think they had to! I've tried to take every opportunity where I don't know what is going to happen. When you called me to do Manero's, I'd never done parties like that – only for my birthday or for whatever girl I was with. I'd done interesting stuff though. I ran a room at the Chelsea Hotel, and when Café Select had just opened I did an ex's birthday party there. But Manero's was my first weekly. I didn't know what to expect, and that was an adventure – you didn't know what would happen.'

It was an adventure in trying to keep it all together! And you're quite adventurous in the way you dress. When I first met you, I knew you were from New York – you had your own sense of style. And I've seen that develop into wearing the craziest Raf [Simons] jumper that Raf has probably ever made. What draws you to that particular way of dressing?
'I think part of it is subconscious – all the magazines I've been reading since I was a kid, all the books, all the movies, interest in all these things... that style is a heavy component of it. In my mind you have got to develop. It seems whack to me to just become stagnant. I have an open mentality with everything, and it shows most through style. When my parents were younger they were very stylish and I think that played a part. The first pet I ever had was this cat, and I named her Fashion. I was six years old. I don't know what that means. I also think the people I am a fan of have developed a style. Miles Davis – if you look at a mood board of Miles there is a change. If you look at a mood board of Andre3000, there's always a change and it keeps changing.'

Out of the younger kids, who are you a fan of?
'Lil Uzi Vert, a rapper from Philadelphia. He looks amazing, like an anime character, like Trunks from *Dragon Ball Z*. Also his rap style is very progressive, it really flows; really witty. I also like how he is super-nuanced and weird but from the 'hood – that reminds me of myself. I'm not a street guy but I grew up around street guys, around violence, drugs and stuff like that. But I was lucky: I had a bubble that my parents kept me in. They kept me very educated and kept it so I had stuff to lose, so I didn't do dumb stuff. There is something to be said about being a young black guy from the 'hood that listens to whatever music you want, does what you want, likes what you want and then you kind of become, in a way, the star of the 'hood. The OGs respect you for the fact that you do your own thing. I see that in Lil Uzi and I see that in the whole A$AP Mob – I'm a big fan of those guys.'

What do you think of people who are cynical about music nowadays?
'I think it's cyclical. My dad told me stories about his father not liking James Brown! I think people get stained by how things were when they came up, and then when it becomes different they don't like it. Music has changed because now there's less music in school, less opportunities to learn core instruments for free. And at the same time there are all these music programs, so anyone can pick it up now and figure it out. Now there's much more music and it's cheaper to make, so there's lots more stuff for you to sift through. There's great music being made every day.'

Everyone used to get signed because there were so few acts! If a previous generation doesn't have disdain for what's happening, it doesn't leave room for growth. An older generation has to dislike something in order for kids to go, 'OK, well that's our thing.' I think that's a huge part of why it's natural for people to go, 'It sucks!' It needs to suck to someone for someone else to like it. There is a weird side of [liking something] that is fanaticism – some of the people we have met along the way have been fanatical. How does that sort of reaction make you feel on a personal level?
'It's a sign of the times. Instagram is the new TV. For some people they think I'm some kind of star, and they're looking at me like we used to look at the people on TV. I'd rather someone be obsessed with the culture I'm trying to emit than just me; I'm just the person. But if they like me just 'cause I'm friends with Frank Ocean or Rocky...'

Have you ever sent a fan DM to someone in you've admired? Drake?!
'No! I never have. I did a post to [US indie band] Bon Iver just saying, "Your album is amazing – next time you're in London let's play basketball"'

How does it feel to be working with Kanye, who you've been a fan of for so long? They say you should never meet your heroes...
'I just see it as a blessing. With Kanye or Frank Ocean, their music is so personal. Like that lyric that 'Ye says, "I'm on TV talking like it's just you and me" – you know what you are going to get. Whereas an artist whose lyrics are in the periphery doesn't mirror onto them, you don't know what you're going to get. For instance, working with Frank Ocean. You were like, "Listen to these two records, I think this guy is gonna go."'

They were The Weeknd and Frank Ocean. You were right – Frank went before The Weeknd.
'Any of these people I've worked with, all these titans of art and culture, just showed me I wasn't crazy – that we weren't crazy. All those times when we were out until five, waking up going to work, doing a meeting on my lunchbreak then back at it. My purpose is coming to life.'

DROMe

NAME: Aoi/DE
AGE: G.O.L.D
LONDON → LOS ANGELES
WHO ARE YOU THE BIGGEST FAN OF ?
PAUL WILLIAMS / MILES DAVIS/BJORK
WHAT FIRST ATTRACTED YOU TO.....
BJORK 'ALL IS FULL OF LOVE' VIDEO
WHAT IS YOUR FAVOURITE THING ABOUT THEM ?
BRAVE, BRAVE, BRAVE & STYLISH
WHO IS YOUR BIGGEST FAN:
IF I HAD ONE IT'D MYSELF BUT ALSO MY BIGGEST CRITIC

ACYDE / Creative

Acyde wears beige laced coat by CRAIG GREEN; *white shirt by* HAIDER ACKERMANN; *leather and Japanese duck satin slides with crystal embroidery by* GUCCI; *vintage beret from* ROKIT; *jeans Acyde's own*

NAME: CHAOS **AGE:** Born 2016!

WHO ARE YOU THE BIGGEST FAN OF ?
Karl Lagerfeld.

SINCE WHEN ?
Since our fashion memories can remember!

WHAT FIRST ATTRACTED YOU TO.......
How Daring he is.

WHAT IS YOUR FAVOURITE THING ABOUT THEM ?
He is never Bored + never Boring

YOUR FAVOURITE FAN ITEM..
His initaled Chanel iPadcase, we have the same initials! A vintage crochet blanket from Him.

HOW HAVE THEY INFLUENCED YOUR LIFE ?
He taught us that you can have total freedom in Fashion.

HAVE YOU MET YOUR HERO ?

IF YES ELABORATE..... YES.
We have been lucky enough to work with him for the last nine years!

CHAOS / Accessories brand

Elevating the humble phone case and luggage tag as high-end objects of desire

Writer HARRIET VERNEY

Chaos is the novel accessories company set up by stylist Charlotte Stockdale and her friend and longtime colleague Katie Lyall. 'We supply direct to the consumer,' explains Charlotte, 'with the occasional pop-up experience if they want physical Chaos. Which is every fucking day for us!'

The two met 15 years ago when Katie was fresh out of college and interning on a shoot where Charlotte was styling. The first sign to the wider world that Chaos was upon us came last September when they merged Instagram accounts during Paris Fashion Week. A month later Chaos dropped its first batch of luxury phone cases along with distinctive zip-up chains that hang around your neck (or wherever). The Chaos cases have been treated to a pop-up shop at Selfridges and hung out of the back pocket of pretty much every supermodel you can imagine. Charlotte and Katie treat the phone case as an It-object much like you would a handbag, and there is nothing that isn't high-end about the Chaos merch: the cases and luggage tags are made from deerskin and chenille, while the charms and hardware are plated with gold and silver.

Having worked on the famous Fendi fluffy gonks that gleefully swing off thousands of handbags, as well as Anya Hindmarch's leather stickers slapped onto backpacks the world over, it's obvious the Chaos sisters are supremely qualified at creating cult objects. 'We worked for so many people to create things people love,' reasons Katie, so it was high time they devoted that energy to their own enterprise. 'And what's good,' says Charlotte, 'is that there's two of us, so one can say "that's crap" – or not!' So how do they come up with their ingeniously desirable designs? 'There is a certain amount of instinct in it,' says Charlotte. 'But instinct basically comes from what you yourself want. That's what fashion is, really. The dream of fashion is we pay crazy prices for crazy things we really want. Basically, it all comes down to lust.'

Chaos is available to buy at chaos.club

Gigi wears gunmetal-plated zip lanyard and personalised leather GH phone case both by CHAOS; *white satin shorts by* MARC JACOBS

CHAOS

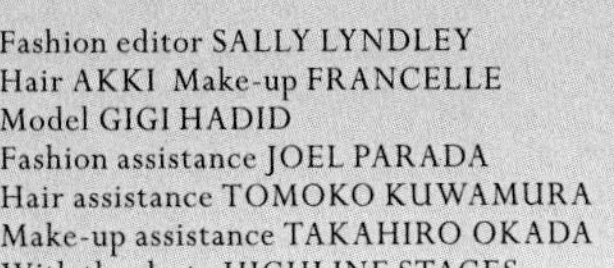
Fashion editor SALLY LYNDLEY
Hair AKKI Make-up FRANCELLE
Model GIGI HADID
Fashion assistance JOEL PARADA
Hair assistance TOMOKO KUWAMURA
Make-up assistance TAKAHIRO OKADA
With thanks to HIGHLINE STAGES

Gigi wears gold-plated zip lanyard personalised with GH charms and leather Ugh! phone case both by CHAOS; *white cotton elastane Bianca bodysuit by* REDWOLF PDX

JAMES THESEUS BUCK AND LUKE BROOKS / Designers

The ego-free duo best known as Rottingdean Bazaar work under a variety of names to amplify the totemic nature of fashion

Writer EDIE CAMPBELL

Fans do weird things when overcome by their obsession: they undergo extensive plastic surgery to look more like their heroes; write letters in menstrual blood and sprinkle them with pubes; when their idols break a leg, in solidarity they break their own. So here's my marginally less creepy contribution to the world of fans. This is what I love about designers Luke Brooks and James Theseus Buck, from a fan.

First of all, I love what they make. And they make lots of different things under different names. My own obsession began when I discovered Badge Taste. Essentially, it's a simple concept: they take an object and make it into a badge. The objects they choose are leftover bits: dead moths, balloons, cigarette butts, hair, old socks, ring pulls, cheap lace thongs, lipstick marks on bits of loo roll, burst sachets of ketchup. The kind of stuff you find when you put your hand down the back of the sofa.

But in making these things into a badge, Luke and James elevate the object. The process freezes it in time and space, presenting it as an artefact. In a way, it's alchemical. They transform the detritus of life into talismans. Incidentally, talismans are an essential part of obsessive fandom. It is this talismanic power that enables someone to rationalise spending $600 on a bottle of water Justin Bieber drank from.

The idea of talismans is something that Luke was playing with during his MA at Central Saint Martins. For his MA collection, he took a pair of boxer shorts he'd stolen from a boy he loved when he was 15, and crocheted them onto the front of a sweatshirt, a monument to a lost love. This same train of thought runs through the clothes Luke and James make together under the name Rottingdean Bazaar. In July 2016, they showed a collection during Men's Fashion Week: white tracksuits and T-shirts with flattened things on them. They kept it simple for a reason. 'I know I could show a lot of the things we've done to my grandma,' says Luke, 'and she'd get it instantly. Whereas if I showed her some beautiful abstract gown, she'd be confused.' One jumper had a pair of large white knickers and grim beige tights heat-sealed onto the front. And alongside it, a jumper with a large and tired-looking bra crocheted onto the chest. They were like mini-monuments to the way people strip off their clothes all at once and discard them in a heap on the floor when there's no one watching.

This idea of turning objects into monuments runs through a lot of their work together. But it is always offset with a healthy dose of the absurd. How silly it is that a single object can come to take on so much meaning when ultimately it's just a pair of boxers. But also how absurd 'glamour' is, when most of the time most people are wearing grim bras and have holes in their socks. James and Luke are not selling an aspirational fantasy, and that's admirably inclusive and honest. Although they handmake things out of grass and (their own) hair, the finished object doesn't feel 'craftsy', and what they produce is ultimately very commercial. These clothes aren't made to be bought and only worn once. The jumper smothered in semi-flaccid balloons is machine-washable.

Aside from making their collections, they've also art-directed and styled shoots for *1 Granary* and *Man About Town* magazines. In part that's because there is more freedom now than ever before to move across different media, and the traditionally delineated roles of the designer, editor and stylist are becoming much looser. But it is also because there is a curiosity to their work, an interest in experimenting and developing in different ways, rather than a tortured-genius introspection. They work a lot with Arthropod Arts, a children's art group in Rottingdean, the seaside village they live in on the south coast. But what they do with the arts group isn't about teaching kids, it's about examining the kids' own creativity. For their story in *Man About Town* they commissioned the group to make clothes inspired by the performance artist David Hoyle, and then shot David and the kids in locations around Rottingdean. There is an openness to how Luke and James work. They love the collaborative process, and reject the idea that designers are pitted against each other. As James put it, 'I think we feel really comfortable with the set-up we have at the moment, that we can go and work with other people. It's not totally "this is my universe". I think that's part of the reason we didn't give it our own names. Rottingdean Bazaar sounds more like a community.'

James (left) wears oversized T-shirt with laminated clothing by ROTTINGDEAN BAZAAR; *vintage military trousers from* VINTAGE SHOWROOMS; *black hat and daisy sandals all by* PRADA. *Luke wears oversized T-shirt with laminated clothing by* ROTTINGDEAN BAZAAR; *black trousers by* PRINGLE; *socks by* FALKE; *lace-up leather shoes by* VALENTINO; *glasses Luke's own*

ANJA RUBIK
/ Model / Editor

She's the face and bare chest of Anthony Vaccarello's first Saint Laurent campaign which appears on nearly every corner in Paris. Anja's personal message to her fans is this: 'Don't go mainstream!'

Anja wears emerald green devoré leopard-print velvet and silver embroidery dress, gold and red brass and viscose Loulou pompom earrings and black leather ankle-strap shoes all by SAINT LAURENT BY ANTHONY VACCARELLO

Anja wears camouflage side-tie bikini briefs by LA PERLA; *gold and red brass and viscose Loulou pompom earrings and black leather ankle-strap shoes all by* SAINT LAURENT BY ANTHONY VACCARELLO

NAME: ANJA RUBIK **AGE:** 33

MODEL, CHIEF EDITOR OF 25 MAGAZINE

WHO ARE YOU THE BIGGEST FAN OF ? MARY KOMA MY FRIEND/SINGER

SINCE WHEN ? SINCE I MET HER

WHAT FIRST ATTRACTED YOU TO....... HER ODDNESS

WHAT IS YOUR FAVOURITE THING ABOUT THEM ? HONESTY & ENERGY

YOUR FAVOURITE FAN ITEM.. WU TANG CLAN T-SHIRT

HOW HAVE THEY INFLUENCED YOUR LIFE ?

HAVE YOU MET YOUR HERO ? MY DAD

IF YES ELABORATE... YOU'RE MY SOUL MATE

FAVOURITE SONG ? "THIS MESS WE'RE IN"

FAVOURITE BAND ? PJ HARVEY MASSIVE ATTACK

FAVOURITE BOOk ? "THE MASTER AND MARGARITA" BY MIKHAL BULGAKOV

NAME: STAZ **AGE:** 24

OCCUPATION: MODEL/ MUSICIAN/MUGICIAN/NOYD OF THE PARANOYDS **RESIDENCE:** LOS ANGELES!

WHO ARE YOU THE BIGGEST FAN OF:

NIRVANA xx

SINCE WHEN: AGE 12th

WHAT FIRST ATTRACTED YOU TO:: SMELLS LIKE TEEN SPIRIT SPOKE TO MY PRETEEN FEELINGS. EVEN THO ITS MY LEAST FAV OF THEIR SONGS NOW

WHAT IS YOUR FAVOURITE THING ABOUT THEM:

SERVE THE SERVANTS & DRAIN YOU

FAVOURITE FAN ITEM:

MY ORIGINAL INCESTICIDE SHIRT + ALL THE BOOTLEGS

HOW HAVE THEY INFLUENCED YOUR LIFE. ITS O.K. TO SELL OUT A TINY ... STAND UP FOR WHAT YOU BELIEVE IN. JUST KEEP YOUR SENSE OF HU... & STAY TRUE 2 U

HAVE YOU MET YOUR HERO: YES! I AM SO LUCKY TO HAVE MET MANY OF MY HEROES

IF YES ELABORATE:

1) I FOUND JOHN WATERS AT THE CHELSEA ART WALK AND PRACTICALL... LEPT ON HIM 2) KATHLEEN HANNA CAME OUT TO GREET FANS AT THE ECHO PLEX 3 YEARS AGO. SHE IS THE FUCKING COOLEST. 3) I DIDNT MEET HIM BUT KRIST NOVESEL... SAW ME WAL...

WHO IS YOUR BIGGEST FAN: LAILA'S MOM MOM & MY BEST FRIEND

WEIDEST FAN MESSAGE EVER: "FROM HERE I CAN TELL YOUR FEET ARE AMAZING"

FAVOURITE SONG: YOU REALLY GOT A HOLD ON ME - THE MIRAC... BE MY BABY - THE RONETTES

FAVOURITE BAND:

CURRENT DAY: SHANNON AND THE CLAMS 4 ABSOLUTELY PERFECT ALBUMS. HOW!

FOR LIFE: NIRVANA

LISTEN 2 UR HEART. FOLLOW UR INSTINCTS

YOU know whats BEST & RIGHT FOR YOU

TAKE CARE OF YOURSELF AND GIVE THE FUTURE YOU PRESENTS & FAVORS

DONT DO DRUGS! (or AT LEAST BE REALLY REALLY CAREFUL BUT MOSTLY NO)

EVEN IF YOU DONT FEEL IT NOW - YOU ARE SO COOL! YOU'LL REALIZE IT SOMEDAY!!

Staz wears striped viscose stretch jersey dress by GIVENCHY BY RICCARDO TISCI; *black and navy belt by* SPORTMAX; *harlequin patchwork jacket in various couture fabrics and leathers by* RONALD VAN DER KEMP

STAZ LINDES / Model

Staz Lindes is one quarter of LA band The Paranoyds whose fans include Jeremy Scott and Hedi Slimane. Hedi even cast her in his Saint Laurent show for spring 2016 and put a tiara on her head after meeting her a month before at a Paranoyds gig. Fitting, then, that the elfin blonde has just been announced as the new face (and lips) of YSL beauty.

Fabio wears suit jacket by BALENCIAGA; *printed silk shirt by* BRIONI; *white T-shirt by* DRIES VAN NOTEN; *printed silk scarf by* COACH 1941

FABIO PIRAS / Fashion guru

The next generation of designers is in safe hands, thanks to the man in charge of the fashion MA at Central Saint Martins

Writer MURRAY HEALY

Two years have passed since Fabio Piras was appointed course director of the fashion MA at Central Saint Martins, but he still hasn't completed the business of making himself at home in the office that comes with the job and, bar a scattering of hardbacks, the bookcases are currently empty. 'I'm in the process of tidying up. Making space, building shelves – trying to make sense of things. That's why it looks like some sort of Ikea display in here,' he smiles, sitting behind the desk from which he launches his assessments of his students' work during their all-important crits. The legacy of his predecessor, the late, legendary Louise Wilson, who first invited Fabio to teach here when he was an emerging designer in the early Nineties, can still be felt around the building, not just in the obvious ways – in the status of the fashion MA as a star-making vehicle, a jewel in the crown of the school – but in more mundane details, too. 'There are drawers I haven't opened yet,' Fabio continues. 'From time to time you find some abusive note written by Louise. It's what happens when you take over from somebody who didn't have time to move out.'

I've arrived today feeling less familiar with Fabio's past than I'd like. I've heard stories of his brilliance as a teacher from his former pupils, but I've yet to see any of his work from his previous life as a designer. The evidence of those days has disappeared in that curious blind spot in the all-seeing scope of the internet, that moment in the Nineties just before everything started to migrate online, leaving a gap which has yet to be filled: too early to be documented contemporaneously, but still too recent to be rediscovered and uploaded. So at the outset I admit to him that I haven't been able to unearth any record of his work. He flashes a big grin. 'I know! Isn't that depressing – to feel that you don't have a past?'

Or maybe it's a freedom? 'I don't know,' he says. 'It's a relief.' A few years ago when he was clearing out his studio he decided to open the boxes of old VHS tapes of his catwalk shows

and get them digitised. 'And I wish I hadn't. Whether it was good or bad, creatively there was a validity to it in its day, and you remember the good things. So something you remember being fantastic comes on the screen and you go, "Oh my God, *no*!" And you sit there criticising it to death, and it's not a memory any more, it becomes a terrible new reality.'

He hadn't set out to become a designer. As with so many designers of his generation, it just sort of happened. His interest in fashion began in his childhood in late-Seventies Geneva, sparked by a daytime show on French TV that would cover the seasonal collections. 'That for me was *the* show. You'd see Saint Laurent, Jean-Louis Scherrer, Paco Rabanne... I was mesmerised.' His favourite was Per Spook, the Norwegian designer who ran Louis Féraud. 'He was very modern – one of those minimalist designers using big patterns and really graphic elements. I was completely obsessed with him. I would draw my own collections that were very Per Spook meets the Russian ice-skating team. Collection after collection after collection.'

He presented some drawings to a couturier in Switzerland who dissuaded him from working in fashion. 'He thought they were shit and told me maybe it was not my career.' So Fabio focused on studying languages instead. He wasn't interested in sewing or making clothes for himself. 'I have never "dressed" myself, to this day. It's always a uniform. So it's black.' Today he's wearing a black jumper and jeans. 'If it's not black, it's navy; if not navy, grey. A colour is really difficult for me, and I'm not comfortable with prints.' In contrast, fashion was something other, detached, sublime. 'My preoccupation was the image of fashion. Womenswear tends to be a fantasy that represents my aesthetics.'

His interest in fashion wasn't completely extinguished, however. There was one newsagent in the city that stocked a handful of copies of *The Face* magazine, and Fabio would go and queue for it every month because the owner refused to reserve it for him. *The Face* made London look like the most exciting place in the world, so he got himself on a flight there. 'And the day before I was due to fly back to Geneva, I decided to stay. That was 1985.' He went out, hung out, enjoyed the city, doing casual work to get by. 'But after two years you start to question what "enjoying it" means.' He decided to apply to Saint Martins. 'Where else but that college? It just seemed obvious. But my aim was not to work in the fashion business as a designer. I wasn't interested in that. It sounds really crap, but it was about expressing yourself through the medium of fashion. You just wanted to be a name. You wanted to be *you*. I needed Saint Martins to change me into the person I knew I was.'

The womenswear BA at Saint Martins was an entirely satisfying experience. 'It was amazing. I applied when I needed to apply, when I needed to explode. The MA was a different story for me. It was much less enjoyable, and it wasn't the MA we know today.' Back then, the BA was *the* course, with star graduate John Galliano still dominating the public perception of the school, along with the hedonism of its location in Soho. 'The MA was a way to be more professional and build a portfolio that could get you a job. It was unnecessary for me to do the MA; I just wasted it. But it's good for me to have had that experience – it helps you direct your students.'

Louise Wilson became director of the MA course in 1992 and, a couple of years after he'd graduated, she asked Fabio back to teach on it. At the time he was working as part of a collaborative label called Commune with other Saint Martins graduates, based in a squat near the old King's Cross gasworks, across the road from the warehouse that now houses Saint Martins. 'It was the early Nineties, the time of that whole Margiela aesthetic. So the studio was all wood and fireplaces, because that was the only way to heat it, and everything was painted white, and we had these presentations there. Which suddenly worked, because in London at the time that scene hadn't emerged yet – this was just before McQueen had his first show at Bluebird Garage.' (At the time it was still just a disused garage in Chelsea, years before Terence Conran would convert it into an expensive restaurant.) 'That kind of scene, that almost poetical way of expressing yourself in a squat and showing a collection in the smoke of coal and wood, was something that hadn't been done before.'

'It was about expressing yourself through fashion. You wanted to be a name'

At the time Fabio had been for one job interview, at Helmut Lang. 'I was completely obsessed with Helmut Lang, like many people at the time. I did this whole project and sent it to him personally: "This is for you." I just wanted to get to know him. I am quite an obsessive person!' It worked in so far as getting Fabio through the door. 'He called me in but he didn't offer me a job. He said someone like me should be doing his own thing, and he was right.'

So after a couple of seasons with Commune, Fabio set up as a designer under his own name producing minimalist womenswear, and menswear too, briefly. He sold internationally and Liberty was a major stockist in London. 'It was madness, of course. But who in their right mind would wait till their forties to set up their own business? You have to be someone who is young and has the necessary stamina, and who doesn't know [what they're doing] in order to make those mistakes and survive them.'

His first mistake, he reckons, was being seduced away from Commune by a backer. 'If you start something, you should see it through. You don't abandon it because someone comes along and says, "I'm going to invest in you." It's like quitting a boy band. Commune was struggling and wasn't meant to be forever, but leaving was a mistake.' It was a painful mistake, too: within a year he had to buy his new backer out. 'It was a complete nightmare for me. I felt I was being taken somewhere I didn't want to go, and we were in a contract together that I couldn't operate in.'

The actual business of creating his collections presented its own challenges. His studio had no heating so in winter it would be full of assistants in coats and gloves. 'It was so cold. I had this wonderful machinist – we had to cut the fingers off her cashmere gloves, otherwise it would have been dangerous. And the toilets were grim.' Any money that was made would go towards the next collection. 'Twice a year you were destitute. And I was a loose cannon – one season was great, the next was super shit.' He remembers one show in the Italian Cultural Institute in Knightsbridge where the models ended up walking with their backs to the audience. 'I look at the video now and think, what planet was I on? Thank God for Japan. They were so faithful, so loyal. So you survived.'

Charlotte Stockdale joined Fabio as a stylist, working on the collections for three years from 1994. 'The style was very minimal, all about the line of the cut,' she remembers. 'The palette was very pale grey, white, lemon yellow and red. Fabio was extremely focused on getting things perfect – such a creative and gentle person.' Charlotte also looked after accessories – she recalls a last-minute pre-show dash around Lillywhites buying white football boots – and the casting, booking a young Erin O'Connor and Jade Parfitt. 'It was very professional and organised, considering there was no money. We were all very serious back then. We'd torture ourselves over whether it should be a white or off-white shoe. Whereas these days it's more a matter of, "Does she look sexy?"'

When an Italian manufacturer offered to take over production of his collections, Fabio felt very pleased with himself. 'You visit the factory and gasp. And you see which other designers they're producing and think, "This is my moment!" But no. It means you're at the end of the queue. And suddenly you're not delivering on time and you start losing orders.' He bowed out of his business, leaving his Italian partners to carry on producing under his name until the contract expired a couple of seasons later. 'It's not like I was *the* name of the moment,' he laughs.

By this point Louise Wilson had got in touch with him. 'We all know about the legend of Louise. What we sometimes forget about that legend is that there was a humanity and a heart.' As she did with so many of the school's ex-students, she took it upon herself to locate him and make sure he was alright. 'She wanted to safeguard me, in a way. So she gave me this teaching contract, working two and a half days a week.' In 1997 when Louise left Saint Martins to work at Donna Karan, Fabio

Continued on page 484

MARC JACOBS
MARC JACOBS
MARC JACOBS

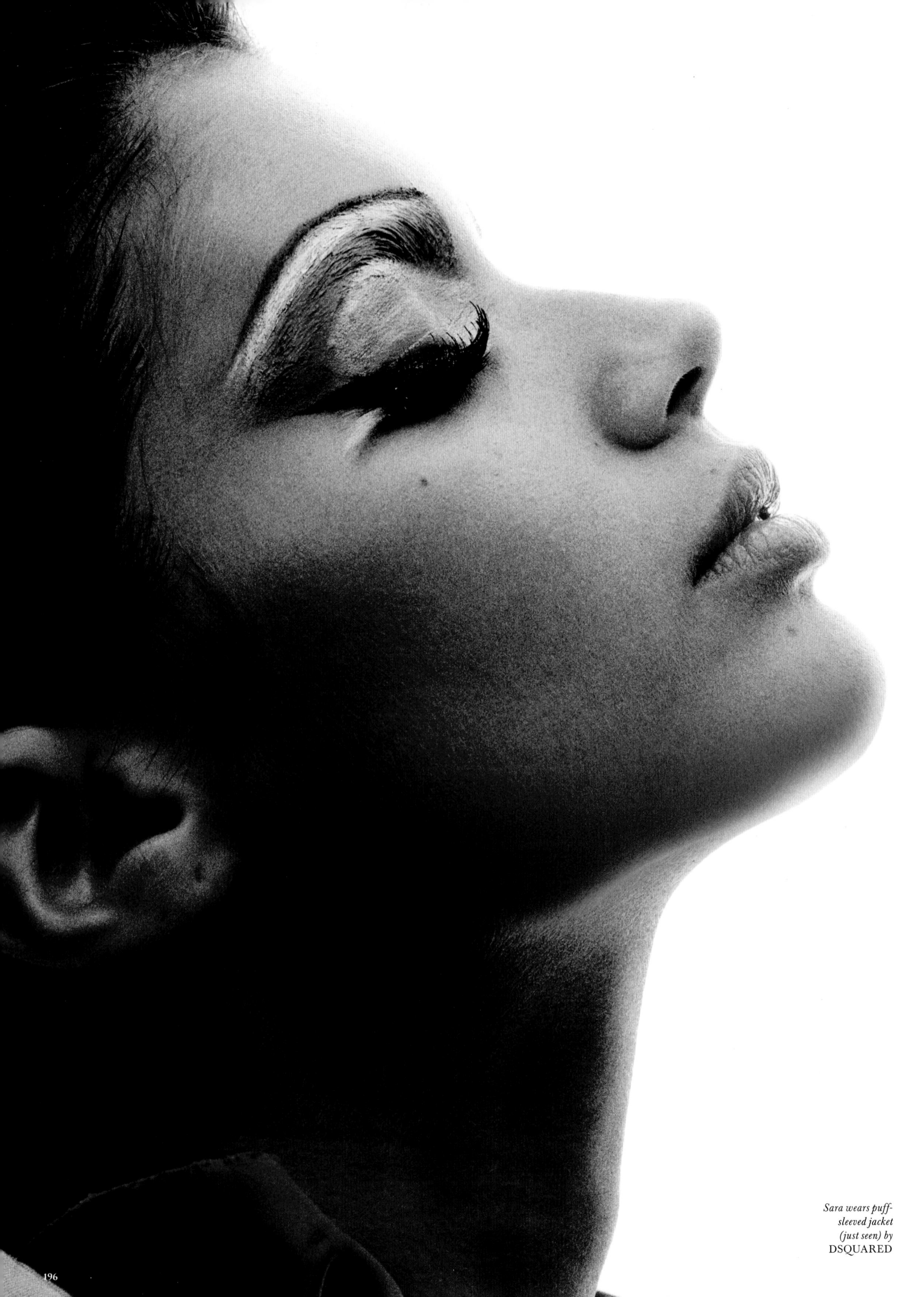

Sara wears puff-sleeved jacket (just seen) by DSQUARED

SARA SAMPAIO /
Model / Actor

Sara wears red shirt, open-front skirt and knickers all by MIU MIU; *pearl-embellished stockings by* MARC JACOBS; *plastic Anglaise knot-sleeved coat by* SIMONE ROCHA

NAME: Sara Sampaio **AGE:** 25

WHO ARE YOU THE BIGGEST FAN OF ?

Angelina Jolie and Eminem.

SINCE WHEN ?

Angelina Since tomb raider, and Gia, and Girl interrupted. Eminen Since foreveeeeer!!!

WHAT IS YOUR FAVOURITE THING ABOUT THEM ?

Angelina is just so captivating and beautiful. And her acting is incredible. And Eminem lyrics really make you feel his life.

YOUR FAVOURITE FAN ITEM..

Probably my Gia DVD

HOW HAVE THEY INFLUENCED YOUR LIFE ?

She pretty much made me want to become an actress.

HAVE YOU MET YOUR HERO ?

never met them, but I have to see eminen in concert before I die.

A PERSONAL MESSAGE FOR YOUR HERO:

Eminem, when we meet can we get married? If not, can we rap "when I'm gone" together?

Angelina, I'm sorry if I cry when we meet, please Don't think I'm weird. And can you get back to Brad? Love you!

SARA

The award-winning Portuguese beauty and Victoria's Angel who walked for Marc Jacobs and Miu Miu this season, among many others

Writer HARRIET VERNEY

It's late in the evening at a photography studio and 25-year-old model Sara Sampaio can be found in her dressing robe, full face of make-up, rollers in hair and bent on her knees talking to a goat. Yes, an actual goat, called Bonnie who also happens to be modelling on the shoot. 'What mascara are you wearing, Bonnie?' Sara asks the miffed goat in between sips of herbal tea. Meanwhile, two burley minders (the goat's, not Sara's) are discouraging the Portuguese beauty from getting too near the Chingford-born animal. But Sara seems genuinely interested in the goat's beauty regime and goes in for the hug. Her display of goat-love is not just for the benefit of an audience, as it turns out. She's an active campaigner against animal cruelty and supporter of the charity the American Society for the Prevention of Cruelty to Animals.

Sara grew up in Porto, an idyllic, ocean-view town in Northern Portugal. While her bedroom boasted classic relics of a Nineties baby's music collection – Eminem, Shakira, Avril Lavigne posters and CDs – it was fashion campaigns for Versace and Intimissimi that really resonated with her. 'The funniest thing is, now I'm friends with all the girls in those ads.'

Aside from nail-biting interviews with goats, Sara is best known for being a Victoria Secret's Angel, donning 10-ton angel wings and skimpy underwear for their shows, adorning their windows and taking on the publicity that comes with Angel territory. Even with her naturally swollen lips, Isabella Rossellini brow and petite gym-honed, unusually elastic body, the coveted VS gig didn't come easily. After being turned down two years running, six years ago she went back in with a more determined attitude. 'The first thing I did when I got in to that audition is say to the casting director, "I'm not going to give you any reason not to book me this year." And then I got it. I'd recommend it to everyone.'

This season saw her walk for Marc Jacobs in 10-inch platform boots, and for Miu Miu, donning a Fifties yellow shower cap, flats and a towelling robe. She has also, brilliantly, won the Portuguese Golden Globe for modelling five times on the trot. It was back in Portugal that she first got into modelling, winning a Pantene 'great hair' competition. 'It's all about the hair,' she laughs. As the winner she got to feature in a TV commercial for the brand. Acting is at the forefront of her ambitions, so Sara thought she'd take a whack at it. 'I was like, I'm going to try. I have great hair, and I've always wanted to be an actor.' Admittedly she does have very good hair.

Currently Sara is watching every Angelina Jolie movie ever (*Gia* is her favourite, *Girl, Interrupted* takes a close second). She knows all the lyrics to the songs in *Moulin Rouge!* and worships the ground director Baz Luhrmann walks on. 'I just *loooooove* Baz,' she purrs.

The tabloid gossip that follows Sara has picked up as much momentum recently as her Angels wings do on the runway. While currently dating Oliver Ripley, a British-born Oxford grad, there was a rumoured dalliance with serial snogger Harry Styles. The pair were papped outside the Ludlow Hotel, New York at a party and emerged the next day in the same outfit. Haven't we all?

The recent interest in Sara has invited a swarm of trolls and a barrage of Twitter hate when she dares voice her opinions. 'Twitter gets on my nerves. Every time I give an opinion about something I get my words completely twisted and I'm like, "I can't engage with this any more." Some of them are just hateful people and you can't go down to the same level as them, but yeah, sometimes you just wanna say "F you", but you can't.' She has taken full advantage of Instagram's trigger-word feature. 'I've banned words like "anorexic", "fat", "skinny" and some curse words. They are hurtful and I don't need to be reading that.'

When it comes to getting her own back on the haters, it's proving people wrong that she really gets a kick from. 'That's what gives me satisfaction. Like when I got my first *Vogue* cover. Or when I walked 90 shows in fashion week. That's what gives me satisfaction,' she says. 'And I'm not stopping here.'

Georgia wears 18kt yellow gold and diamond Serpent Bohème sleeper earring by BOUCHERON

GEORGIA

Georgia wears black nappa leather redingote jacket with gold brocade by REDEMPTION; *black latex Miss T bra by* ATSUKO KUDO; *plonge voile embroidered leather skirt by* CHRISTOPHER KANE; *18kt yellow gold and diamond Serpent Bohème necklace and 18kt yellow gold and diamond Serpent Bohème pendant earrings all by* BOUCHERON

NAME: Georgia AGE: 24

OCCUPATION: [hanger] RESIDENCE: NYC

WHO ARE YOU THE BIGGEST FAN OF ?
Malala Yousafzai Beyonce
Marlene Dietrich David Attenborough

WHAT IS YOUR FAVOURITE THING ABOUT THEM ?
COURAGE & DEDICATION

YOUR FAVOURITE FAN ITEM..
My ALL BLACKS Rugby Jersey

HOW HAVE THEY INFLUENCED YOUR LIFE ?
Most weekends I'll watch a David Attenborough doco, & I'm encouraged to stand up!

HAVE YOU MET YOUR HERO ?
I'm still waiting... waiting waiting waiting.

FAVOURITE SONG ? karaoke song.
I will survive - Aretha franklin,
lose yourself - Eminem

WHO IS YOUR BIGGEST FAN:
MUM

GEORGIA FOWLER / Model

The science prodigy from New Zealand who's catwalking her way around the world

Writer HARRIET VERNEY

'I've always wanted to be something in the limelight,' says Georgia Fowler. 'I was always a bit of a show pony growing up. You know, coming out from behind curtains and stuff.' With her long limbs and enviably lean body, the New Zealander looks more like a racehorse right now as she canters around the studio, with the energy to match.

And she certainly has galloped right into the spotlight. Aside from the Victoria's Secret catwalk, she has trotted down Miu Miu's runway, been seen with her arms wrapped around Leonardo DiCaprio while out clubbing, Snapchatted a game of Scrabble with Harry Styles in his dressing gown, and set tongues wagging and angry mothers tapping away on forums when she posed naked for a French Connection campaign with nowt but a few brushstrokes preserving her modesty.

Georgia grew up in leafy Surrey, so she had what she describes as 'a little plummy Queen's English accent' until the age of five when her dad, a professional golfer, moved the family to New Zealand. After that, 'Life was pretty simple,' says Georgia. 'We never wore shoes.' Why on earth not? 'Because Kiwis just don't!'

Before she became a model her ambition was to be just like her idol Baby Spice, but that dream was crushed pretty quickly: 'I wasn't blonde so I couldn't be her. I was gutted.' Her taste in idols has matured slightly since the Emma Bunton days. 'I'm a fangirl of Angelina Jolie for all the humanitarian stuff she does – she's got beauty but she's also saving the world.' But even though she wanted to be in the limelight, one job that was not among Georgia's ambitions was modelling. 'No, I never thought, "I want to be a model." Every time someone would call me pretty, Mum would be like, "Yeah, pretty ugly" as a joke and put them down!'

However, after her sister was signed to IMG models they signed Georgia, too. She saw it as an opportunity to travel. 'I was a bit of a geek, so I worked really hard in my second-to-last year.' As a result she left school at 16 and went straight to university on a BSc course majoring in psychology. When the modelling took off, Georgia deferred a year, but she is still adamant she will be back at university before long: 'I want to read minds!' she laughs. If she wasn't studying psychology she'd like to be doing engineering 'because I love maths and science'.

But for now her focus is solely on her modelling career. 'At the beginning of 2016 I wrote down a list of jobs that I wanted to do,' says Georgia, 'so I've just been ticking off those goals.' For the spring/summer collections she ended up walking in a dozen shows, Miu Miu, VS and Ungaro among them. 'All these jobs are a dream come true, and that gives me a sense of achievement. I've been doing it for a while, so it shows hard work really pays off.'

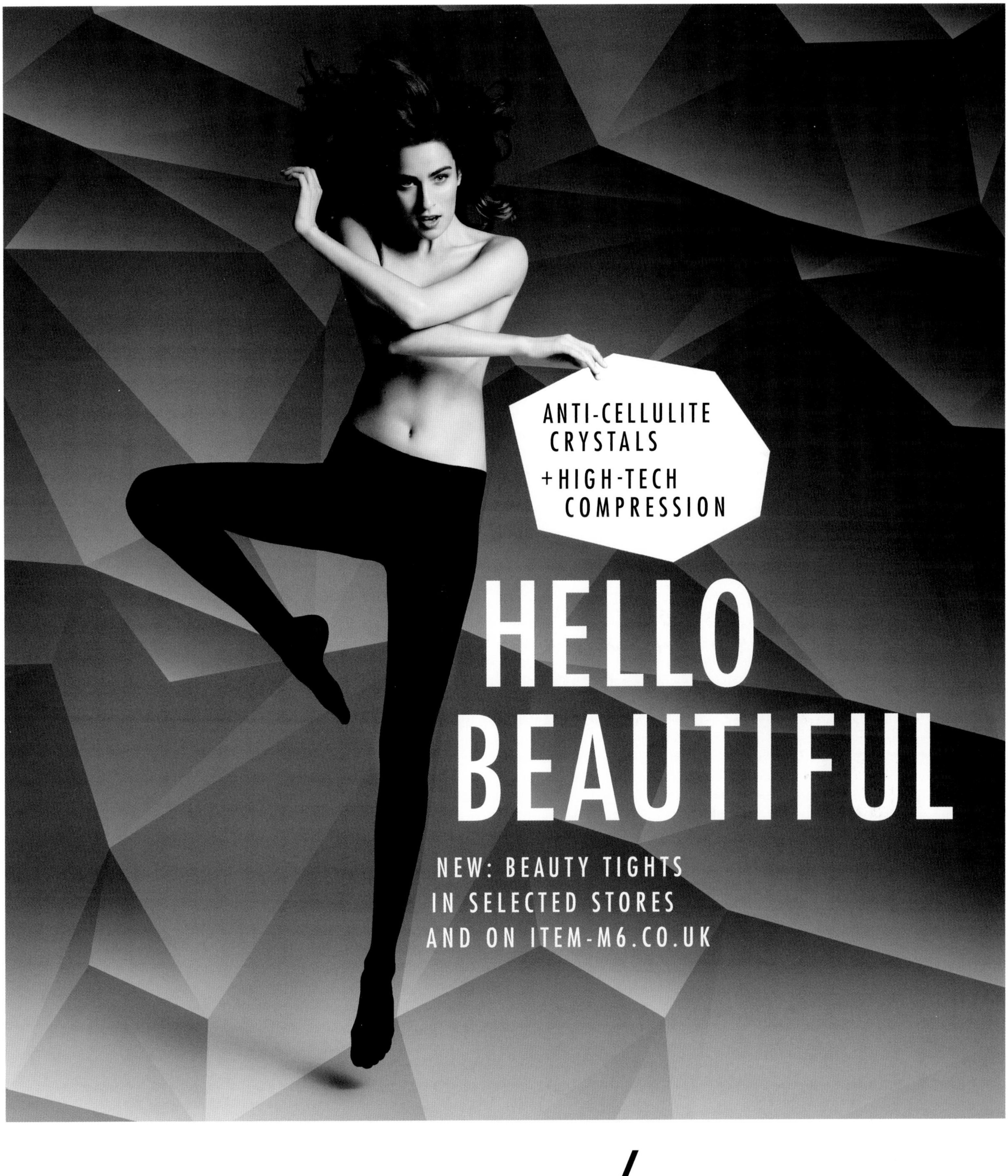

STUART VEVERS / Designer

How Coach's executive creative director is building an all-American alternative to couture through the easy individualism of imperfection

Writer ANDY MOFFAT

The portrait of Stuart Vevers on the right needs some context, as it's the wildest picture you're likely to see of the designer any time soon. Stuart is well known for having a modest public persona. So when Charles Jeffrey turned up to style him at the studio in New York with an ostentatiously-sized crown in his carrier bag, the general verdict from the crew was, 'Good luck with that.' Stuart arrived, Charles introduced himself, unveiled the crown and declared, 'Since you're King of New York, I thought I'd get you to wear this.' Stuart blushed bright red and replied, 'I'd love to!' Mission accomplished.

A month later, Stuart is in London for the launch of Coach's brand-new London flagship store on Regent Street: the sort of photo-friendly party designed to look good on the sites of *Tatler* and *WWD*, which duly covered it, attended by Poppy Delevingne, Daisy Lowe, Nick Grimshaw and Kate Moss, who hosted a karaoke session. It took place on Thanksgiving, underlining the provenance of a brand that in the UK still appears exotically USA. There was a further factor determining the timing of the opening, more material than symbolic, which Stuart Vevers sums up with down-to-earth bluntness: 'We wouldn't have had enough stuff to fill the shop previously!'

The morning after the party, Stuart is back in the store for the first of a string of interviews to further publicise its opening. He can't have had much sleep: last night he went off to catch up with one of his old friends from his early days as a bag designer in East London. And there was a lot to catch up on, as his visits to the UK are infrequent. He has spent most of his career working abroad, for Calvin Klein, Bottega Veneta, Givenchy, Louis Vuitton and Loewe. 'I've been working for 20 years,' he says, 'but I've only spent three of those in London.'

When he moved to New York in 2014 to head up the Coach studio, the brand was known in the US and East Asian markets for its luggage and accessories, primarily for the reassuringly sturdy practicality of its handbags. This 'satisfying heft', as Stuart calls it with a smile, is an attribute he's keen to maintain in the bags: 'things like a heavy stitch, a luggage handle, a chunky zip.' Then there's the turn lock, the signature detail which designer Bonnie Cashin introduced in the Sixties, which Stuart supersized on little shoulder bags in his second season, and used in place of a lid on the bottle he designed for Coach's first scent. He's careful not to be too heavy-handed with callbacks to the past though. 'When I started at Coach I looked at the archive, and then looked away quite quickly. I felt there was a shift happening where people don't care about the old codes of luxury any more. So I use heritage much more now as a touchstone. It basically promises a level of trust. If you've been around for a certain amount of time' – Coach is 76 years old – 'then it means you know a lot about what you're doing.'

The biggest impact of his arrival, of course, has been the introduction of clothing. With no precedent to follow, this has also been his biggest challenge – albeit one he was well prepared for, having witnessed the process of expanding a luggage giant into a fashion house up close when he worked with Marc Jacobs in his early days at Louis Vuitton, where Stuart was head of accessories. A natural way in ready to wear for Coach emerged in his first collection for autumn 2014 in the shape of the Sheepherder, a big, sturdy, unlined shearling coat that proved an instant hit, in both reviews and sales. Ever since it's the leather coats that have proved to be the signature ready-to-wear pieces, such as the fireman's coat, with its distinctive big buckled fastenings, in spring 2015. 'It just makes sense,' says Stuart of his early emphasis on outerwear. 'Coach is America's house of leather, so leather and outerwear make loads of sense. From Marlon Brando to James Dean, a leather jacket is a fundamental cool reference of American style. And shearling felt right because it's got a luxe feeling but it definitely doesn't feel precious. It comes from a real, functional place – which most things in American style tend to, whether it's denim or workwear or a biker jacket.'

Grounding the language of Coach's clothing in American traditions of workwear has seen Stuart steer clear of the more obvious clichés of femininity in his womenswear. His footwear has included clogs, sandals, creepers and boots – usually with a thick, solid sole. 'I've never really shown a heel, and if I do it's a short one. But she's usually stomping. There's something grounded about the Coach girl.' Worn with leather coats and styled with bandanas and studs, these tough girl-gang aesthetics were tempered in Stuart's third and fourth seasons when he introduced dresses, first in sheer silk fabrics and then colourful *Little House on the Prairie* florals. But even these followed Stuart's hard line on keeping everything utilitarian in the shape of a simple shift dress. 'So it's not about formality or fit – you can slip it on with the ease of a T-shirt.'

Informality is key to Stuart's process of claiming American style for Coach. 'I felt an American take on luxury should offer a genuine authentic alternative [to European luxury], not just be a diluted version. So it became about ease, informality, authenticity. It's all about feeling less precious.' This is most explicit in the 'Rip and Repair' process which Stuart introduced in autumn 2015, whereby leather is patched or torn and whipstitched. 'If something isn't precious,' says Stuart, 'that for me creates more desire right now than being fully resolved and perfect.' Realising that 'imperfect' is just another way of saying 'unique', Stuart has developed 'Rip and Repair' as a signature style. 'For our varsity jackets for fall '16, we did one-of-a-kind pieces where we found vintage patches and made special jackets with them in our New York workshop.' Each jacket came with a specially made booklet, 'handwritten, about where the patches were from and what they were'. This approach also serves to counter Coach's continent-spanning ubiquity. 'Yes, Coach is a big brand, but there's moments of discovery and uniqueness. And for Coach as an American brand, I guess customisation is an authentic answer to what couture is in Europe.'

In the Regent Street store he has devoted an area to customisation, where purchases can be stamped with a choice of a hundred motifs: everything from false teeth and old computer-tape spools to smileys and palm trees. 'We've taken the idea of monogramming,' says Stuart, 'and made it more lighthearted.' It's proving popular: in the week the store has been open, three quarters of sales have been stamped. 'So far the most popular is the banana.'

Also included in the stamp motifs is Rexy, the tyrannosaurus rex introduced by Stuart on a keyring before evolving into bracelet charms and knitwear motifs. A giant multicoloured Rexy guards the front of the Regent Street store, and there were even dancers dressed as T. rexes at the launch party. 'Rexy always made us smile in the studio,' says Stuart, 'and she seemed to have the same effect on our clients, so it grew organically from that. Sometimes the client just chooses for you. That Rexy keyring was just flying out of the stores.'

Stuart wears pea coat and jumper both by COACH 1941; *white solid poplin dress shirt by* RALPH LAUREN PURPLE LABEL; *crown by* CHARLES JEFFREY

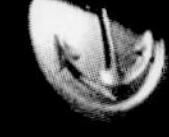

WHO ARE YOU THE BIGGEST FAN OF ? FIVE STAR

SINCE WHEN ? 1986

WHAT IS YOUR FAVOURITE THING ABOUT THEM ?
THE MUSIC THE MAKE UP, THE LOOKS, EVERYTHING!

YOUR FAVOURITE FAN ITEM..
12" SINGLE OF 'THE SLIGHTEST TOUCH' SHEP PETTIBONE REMIX

HOW HAVE THEY INFLUENCED YOUR LIFE ?
THEY MAKE ME HAPPY

HAVE YOU MET YOUR HERO ?
NO - BUT I SAW THEM ON STAGE AT G.A.Y., WELL 3 OF THE 5

A PERSONAL MESSAGE FOR YOUR HERO:
DEAR FIVE STAR,
I'M SAD I'VE ONLY SEEN THREE OF YOU ON STAGE. BUT THANK YOU FOR THE SONGS, VIDEO'S & AMAZING LOOKS.
LOVE ALWAYS, STUART X

Dilara wears baby-pink satin top with lace cuffs and baby-pink snake skirt (just seen) both by DILARA FINDIKOGLU; *heart purse (worn as hat) by* VIVIENNE WESTWOOD; *black latex choker by* ATSUKO KUDO; *embellished necklace by* PRADA; *black leather belt by* J&M DAVIDSON

DILARA FINDIKOGLU
/ Designer

The Turkish-born tearaway recharging fashion with a political punch

Writer MURRAY HEALY

'There's no revolution in any industry at the moment, not even in fashion. Everyone's really safe and no one wants to take risks.' After barely a year in the business, this is the conclusion Dilara Findikoglu has come to – although the same might not be said of the young designer herself. She was branded a rebel the moment she graduated from Saint Martins (early reviews called her a 'punk feminist' and 'rule-breaker'), thanks to the circumstances of her graduation. Every year, the 100-plus students finishing the fashion BA create a final collection in the hope that it will feature in the annual press show. But in 2015 Dilara was not one of the 40 students selected, and she wasn't happy about it. 'I felt really fucking horrible for about a week,' she says. So she took it upon herself to create an alternative show with fellow students who'd been rejected by the system. Titled Encore CSM, the event was staged in the forecourt outside the main entrance to Saint Martins. And in pointed contrast to the press show, it was devised to be as accessible as possible: any graduating student could take part, and anyone passing by could watch. Such was the novelty of the event, it threatened to upstage the official show. 'We got loads more press than they did,' beams Dilara. 'And the tutors supported it.' Not every eligible student was willing to take part, though. 'Some were like, "What if it's controversial and the tutors get angry?" There's a fear of offending someone, she continues, that people are loath to get involved with anything slightly unorthodox. 'They worry too much about what might happen.'

This is another observation that doesn't apply to Dilara herself. When it comes to her references, she'd sooner look to politically charged events from history and the news rather than fashion archives. The title of her spring/summer 2017 collection, 'Dear Past, Thanks for All the Lessons', was inspired by an image from her native Turkey that was in the news as she started on the collection. These words were featured on a T-shirt worn by Çilem Doğan giving a defiant, handcuffed thumbs-up to camera as she was escorted to jail after killing her violent, abusive husband in an act of self defence. By the time Dilara had finished the collection, Çilem had won an appeal to the Turkish High Court, walking free with the words 'We will fight for women's rights. We will say, "Women shall not die."' 'She's like a hero to me,' says Dilara. 'I'm not saying that it was amazing that she killed him. But to protect herself like that and be supported by all those women, and then to get released… That's a really big statement for women in Turkey, and for human rights in the Middle East in general.'

'Dear Past, Thanks for All the Lessons' might also stand more generally as a description of the way Dilara uses history in her work. As explained in the show notes, her spring collection is about 'the body of a woman and its cultural representation, today and in centuries gone by' – in 16th-century England, for example. 'I found it strange that Elizabeth I wasn't married, which was quite a scandalous thing back then. And yet while this super boss woman was ruling the country, women still weren't allowed on the stage.' That manifests in the collection as Shakespearean corsetry and doublet-style tops. The clothes are embellished with line drawings by her friend, the tattoo artist Liam Sparkes, highlighting the collection's theme of women's skin – which is why a Soho strip club was chosen as the location for the show. 'The whole collection is about skin and how a woman's body is treated in different cultures. Like, Mexican gangs and how they treat women. The men love women – their mothers and stuff – and they accept women, too. But if women want to leave, they kill them. It's really fucked up and brutal. They have amazing tattoos on their faces, with the names of their gangs written on their foreheads.' This is where the tattoo embellishments began. 'I looked at various aspects of their culture, but obviously I looked at how they look, too!'

Becoming a fashion designer has been a long-standing ambition for Dilara. Her first love was John Galliano (with whom she would later intern at Margiela), and then Alexander McQueen and Hussein Chalayan. So Saint Martins, the institution that linked them, was always going to be her destination. 'From about 13 I wanted to study there,' she says, but her parents weren't so sure. 'I don't come from a super-strict Muslim family, but they are much older than me and were a bit old-fashioned. They had friends whose children had studied in other countries, but they were all boys. So it got a bit difficult when I was a teenager. I was a rebellious kid.' She would regularly dye her hair different colours (she still does: today it's bright red) and got her first tattoo when she was 16; she now has many, and I can see the words LET GO on her right forearm. 'So they thought I was going to be some sort of fuck-up, you know?' They're a lot more accepting now. 'They're *so* supportive. My dad's a businessman so he loves that I'm doing business. When I was in Paris doing my showroom he'd call me every day: "So, how many orders did you get?"'

But there was a crisis moment during her Saint Martins days when political events in Turkey tried her enthusiasm for her subject. In May 2013 demonstrators in Istanbul occupied Taksim Gezi Park in protest at government plans to build a shopping centre there. When they were driven out by police armed with tear gas and water cannons, further protests spread across cities in Turkey. Aimed more generally at government repression, they carried on through the summer and were met with an increasingly violent response from the authorities. 'I was in London while that was happening and I was so upset,' says Dilara. 'I'm not a nationalist, I'm super humanistic: I live here and I love this country, it's my country as well. But something like this happens and your family and friends are there fighting…' She felt so far away when she saw the photos of people demonstrating in their thousands, but still managed to find a way to support them. 'Because I couldn't be a part of the riots, I put this friend who works for the BBC in touch with people in Istanbul. Because Turkish media weren't showing much of it, as obviously they have to lick the government's arse.'

Her frustration affected her studies. 'Every day I was going to school really upset and not putting much effort into my work.' She lost patience with her fellow students: 'I was like, "How can you be happy just making clothes when there's so much going on?"' But then a course project set by Grayson Perry proved to be a turning point: she found inspiration in the way his pottery brings autobiography and sociopolitical commentary to a field that's usually assessed purely in terms of aesthetics. 'I realised I had to mix these other things in my work. I don't want to be just another brand that makes lovely clothes and people wear it and it's just *nice*.'

Which is how Dilara's clothes ended up with their political edge. 'You have to change things. I'm not a politician, I do fashion, so all I can do is put those things in my work. I can use what I'm really good at to make people aware of other things. Because it's not just about clothes.'

SONIA BEN AMMAR
/ Model / Actor

Sonia wears black lace dress, gold metal resin and glass pearl necklace, metal strass and crystal earring and metal and resin bangles all by CHANEL

Sonia wears pink polyester dress with ruffles and lace trim by MARC JACOBS; *glittery socks by* CALZEDONIA; *pink suede Flora shoes by* GIUSEPPE ZANOTTI

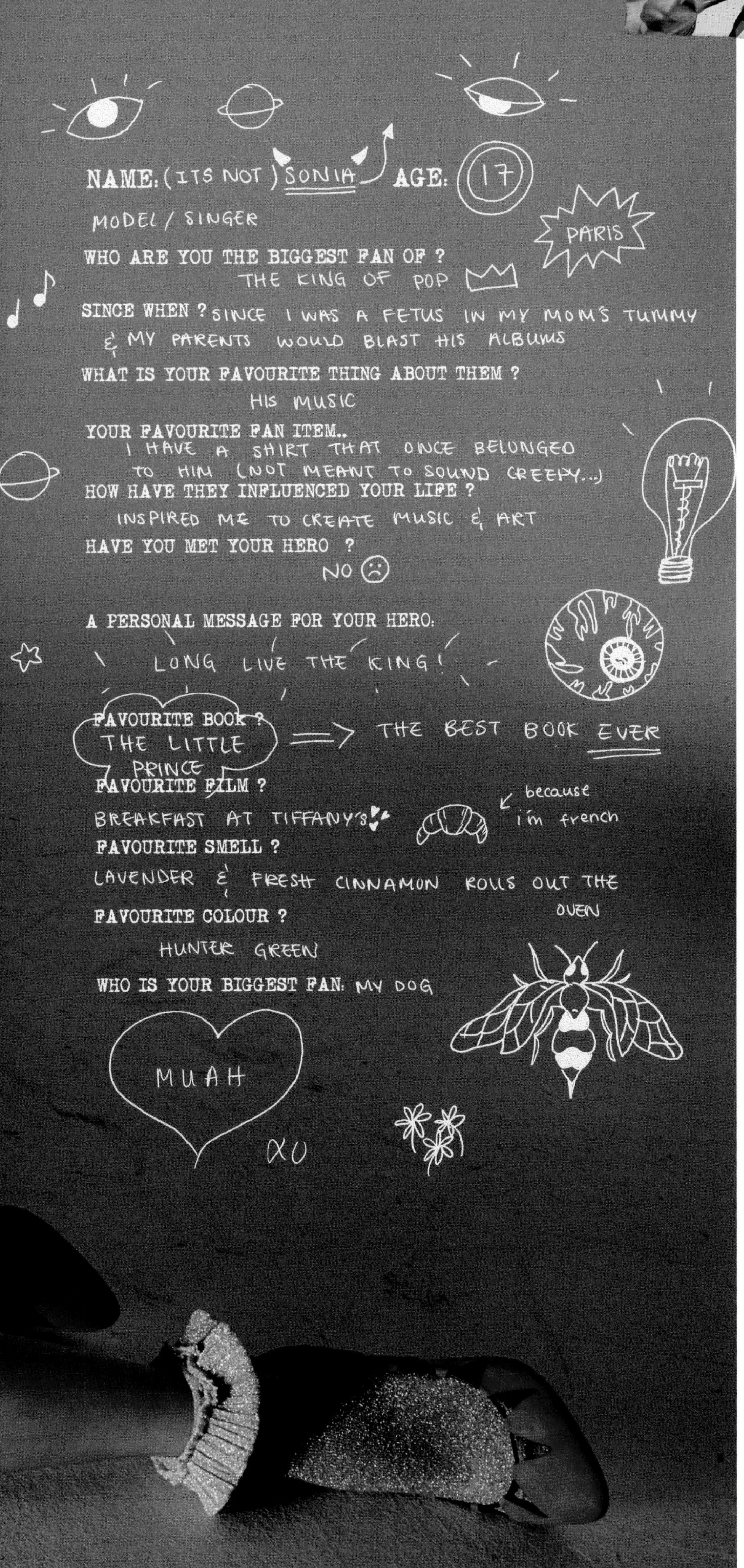

NAME: (ITS NOT) SONIA AGE: 17
MODEL / SINGER
PARIS
WHO ARE YOU THE BIGGEST FAN OF ?
THE KING OF POP
SINCE WHEN ? SINCE I WAS A FETUS IN MY MOM'S TUMMY & MY PARENTS WOULD BLAST HIS ALBUMS
WHAT IS YOUR FAVOURITE THING ABOUT THEM ?
HIS MUSIC
YOUR FAVOURITE FAN ITEM..
I HAVE A SHIRT THAT ONCE BELONGED TO HIM (NOT MEANT TO SOUND CREEPY...)
HOW HAVE THEY INFLUENCED YOUR LIFE ?
INSPIRED ME TO CREATE MUSIC & ART
HAVE YOU MET YOUR HERO ?
NO
A PERSONAL MESSAGE FOR YOUR HERO:
LONG LIVE THE KING!
FAVOURITE BOOK ?
THE LITTLE PRINCE
THE BEST BOOK EVER
FAVOURITE FILM ?
BREAKFAST AT TIFFANY'S
because i'm french
FAVOURITE SMELL ?
LAVENDER & FRESH CINNAMON ROLLS OUT THE OVEN
FAVOURITE COLOUR ?
HUNTER GREEN
WHO IS YOUR BIGGEST FAN: MY DOG
MUAH
XO

The Parisian beauty whose romantic entanglements have been all over the tabloids has just recorded an album 'about love and stuff'

Writer HARRIET VERNEY

If Sonia Ben Ammar could snog anyone famous it would be Johnny Depp circa *Cry-Baby*. She also wouldn't say no to a snog with Leonardo DiCaprio circa *Romeo + Juliet*, and thinks a 73-year-old Mick Jagger definitely still has 'sex appeal' but wouldn't snog him. She has, though, famously snogged Brooklyn Beckham after their families holidayed together in the Maldives. Sonia went on to enjoy a brief *Daily Mail*-covered dalliance with the eldest son of Posh and Becks.

Sonia is the perfect hybrid of an all-American gal-next-door type and Parisian pony, which is why she ended up walking in the Chanel pre-fall 2017 show and starring in Miu Miu's campaign for spring. She looks like a young Sophia Loren, a classic oil-painted beauty. She has dark brown hair, ice-blue eyes set wide apart that never break a fixed gaze, and an upturned pout. She giggles loudly when we take the rollers out of her hair on set and runs and jumps on the LOVE bed in a near see-through baby-doll dress when it's time to be interviewed. She didn't even bat an eyelid when asked to pose with Bonnie the goat, despite the fact the goat clearly hadn't showered for weeks.

A year on from the fling that flung her into the spotlight, the 17-year-old French-born Sonia is currently in the process of writing and recording her debut album in LA. She says it should appeal to more than her online teenage fanbase. 'It's about love and stuff. But I think I sing about some darker stuff too, like betrayal and things that everyone can relate to.' Does any of it refer to Brooklyn? 'No,' she says. 'I don't name names.'

The music bug struck after a stint on what Sonia calls 'Paris's equivalent to Broadway', where she played a female version of little Gavroche in an adapted version of *Les Misérables* titled *1979*. The schedule meant touring France for a year, nightly crowds of nearly 5,000 and a special schooling where lessons were conducted only in the morning. It was all a bit crazy, she says, except missing school, which was 'incredible'.

Her acting abilities come from the dominant Ben Ammar gene. While Mum dabbled in acting when she was younger and has taken to writing screenplays, Dad (Tarak Ben Ammar) is the acclaimed producer behind the films *The Life of Brian, Hannibal Rising* and *Femme Fatale*. He also famously managed Michael Jackson's *HIStory* world tour. He surely must know first hand how to deal with an onslaught of media interest? 'I've never actually asked him about it, but I wish I had lived in the Eighties. Actually, I wish I'd been born in the Eighties.'

So how does she react to all the fan accounts dedicated to her that popped up when she started dating Brooklyn? 'It was definitely weird. But I knew it was going to be part of it and you've just got to accept it. Even if there's hate stuff being said or bad stuff, you're just like "whatever".'

Richard wears his own glasses by WARBY PARKER

WHO ARE YOU THE BIGGEST FAN OF ?
TATTOOS

SINCE WHEN ?
SINCE I SAW THE STRAY CATS AT THE LYCEUM

WHAT FIRST ATTRACTED YOU TO.......
THEY LOOKED LIKE CARTOONS FOR BAD BOYS NGIRLS

WHAT IS YOUR FAVOURITE THING ABOUT THEM ?
MY MUM HATED THEM WHICH MEANT I WAS ON THE RIGHT TRACK!

YOUR FAVOURITE FAN ITEM..
JAPANESE DRAGON ON MY THIGH

HOW HAVE THEY INFLUENCED YOUR LIFE ?
I BUTTON UP MY SHIRTS IN CORPORATE AMERICA

RICHARD HABBERLEY / Model agent

After 30 years in the business and now happily installed at DNA, the East End star-maker of the catwalk has seen it all

Writer PAUL FLYNN

'The faces may change,' says Richard Habberley of the modelling industry, 'but the people don't.' Habberley is the man who knows. He is a supremely well structured fellow, built and inked like a thoroughbred, sporting spectacles and in possession of the sly humour of one who has seen so much come and go in his time negotiating the extreme tenets of beauty that, for now, all there is to do is sit back, work hard and enjoy the view. Richard books at DNA Model Management in New York, his home for the last two decades. His wit and wisdom is still watermarked with the inscrutable Britishness of his East London upbringing. He is the son of a Bethnal Green carpenter. As a model agent, he is another sort of craftsman, one of the industry's few certified star-markers.

Richard's backstory comes replete with first-hand proximity to legend, a useful training circuit for later life. His first boyfriend at 17 was the dancer Michael Clarke. Of the relationship, he doesn't recall much. 'When you're 17 years old and you're going out with someone who's 20, it's all a bit confusing. It's quite hard to know what's going on when you're tripping all the time.' Leigh Bowery would stand at the door 'and listen to us while we were at it'. There was a part of Bowery, he says, that reminds him of the tales of Warhol's endless time spent on the telephone. 'Everyone talks about fake news now,' he laughs. 'That's nothing new, is it? It's just gossip. Leigh Bowery spent his life delivering fake news over the phone. Running a nightclub in our times made you the equivalent of a leader.'

Richard once saw Pete Burns lamp Boy George down a staircase at the Camden Palace. His best friend as he negotiated the outer reaches of mythological Eighties London nightlife was the artist Trojan, who cut off his earlobe as a fashion statement and died prematurely, just as his talent was beginning to blossom wildly in his early twenties. 'Our birthdays were only a week apart,' says Richard. 'I think with all the people I grew up with, there were the real performers and there was the audience. You needed both. I would say that I was more of the audience.' There was always someone pulling more of a look-at-me pose. 'Trojan was much quieter, too. He was very thoughtful but he was very funny and caustic, like everybody.'

The marvellous coterie Richard found circumnavigating the London nightlife of his early years would prove useful, incubating his later dealings in the fashion industry. 'A nightclub is the same as creating a great fashion story, really,' he says, 'because there's that moment where you've got a grotty old warehouse and it's transformed into something with all these glittering little objects, these fabulous creatures that are just there. When the night ends, they all vanish and you're left with the grotty old warehouse again. You create this moment and then it is gone.'

He likes the transitory nature of it all. Since falling into work as an agent in the mid-Eighties, there is little that he hasn't seen. It started as it meant to go on and his entrée into the industry is delightfully casual. Richard was standing in the corner of the offices at Select's Chelsea agency one morning when he overheard a booker having a full-on meltdown. 'She said, "Oh, I've just become a born-again Christian, I can't lie any more." The agency owner looked up horrified and said, "Well, you can't do this job," and I said, "Can I do it then?"' Richard Habberley's glorious tenure in the fashion industry had begun.

Despite changing circumstances, Richard doesn't feel there's much difference between

then and now. He can usually spot a girl's future during their first meeting, when he'll sit them down and ask the magic booker's question: how would you feel if someone wants to cut your hair? 'Because for most young girls, that's going to be the biggest trauma that they face. You get some girls who will instinctively at that moment reach and grab their hair and hold it and you see their face slightly furrows and they don't want to do that. Those are the girls that probably won't succeed. The ones that don't reach for their hair and look straight at you and say, "I don't mind – they can cut it, they can dye it," those are the ones that already have what it may take to make it. That's the first thing I ever notice with them.' He says of all the physical attributes any girl can share, the easiest to identify is the proclivity to work hard and to work for the right reasons. 'Linda [Evangelista] would stay up with Azzedine Alaïa until four in the morning with him sticking pins in her and she'd give interviews saying, "I loved it because that was my job and I was a part of a process" – as opposed to the ones who bitch and moan, who don't get why it's happening, "I don't want to do that." The industry is not about people being there to make you look pretty.'

The current success of the Instagram girls, Richard thinks, is little more than something to keep the wheels turning, a new obsession that will probably pass. 'There always has to be something that causes some friction and discussion in the industry and at this moment that is the thing. In five years' time we won't be talking about that.' His matter-of-fact attitude to all this shouldn't betray his genuine romance for the work. 'The modelling industry is something that's very hard to understand.' He says that after 30 years of working within it he has yet to uncork what drives a particular notion of beauty at one particular time. Knowing would interrupt the game, anyway. 'It's a bit like quicksilver. It's something you see shining in the desert and you go over to it and you find this little group of people who are all running around like they're erecting a circus and you pick it up and feel it in your hand and it feels really good and you want to be a part of it and it's full of all these beautiful things. Then it slips through your hands and falls in the sand and you're left standing on your own and it's gone. They've all vanished.'

Richard thinks we're probably asking the wrong questions about the Instagram girls right now, anyway. 'Is it valid or is it not valid? That's not the question.' He points out that his most successful model of the season, Julia Nobis, has six concurrent campaigns and no social media presence. 'If you said to most people, "Who is Julia Nobis?", they'd have no idea. If you asked, "Who's Gigi Hadid?", they'd know. Because everybody knows. So why do those six brands choose Julia Nobis to be the face of their campaign? The advertising industry itself is in some form of discussion figuring out how they're going to move forward, and I think maybe they don't know yet. I'm not a millennial so I don't know, either. While I think it's a consideration for advertising agencies, at the same time none of it makes any sense, which is how it's always been. It's if the face fits.'

Fashion cannot be aggregated by science. It is so much more tempestuous and exciting than that. 'If you have a mind that is about spreadsheets, numbers and defining what is a model, that's very reductive. You're going to reduce it to nothing and you're not going to get the essence of what it is, because it's about creating a fantasy and creating an illusion. It vanishes. So growing up in a world where there was a lot of that going on in nightclubs helped.'

'The queen has been identified. Now we all push her forward'

By way of an example, he recalls Gisele's upending of the industry during the Nineties, something he witnessed at close range as her agent. 'There's a movement and there's a group of girls that are the faces of that movement, the human embodiment of the look that the designers, the stylists, the photographers are going for. Then what will happen is that one of those faces will suddenly be the one who steps forward to define it, completely. All of a sudden everything will click and she'll become that girl the main drive is pushed towards. She'll be the one everyone wants.' This, he reckons, is probably the most satisfying time in his job. 'All the times I've been around it, at that point you kind of sit back: "Oh, this is it!" I suppose it's like in an ant's nest or a beehive, where everybody knows their job. The queen has been identified, Now we all push her forward.'

Richard knows what it is to be attracted to a face, a body, a world that is somewhere beyond comprehensive agreement of what beauty means. 'I used to look through the magazines and then I would see Jenny Howarth or Leslie Winer in a magazine and I would think, "Oh, they're fucking cool and I like what they're doing." And that was where I caught on to it, where those girls talked to me all of a sudden. That was what I wanted to be a part of. It's about what hooks you in at the beginning.'

Some questions will always rear their heads for the industry. Sexuality, body size, drugs, inappropriate men with access to huge bank accounts. 'Addiction is equal opportunities, across the board,' says Richard. 'It's believed to be higher in our industry than in other areas, but I think that's because the media are more interested in beautiful models with a problem than a 14-year-old homeless girl in Bristol with a problem.' On gender, though, he has seen positive moves. 'I suppose the difference now, if I'm thinking about Trojan, is that there was a whole bunch of them that stripped away traditional masculine ideals but didn't want to look like girls, they just went somewhere else with it. The same with Pete Burns. You took your life into your hands walking down the street like that.'

He is pleased that a new generation is breaking down old gender rules in a more deliberate way, that it has become a defining conversation of its day. 'Of course. I love it. There are models who may surprise you. As far as sex and gender goes, there are models that were born a different gender than maybe you think they were and you don't know. And they've been working for a while.'

Times have changed, at least in this regard. 'When I was growing up, if you were a boy that was really a girl then your career choices were basically in the sex industry. That was pretty much it. You had to work outside of society.' There is one side-effect of all this that he laughs about. 'Being gay is really pedestrian. Oh, completely. Maybe we grew up in the last generation where there was something outside of society about homosexuality. My dad believed that homosexuality was the same as paedophilia because that's what the *News of the World* told him. And so, yeah, now there's a gay bar in every small town across America. Fashion-wise, I think that has created, say with bears, a situation where gay men have wanted to take all the worst attributes of straight men and dress like them. They want to dress like someone who works in a factory in Omaha.'

This is not the idea of fashion that Richard Habberley has spent his life in thrall to. The one thing that remains above all else in his industry is the thrill of the new. 'What you really want to be is open to the next thing as opposed to what's going on now. The thing that people really struggle with – and at the same time is really the overriding thing – is that it's about beauty, which can come in so many shapes and forms. It's about being open to that, not about gender and not about anything else apart from this quite pure drive towards what is deemed to be beautiful at any given moment.'

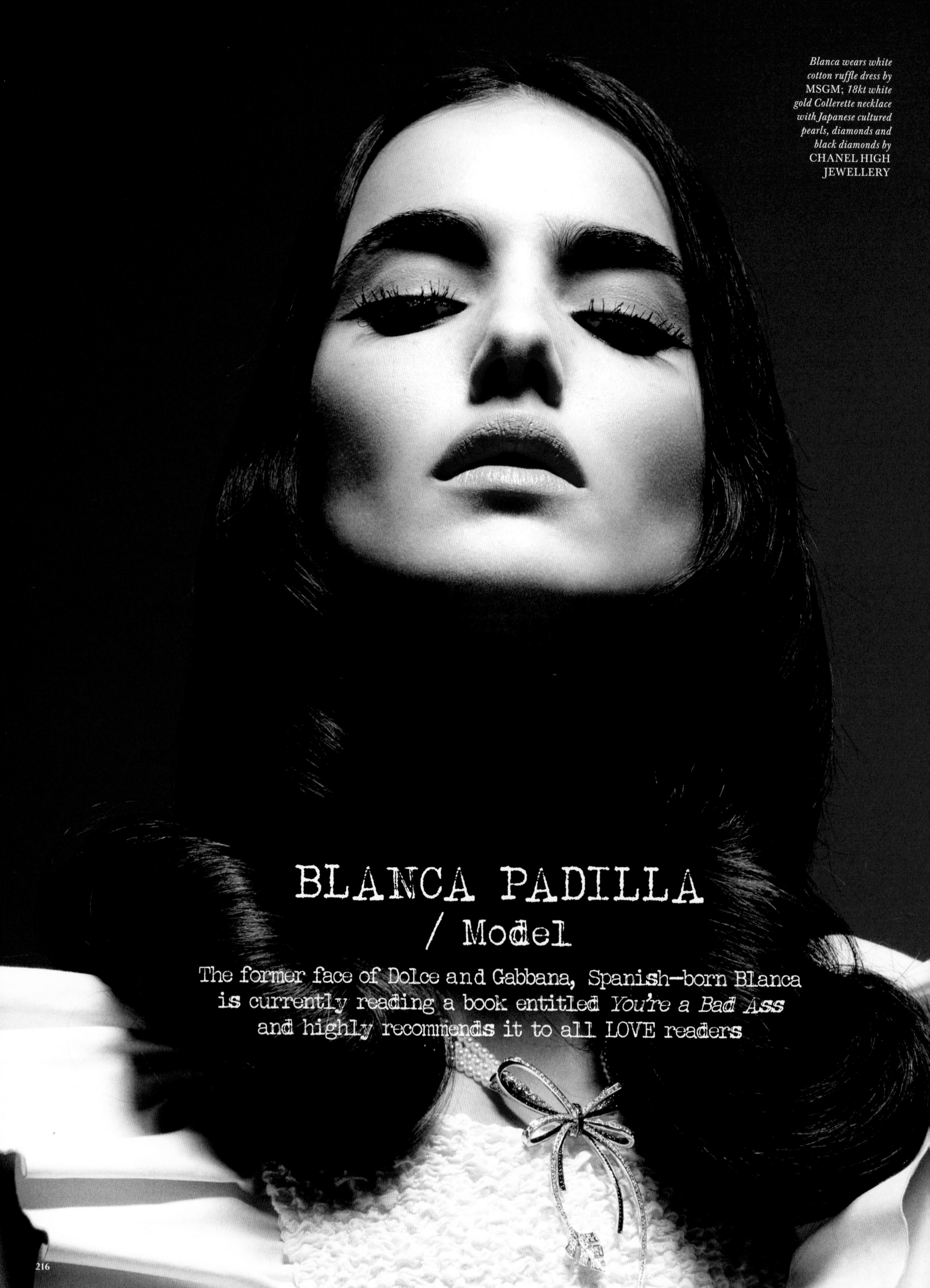

Blanca wears white cotton ruffle dress by MSGM; *18kt white gold Collerette necklace with Japanese cultured pearls, diamonds and black diamonds by* CHANEL HIGH JEWELLERY

BLANCA PADILLA
/ Model

The former face of Dolce and Gabbana, Spanish-born Blanca is currently reading a book entitled *You're a Bad Ass* and highly recommends it to all LOVE readers

WHO IS YOUR BIGGEST FAN:
My mum

Blanca wears white cotton ruffle dress by MSGM; *cape (on floor) by* NAMILIA; *18kt white gold Collerette necklace with Japanese cultured pearls, diamonds and black diamonds by* CHANEL HIGH JEWELLERY; *18kt white gold Perle Couture earrings with diamonds and Japanese cultured pearls by* CHANEL FINE JEWELLERY

Hailey wears cascade glitter embroidery one-sleeved sparkly jersey dress by LOUIS VUITTON; *platinum Soleste ring with diamonds and tanzanite, 18kt white-gold T Line diamond bracelet, 18kt gold T Hinge wrap bracelet with diamonds and 18kt rose-gold Sugar Stacks ring with pink sapphires and 18kt gold and platinum square red diamond ring with white diamonds all by* TIFFANY & CO; *gold Serti Sur Vide earring and gold Staple full pavéd earring both by* REPOSSI; *plain ring Hailey's own*

WHO ARE YOU THE BIGGEST FAN OF ?

Shawn Mendes

WHAT IS YOUR FAVOURITE THING ABOUT THEM ?

He is the reincarnation of John Mayer

YOUR FAVOURITE FAN ITEM..

don't own anything of that sort..... yet. //

HOW HAVE THEY INFLUENCED YOUR LIFE ?

He has changed my entire world for the better!

HAILEY BALDWIN / Model

Kendall's best friend is keen to make the jump from the catwalk to Hollywood, just like her dad

Writer HARRIET VERNEY

The first time model Hailey Baldwin ever snuck out from home was when she was 16 and there was a very important Drake gig happening that evening in Brooklyn – a gig that her parents (actor Stephen Baldwin and graphic designer Kennya Deodato) did not want her to go to. With her sister Alaia as the designated driver and friend and accomplice RJ in tow, the three of them crept out under the premise of a quiet dinner in the city. After the gig little Hailey carried on partying into the night celebrating Drake's birthday. 'It was so fun!' she says. 'I'll never forget it as long as I live.'

That was four years ago and her parents have never found out (not unless they're reading this). The legal drinking age in the States is 21 which means technically she can't order alcohol in a bar till the end of this year, although she says she's 'not really a drinker' anyway. For her best friend Kendall Jenner's 21st birthday party in LA, which is still yet to happen when we meet, Hailey says that she'll be sipping 'bottled Fiji water and some Red Bull'. What has she got Kendall for her birthday? 'A custom bottle of 1942 Tequila – it's engraved and says "Kendall's 21st" and the date.' Theirs is a well documented friendship, with Kendall being a mutual friend of Hailey's rumoured on/off boyfriend Justin Bieber. Hailey was 14 when she first met Kendall. 'I was actually closer to Kylie first and Kendall after. We ended up becoming much closer because she would come to New York to work and I live here.'

When Hailey walked into the LOVE studio she was hidden behind a massive suitcase about eight times as big as her. She is an incy-wincy, teeny-weeny honey blonde, with a figure that shows the effect of the years she spent doing ballet to an almost professional level. Her plump pink pout is most definitely real – you only have to look at pictures of her mum at the same age to tell. And when she isn't on her phone, she is a pro at holding an enviably immobile resting bitch face – until she breaks into a girlie grin that can't contain itself, especially when she is telling you really good gossip (none of which we can print here, sadly). 'I don't like to force a smile if it's not what I'm feeling in that moment,' she says of the accusation that she never smiles. 'I'm not going to cheese while I'm walking down the street and weird paparazzi are taking photos – that doesn't make me happy.'

The paparazzi's interest in her only increased when she began dating long-time friend Justin. His fans, she says, were 'passionate'. Were they ever weird with her? 'To be honest, everyone's been pretty nice to me. There are still going to be people that get mean or get weird because they can, because they're behind a computer screen. But people are even mean in *Daily Mail* articles. So it doesn't really matter if they're a fan of somebody or not – people are just mean in general.' Right now she says she is a fan of singer Shawn Mendes and the Jonas Brothers, Nick in particular. She was at school with Nick and she wasn't his only fan on campus. 'The woman who worked in the office when you walk into the school told me that she would pay Nick a dollar to sing a Broadway song for them.'

With work keeping her busy, dating isn't really on her mind at the moment anyway. 'I think a lot of people date for the aesthetic of dating, which is weird. I'm just not big on dating around a lot – at all, really.' Does work get in the way? 'Yeah, for sure. I don't wanna date someone that doesn't have their own thing going for them, because I think that's when things can get kind of weird. But then when both of your schedules are so crazy, it's super, super hard to find the time. One of you has to be in the position of sacrificing. You have to take time off and relax, but I never know where I'm going to be week to week.'

Those weeks are filling up fast. She is now in her second year of starring in the Guess campaigns (which she says are her favourite photos), has become a D&G catwalk regular, walked for Tory Burch in New York and Matty Bovan and Julien Macdonald in London last season, and has endorsements coming out of her ears. She says she has a bucket list of things she would like to shoot in her career. One item on the list was ticked off this year when Karl Lagerfeld photographed her for his own-brand campaign. 'He's really quick. He takes the photo and goes, "We got it." He knows what he's doing.'

Another item on her bucket list is walking in the Victoria's Secret show. She was called to a casting for it this year but didn't make it to the catwalk. Because so many of her friends are veterans of the VS catwalk, she says, 'People assume it's really, really easy to get in the show, but it's actually really difficult.' The casting 'was really, really intense. I was really nervous: I was shaking, and in my head I was like, "Stop shaking or they're not gonna give you the show." Then I didn't get it, and I thought, "It's because I was shaking in front of them!"'

Has she ever cried because she didn't get a job? 'One hundred per cent. Sometimes I just get frustrated because I see certain people do certain things. And I know I can do that – so why do I not get to do the same things?'

Acting is next on the list for Hailey. She is about to star in rapper Travis Scott's music video, directed by Hype Williams, and is auditioning here and there for the right kind of acting role. She has come in for some stick for this particular ambition and can't understand why, when all she's doing is following in her family's footsteps. 'My uncle Billy modelled before he acted, my dad modelled before he acted. We don't have any female models in our family, but even Kim Basinger, who's my cousin Ireland's mom, was a model before she acted, too. So it's pretty normal. No one questions Cindy Crawford's daughter for wanting to model like her mom, so I don't understand why people flip about us. Even with Gigi, her mom was a supermodel. So why do people question when all we wanna do is what our family has already done before us?'

JONATHAN SAUNDERS / Designer

Diane von Furstenberg's first-ever chief creative officer talks about his new life in New York – and pays tribute to his friend Richard Nicoll, who sadly died shortly before this interview

Writer PAUL FLYNN

'A Glaswegian in New York is a funny old combination,' says Jonathan Saunders, staring out from a roof terrace on the gloriously familiar new skyline he now calls home. It's a long way, physically and metaphorically, from Cambuslang. 'I'm imagining my Glaswegian schoolmates thinking, how the hell did he do that?' Since taking the chief creative officer's role at Diane von Furstenberg, Jonathan's life has been imbued with a new sense of purpose. His 14-year-old dog Amber is being passengered over to his West Village home as we speak. His partner Justin moved a month previously. 'Now he's here and Amber's here, I feel like it's all falling into place.'

Back in London, Jonathan Saunders was one of the most beloved fixtures among a close-knit assemblage of young designers who created their own passage onto fashion's world stage. They caroused between putting together shows with piecemeal resources and the hostelries of the East End, lending the honest pursuit of making people look better feel like a fun, free and inviting enterprise. His disparate peer group negotiated the complicated transition into adulthood full of dreams of revising their industry for the 21st century. They were the rock stars of their day. Not all reached their full potential, getting to work alongside and shape the future of household-name brands. Jonathan did it.

At 38, Jonathan has a significant position among the top tier, very much on his own terms. He is part of the elite. 'Am I?' he says, looking genuinely surprised by the supposition, making some sense of his wistfulness on what old Glasgow allies would make of his new life. 'I guess so. I never thought about myself like that.' He brings to the house of DVF a unique gift for colour, print and texture, one that always defined his own line. In return, the house of DVF brings to Jonathan resources, infrastructure and a global clientele he could once only have dreamed of. He first met Diane to talk about the job in Claridges ('casual'). His role involves a carefully aggregated release of ego on both sides. 'Diane has always known what I did,' he says. 'It's about being humble enough to listen to people and to be strong enough to have your own point of view. I feel ready for that.

'It's the scale of the thing,' he says of his new home. 'I've been proving things to myself since I was 16. I guess when you are in your late thirties, as I am now, you start to understand your value and you become a lot more confident with it. I remember in London for years and years trying to be creative while working on a shoestring and trying to show people this illusion of grandeur, that you were this designer brand, when you were basically creating things in a spit-and-sawdust way. All those years I found really tough to work through. Now I realise that all that experience I went through has enabled me to come here.'

If Jonathan is in reflective mood, it cuts deeper than his big move and the fact that he's approaching 40. Fashion found him partly by accident. At 15 as a Glasgow schoolboy his awakenings coincided with discovering the city's nightlife, making new friends, finding a life away from his strict religious homestead. 'I had Glasgow guilt and Jehovah's Witness guilt,' he notes. 'That's a double whammy.' He got his first Saturday job at the Katharine Hamnett store in Princess Square as a teen. He flyered for the Sub Club and began hanging around with the city's gilded shop, club and hairdressing folk.

By the time he arrived at Glasgow School of Art, Jonathan was well versed in the work of his heroes Margiela, Hamnett and Helmut Lang. 'What was great about fashion then was that it was touchable and attainable. Obviously there were aspirational pieces that designers created, but there was a wearability and reality to it.' It is this cross-pollination between wearability and expression that he intends to see through to a natural conclusion at DVF. 'Fashion became almost a demi-couture thing in the following decade. I've just recently been thinking about why I'm so interested in this kind of area within fashion. And I figure that it's probably because that influential moment was when I was building in my mind what I was going to be.'

He studied product design for two years and graduated in textiles ('craftsmanship has always intrigued me and that's what I learned there') before making the decisive shift to London to complete his studies with an MA at Central Saint Martins. Having trouble making ends meet, he had to sell his Glasgow Art School collection, a series of deconstructed kimonos, which makes a particular kind of sense given the wraparound DNA of the brand he now has creative charge of. 'Then I met Richard,' he says, of his great friend and inspiration Richard Nicoll. 'I had no experience of London; I was so broke and I was very intimidated by it. Glasgow's very small. I didn't know much about fashion, even though I'd religiously followed *Dazed* and *i-D* and *The Face*. I was so excited by it but it felt like a world that I couldn't touch. Then Rich introduced me to a lot of people and finally made me realise I can do this, actually.'

Richard's passing at the end of 2016 sits soberly over the conversation. 'His influence on me was massive,' he says. 'His taste felt so developed and specific; there was a sophistication I hadn't seen before. His confidence with what he loved and what he thought was relevant was really inspiring. He also envisaged a whole world, and I didn't know how to realise that until we met.' After Richard died, Jonathan began thinking about his old friend and mentor's graduate collection. 'There was a film of our friend Barbara, dancing in this funny disco scene, with this beautiful silver curtain. She had a Giorgio di Sant' Angelo kind of swimsuit on and she looked so beautiful and so sexy and free, in this future-disco world he created.' It is still one of Jonathan's favourite memories of Richard. 'Everybody was really overdesigning stuff and not really understanding women's bodies at that point. Everyone was making heavy, deconstructed clothes, and he was making this beautiful, sensual work, all very Pina Bausch, about beautiful movement.'

In the end, of course, it is not the work but the man he will miss most. 'Rich had that mesmerising quality where he was so captivating as a person that he managed to sieze everybody's imagination. There wasn't a single friend of his or person who crossed his path that didn't have an emotional connection with Richard.' It is Jonathan's duty now, in work and life, to continue the mesmerising spell. 'There are not many designers that can create a world like that. I guess, you know, the only way to reconcile something like this is to think maybe his job was to influence and to inspire us in the amazing way that he did. He was totally loved.'

A PERSONAL MESSAGE FOR YOUR HERO:
thank you for the inspiration

Jonathan wears black barathea suit jacket by RALPH LAUREN PURPLE LABEL; *lanyard with lighter by* ALEXANDER WANG

WHO ARE YOU THE BIGGEST FAN OF ?
My mama

Maggie wears silk dress, gold rings, necklace, earrings and white high-heeled shoes all by DIANE VON FURSTENBERG; *vintage Legato sunglasses from* FABULOUS FANNY'S; *black choker by* PROENZA SCHOULER

MAGGIE RAWLINS

/ Model / Nurse

24-year-old Maggie Rawlins says that the weirdest message she ever received from a fan read: 'Can I buy your socks?' 'No', was her curt reply

Barbara wears red sequinned ruched blouse with ruffles and red sequinned lace tiered skirt both by RODARTE; *orange latex knickers by* ATSUKO KUDO; *gold-plated earrings by* DSQUARED; *18kt gold T Chain necklace, 18kt gold T Cut Out hinged cuff, gold T Hinge wrap bracelet, gold T Square bracelet and 18kt gold Elsa Peretti Bone cuff all by* TIFFANY

WHO ARE YOU THE BIGGEST FAN OF ?

Cheese

WHAT IS YOUR FAVOURITE THING ABOUT THEM ?

the smell

YOUR FAVOURITE FAN ITEM..

panda (plush)

HOW HAVE THEY INFLUENCED YOUR LIFE ?

they help me sleep

HAVE YOU MET YOUR HERO ?

no ... I'm still single ..

FAVOURITE BAND ?

KOL

FAVOURITE BOOk ?

anything from Leslie L. Lawrence

FAVOURITE FILM ?

White chicks

BARBARA PALVIN / Model

She's L'Oréal's youngest ambassador and Stella Maxwell's best friend, and has cleverly set up a shoe company back home in Hungary

Writer HARRIET VERNEY

Barbara Palvin is refusing to put on any clothes. Resplendent in a nude G-string which has less material than the hairband around her wrist, the Hungarian model has just dropped her dressing gown and climbed into the makeshift, pink-glittered LOVE bed to be interviewed. With one bare tanned leg wrapped around the duvet, she's straight into PG-certificate Paula Yates in *Big Breakfast* mode. Barbara and her perfectly pursed lips may look every inch the innocent, but the reality turns out to be something else entirely.

Barbara was first approached by a model agency in Budapest. 'Do we have to pay for it?' her mother asked the scout. 'It's free,' he replied. Barbara pieced together her hottest look for the interview. 'I put on this pink T-shirt with white flowers with purple cord jeans and a pink scarf as a belt – that was my best outfit.' She didn't wear make-up – 'My parents wouldn't let me.' Hurrah. Barbara's career had begun at the ripe old age of 12.

Her modest family life was quietly uneventful until fashion beckoned. She describes her parents as 'strict – not conservative, but they didn't roll with the times'. Her older sister was 'the smart one in the family'. Her grandmother suggested Barbara become a lawyer or something in the financial industry before her startling looks took her down another path. 'We'd watch these TV shows with lawyers in, starring the most beautiful, smartest women ever. I promised her I'd be that one day.' Barbara never had posters in her bedroom growing up and she didn't obsess over pop stars as her contemporaries did. At school things were a little complicated. She says she was a 'loner' who 'no one liked'. 'They always made fun of me,' she says of her classmates. Did she get into trouble a lot? 'Yeah, for locking younger children in the toilet. We would turn off the lights and they'd get scared. That wasn't very nice of me.' While most of her early teens were spent travelling to Asia with her mother on modelling assignments, after she switched schools the temperature of the classroom changed towards her. 'The first three years I was playing soccer every break. I would just run into the garden and be one of the boys, and suddenly I was the cool kid. I'm still a nice girl, I'm nice to everyone.' Promise?

Barbara became one of the Victoria Secret's Angels at the age of 18. She's the youngest ambassador for L'Oréal, has starred in Armani Exchange and H&M campaigns, the latter alongside her occasional landlady while in New York, Stella Maxwell. 'She's the first person I became friends with in the industry,' says Barbara. 'We're not even friends any more, we're family. She's not wild. She's the nicest girl ever.' Barbara became a *Sports Illustrated* Rookie of the Year in 2016. Her early years were spent on Prada, Louis Vuitton, Christopher Kane and Miu Miu catwalks. Then, inevitably, came the offer of a movie role. Would she like to talk about *Hercules*, the film that she starred in? 'No.' What about the rumoured romance with a car-loving, Formula One British racing driver? 'No,' she responds stony-faced, and then bursts into a very good rendition of Salt'n'Pepa's 'Let's Talk about Sex, Baby'.

Barbara and Stella capitalised on their double-trouble sex appeal by dressing as 'gentlemen' for Heidi Klum's infamous Halloween party last year. Why? 'Because gentlemen are dead.' Right. 'All the girls were hitting on me,' she notes. 'I felt like I could have taken home more girls than any of my guy friends that night. I'm not even kidding. This one girl came up to me and said, "Hey, I'm leaving. Do you want to come back to my hotel ?"' Tempting as the offer was, Barbara declined. 'I said, "Girl, I know I'm dressed like a man but I don't have a thingy down there."'

If she wasn't modelling, Barbara says she would be back in Hungary working for the shoe business that she and her sister own. Does she get bored of modelling? 'Modelling is not work every day. There are weeks when you're not doing anything and I hate myself – that's why I started this company with my sister, to keep myself busy. I'm still friends with everyone in Hungary because I always go home.' Barbara is happy to have a stealth career for now. 'You know, it wasn't like Gigi or Bella or Cara,' she says of her modelling life. 'They came and just took over everything in a second. Whereas my career has always been building up, step by step.'

WHO ARE YOU THE BIGGEST FAN OF ?

David Attenborough

WHAT IS YOUR FAVOURITE THING ABOUT THEM ?

How excited he gets around wildlife

YOUR FAVOURITE FAN ITEM..

All his DVD's - they help me sleep

HOW HAVE THEY INFLUENCED YOUR LIFE ? He taught me more about earth than school ever did + how we need to look after it.

HAVE YOU MET YOUR HERO ?

I wish

FAVOURITE SONG ?

September - Earth Wind + fire

FAVOURITE BAND ?

Tupac

FAVOURITE BOOk ?

I am Pilgrim

FAVOURITE FILM ?

Mary Poppins

FAVOURITE SMELL ?

Roast Pork

JENA GOLDSACK / Model

The French Vogue protégée whose Cornish roots keep her grounded

Writer PAUL FLYNN

Jena Goldsack was scouted by someone she describes as 'a famous Nineties model' six years ago, walking along the high street in Falmouth near her home in Cornwall. 'I'm not going to name any names, but the day after, she was on *The Jeremy Kyle Show* talking about her coke addiction and her prostitution. I was just 16, sitting there with my mum on the sofa going "oh", so it kind of put me off a bit.' For the next few months, friends told her she was insane for not taking up the offer of a London agency meeting. 'Finally, I caved.'

Jena is still a country girl at heart. She says her favourite moments in a fantastic six-year period of work that has seen her rise through the commercial world to get the blessing of Emanuelle Alt at *Vogue* Paris have been watching a volcano erupt in Iceland, and on Jervis Bay, Australia, where she got to hang out with kangaroos on the beach. Her boyfriend, also a model, says he wants to stay in the city. 'He's such a city boy, he can't ever see it. He's like, "You're all so weird down there."' Such is the stigma of hailing from rural Cornwall. 'We are all related, obviously,' she laughs.

Jena says she's stopped trying to explain to friends back home what it is she does for a living. 'My mum always tries to prise answers out of me. If school friends see me out, they'll be like, "Why haven't we seen your tits on Google yet?" I'm like, "Fucking hell." Because it's such a different world, I think people know that if they ask questions then they'll only get more confused. I just try and keep it really separate.' Home keeps her feet on the ground. 'I love going back. It's such a nice relief.'

Jena wears men's tailored jacket by KENZO; *leopard-print Slim Signature shirt by* EQUIPMENT; *pearl necklace and earrings all by* MIKIMOTO; *Pom Pom veil with pearl details by* PIERS ATKINSON

Jena wears black polka-dot print silk dress by CHRISTIAN DIOR; *pearl necklace and earrings all by* MIKIMOTO; *Pom Pom veil with pearl details by* PIERS ATKINSON; *Tania high-heeled sandals by* GIUSEPPE ZANOTTI

JENA

Every thing
But the
Dress

LONGCHAMP.COM

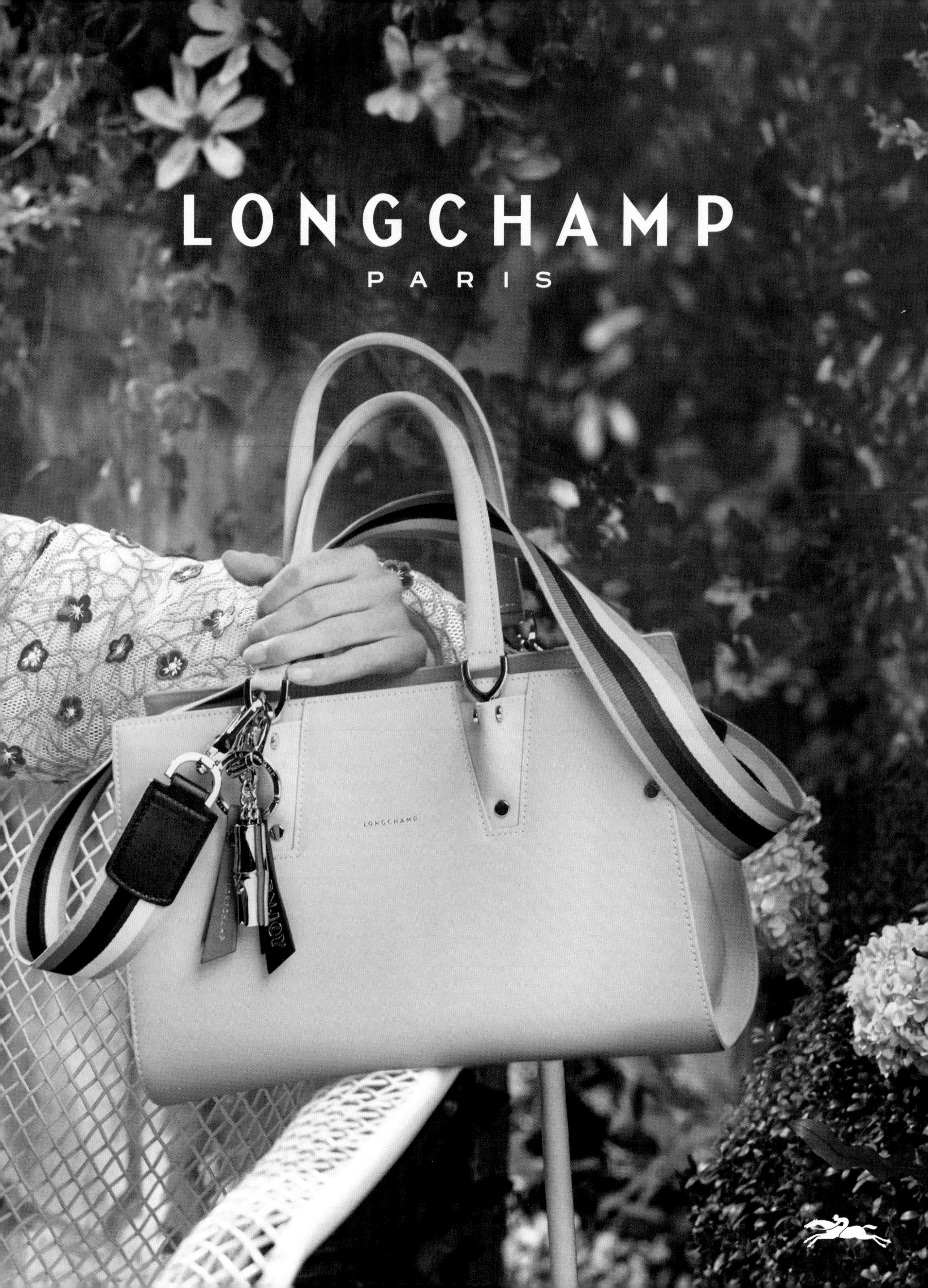
LONGCHAMP
PARIS
LONGCHAMP

War of the Words

An exchange of slogans in the streets of New York, from the demonstrations that greeted Donald Trump's election as president of the United States last November

Photographer HUGO SCOTT

CAN'T GRA
THIS
PUSSY

HOW AM I
SUPPOSED TO LOVE
A COUNTRY THAT DOES
NOT
LOVE ME?
Nikon

TRiUMPhant
Make America Great Again!
TRUMP
AMERICA GREAT AGAIN!

PUSSY
Grabs Ba
MY NECK
MY BACK
MY PUSSY
WILL GRAB BACK
OT OUR PRESIDENT
ABOLISH
ELECTORAL
COLLEC

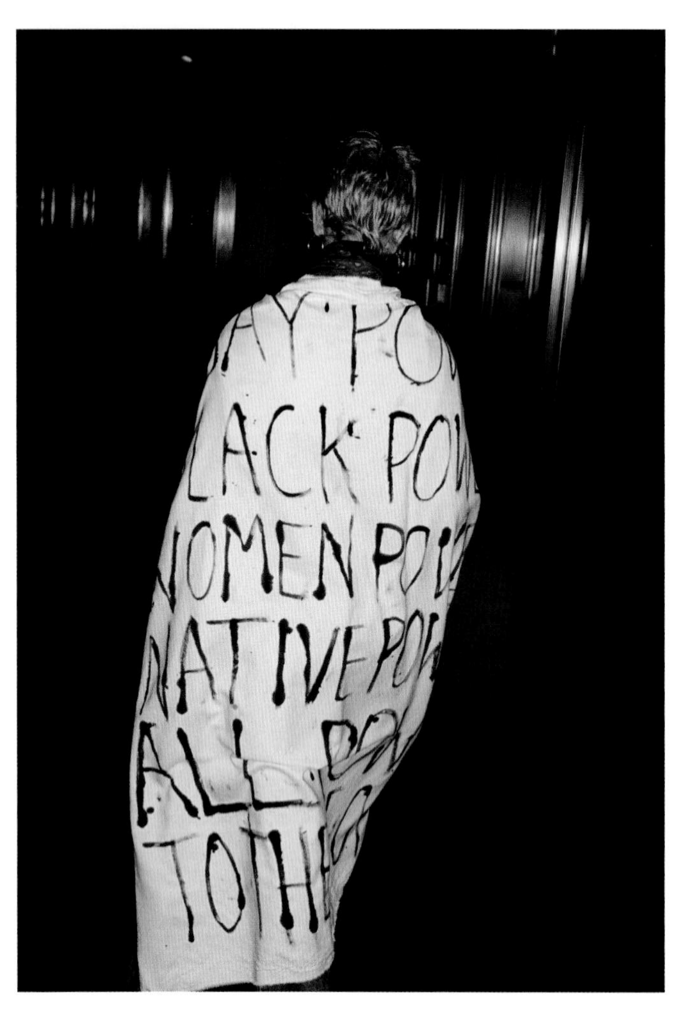
LACK POW
OMEN PO
NATIVE PO
TOTH

IF I WANTED THE
GOVERNMENT IN MY
VAGINA I'D FUCK
A SENATOR!
#FUCK TRUMP

FUCK
that
GUY

8 AM to 10 PM
RUMP TOWER
NYC
TRUMP

IM HERE
IM QUEER
AND YOU WILL
NOT
SHUT ME UP
#NOTMYPRESIDENT

WHEN CONFRONTED
BY A BULLY U
A) RUN
B) STAND DOWN
C) FIGHT!

END
WHITE
SUPREMACY

HITLER
TRUMP
REAGAN
GRAB

Walter Pfeiffer - London, November 2016

Hell's Bells

Enter a state of undress with hearth-rug heart-breaker beauty Bella and slip into something more comfortable

Photographer CARIN BACKOFF
Fashion Editor LYNETTE GARLAND

Bella wears multicoloured Pansy knickers by MISS CROFTON; *striped socks by* MARC JACOBS

Bella wears embroidered silk crepe shirt by ROBERTO CAVALLI; *vintage blue and white check shorts from* COSPROP

Bella wears blue and white striped T-shirt by AG JEANS; *lace and silk mix Cherrie bra and briefs both by* AGENT PROVOCATEUR

Bella wears grey jersey Punto Stoffa cardigan, printed silk shirt, high-waisted black briefs and belt all by PRADA; *vintage grey stockings from* MODES AND MORE

Bella wears blue and white silk Tuyu Nuage shirt by ZADIG & VOLTAIRE; *black polyester Culotte knickers by* FIFI CHACHNIL; *black fishnet tights by* CAPEZIO

Bella wears black velvet goatskin Paris Rocks Velours ballerina shoes by LONGCHAMP; *white vintage rose-print cotton Culotte Retro knickers by* APC; *white socks by* TABIO

Bella wears sheer black dress with lace and pale pink floral shorts both by COACH 1941; *point d'esprit tights by* FALKE

Bella wears red cotton knit Ajour sweater by BOTTEGA VENETA; *blue denim shorts by* GUESS JEANS

Bella wears Sondra pink blouse by KATE SPADE; *vintage cream corset from* NATIONAL THEATRE COSTUME HIRE; *Tearose Brazilian ivory lace briefs by* LA PERLA

Hair ASHLEY JAVIER Make-up SIL BRUINSMA Manicure MAKI SAKAMOTO Retouching PICTUREHOUSE and THE SMALL DARKROOM Model BELLA HADID
Photographic assistance DAVID RUBIN Fashion assistance PRINCIPAL YIP, LAURA NEWRZELLA, ERIKA GOLCHER Hair assistance KIMBERLY GARDUNO

Redemption
redemption.com

WHAT DONATELLA LOVES MOST

Photographer SØLVE SUNDSBØ
Fashion Editor KATIE GRAND

Donatella Versace lists the things she's a mighty fan of, to accompany an overview of her multipanelled and checkered collection for spring

Ondria wears red and navy silk baroque print asymmetric dress and leather high-heeled platform shoes with ankle straps all by VERSACE

ZAYN MALIK
'Everyone knows how talented he is, how handsome, how captivating. What I love is that Zayn is all of these things, but he is also a true gentleman, with the kindest of hearts. Now we are collaborating together on Zayn X Versus.'

VIOLET
'Violet is one of the most incredible artists working right now. For spring/summer 2017, I asked her to write a new track just for me, and Edie Campbell walked out in the first look to the lyrics "This show is for the women taking chances. Take the leap – if we do nothing, we get nothing."'

PALAZZO VERSACE DUBAI
'It's the most incredible place on the planet – the most perfect vision of the Versace life.'

LONDON
'If I had the chance to live two lives at once, right now I would be living in London. I am captivated by the energy on its streets, by the mix of cultures and people who make the city so special.'

PRINCE
'It was my privilege to be able to call Prince my friend. He had an endless flow of creativity and energy, a mind that could not be stopped. I miss him every day, and I will always be his number one fan.'

LADY GAGA
'Fearlessness. Bravery. Individuality. When I think about Lady Gaga, these are the characteristics that come straight to my mind. I am inspired by each new leap she makes into the future.'

BRUCE WEBER
'For me, Bruce Weber is one of the great storytellers of our time. For spring/summer 2017 we travelled to Kentucky to look at the beauty and soul of the Deep South. In every image, he creates a world of love and beauty that I could live in forever.'

GIGI HADID
'Gigi is funny and clever, she fights for what she believes in, and she only does what she wants. When I first met her it was like an instant connection – I knew that we would become friends.'

PAT McGRATH
'Watching Pat work is like magic: the way that her hands move with such instinct, how her eye sees the power of what make-up can hold.'

ANGELINA JOLIE
'Angelina embodies everything that I love about women today. She is the most incredible talent: fearless, provocative and passionate. I am always so proud to create dresses for her.'

Ondria wears black viscose sleeveless jacket, black neoprene leggings, red leather bag with canvas shoulder strap and leather platform sandals with red and navy canvas straps all by VERSACE

Ondria wears red and blue embroidered mesh column gown and leather platform sandals with red embroidered canvas straps all by VERSACE

Ondria wears purple, black and green knitted crop top, yellow, black and purple check-printed pencil skirt and leather platform sandals with navy embroidered canvas straps all by VERSACE

Ondria wears navy, green and yellow leather rain jacket and blue chain-link crop top both by VERSACE

Hair SYD HAYES Make-up MIRANDA JOYCE
Manicure CHISATO YAMAMOTO Production PAULA EKENGER, SALLY DAWSON Retouching DIGITAL LIGHT LTD Model ONDRIA HARDIN
Photographic assistance SIMON McGUIGAN, SAM HENDEL
Digital technician ANNA HENDRY Fashion assistance OLIVER VOLQUARDSEN
Hair assistance PAULA McCASH
Make-up assistance HANNAH MAESTRANZI, VASS THEOTOKIS

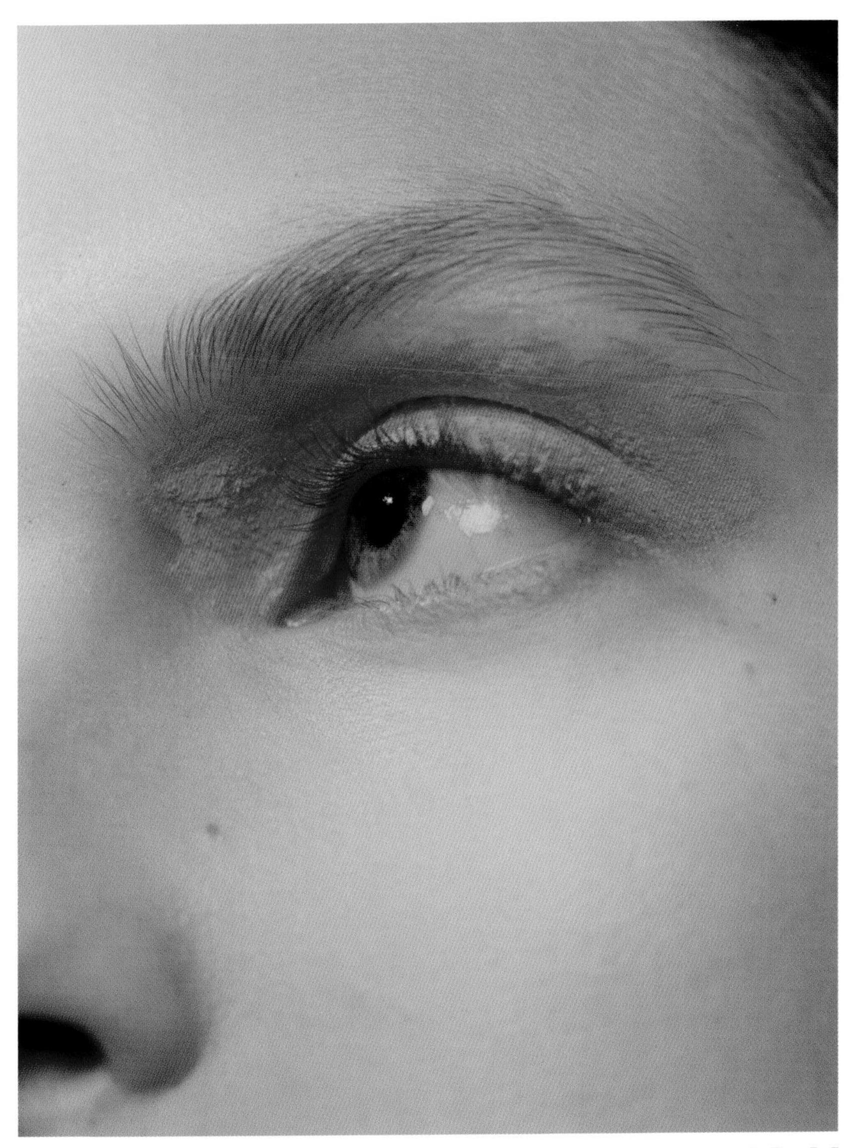

ERIKA CAVALLINI

ELISABETTA FRANCHI

The Fan Club

Binx, Cami, Karlie, Frida, Julia and Julia

Bad girls come out after dark in polka dots, pearls, leather and lace. See you at the parking lot. Bring my/your/a lipstick

Photographer DREW JARRETT
Fashion Editor STEVE MORRISS

Cami wears pink silk lace slip dress, green crepe de Chine silk blouse and gold metal and glass pearl belt all by CHANEL; *pink suede Tina headband by* MAISON MICHEL; *lace socks by* TABIO; *pink open-toe La Baronne shoes by* LONGCHAMP

Binx wears black silk bra by LA PERLA; *polka-dot silk shirt-dress by* MOSCHINO; *crystal hoop earrings by* ELISABETTA FRANCHI; *leather and crystal wrap choker by* RENDOR AND STEEL; *tights by* WOLFORD; *red suede Romy 100 shoes by* JIMMY CHOO

Karlie wears black crepe de Chine minidress with embroidered bow by FENDI; *pearl drop earrings by* KENNETH JAY LANE; *point d'esprit tights by* GERBE

Frida wears silk organza ruffled dress with bows by CHLOÉ; *socks by* TOPSHOP; *pink patent Carnaby pump heels by* BALLY

Frida wears silk organza ruffled dress with bows by CHLOÉ

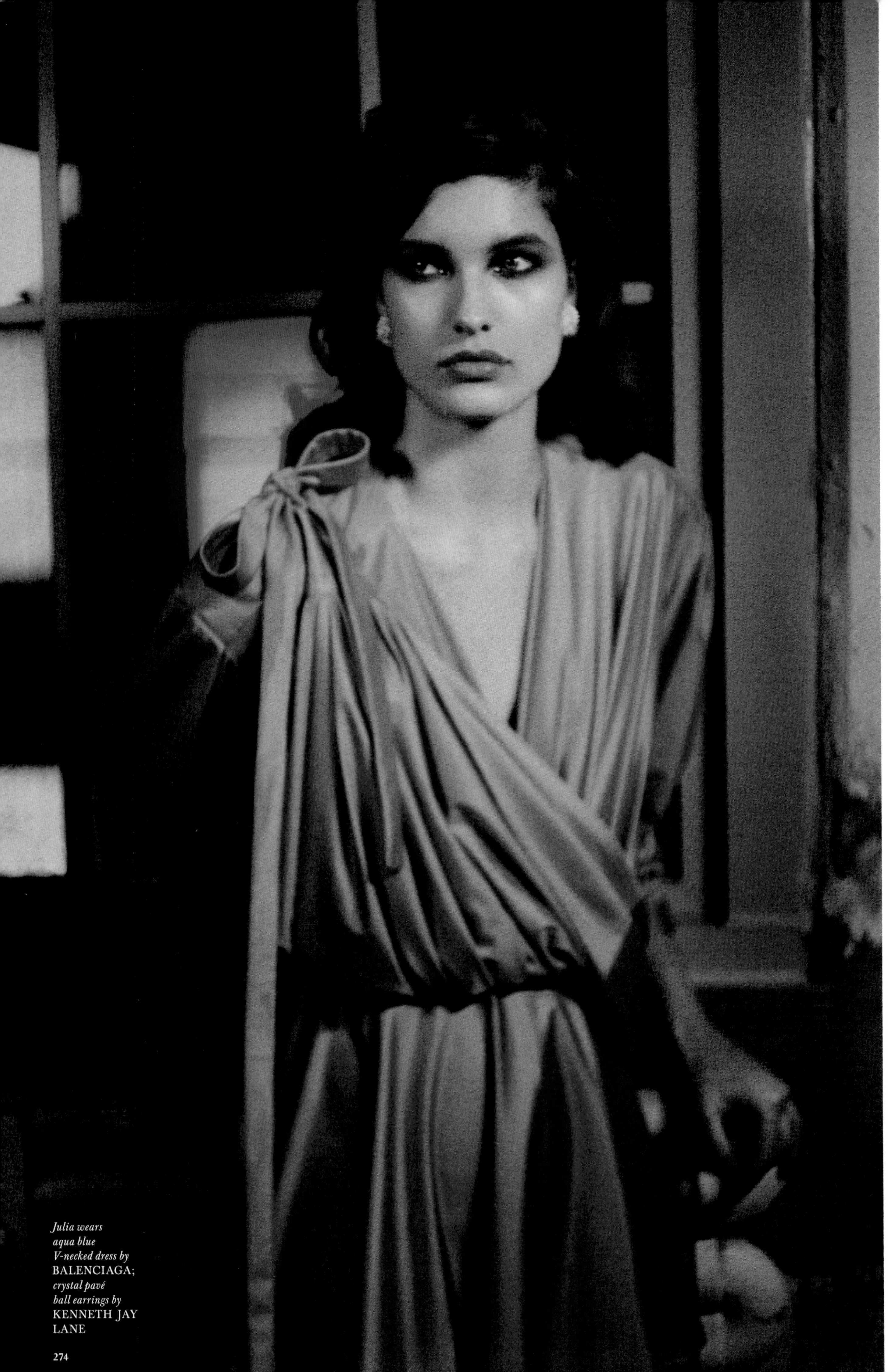

Julia wears aqua blue V-necked dress by BALENCIAGA; *crystal pavé ball earrings by* KENNETH JAY LANE

Julia wears blue Ischia dress by PINKO; *vintage gloves from* COSPROP; *vintage crystal earrings from* SUSAN CAPLAN; *point d'esprit tights by* GERBE; *degradé glitter Romy 110 shoes by* JIMMY CHOO

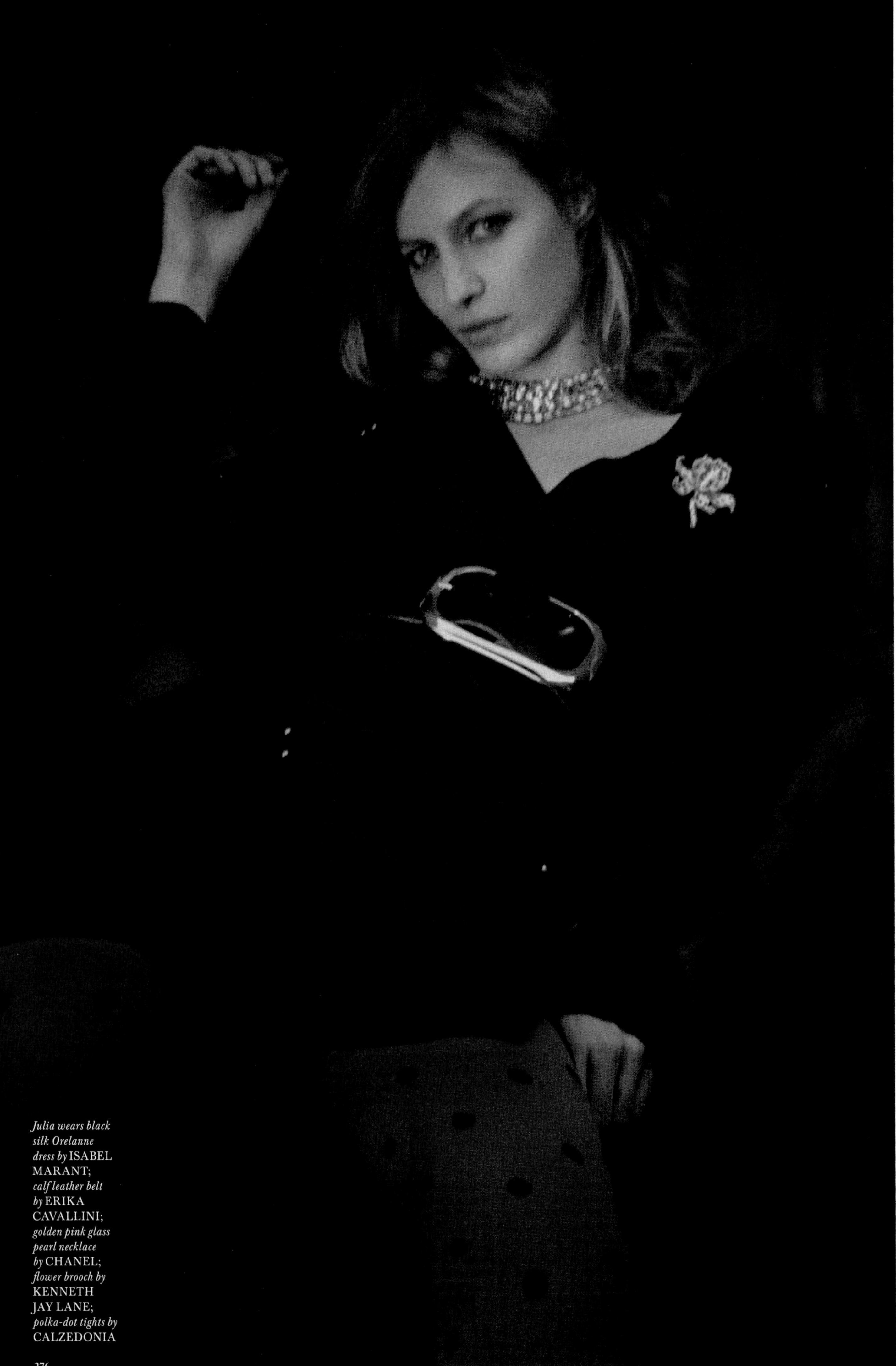

Julia wears black silk Orelanne dress by ISABEL MARANT; *calf leather belt by* ERIKA CAVALLINI; *golden pink glass pearl necklace by* CHANEL; *flower brooch by* KENNETH JAY LANE; *polka-dot tights by* CALZEDONIA

Julia wears fluid python-printed stretch satin lamé top, Parure Petale necklace and earrings all by LOUIS VUITTON

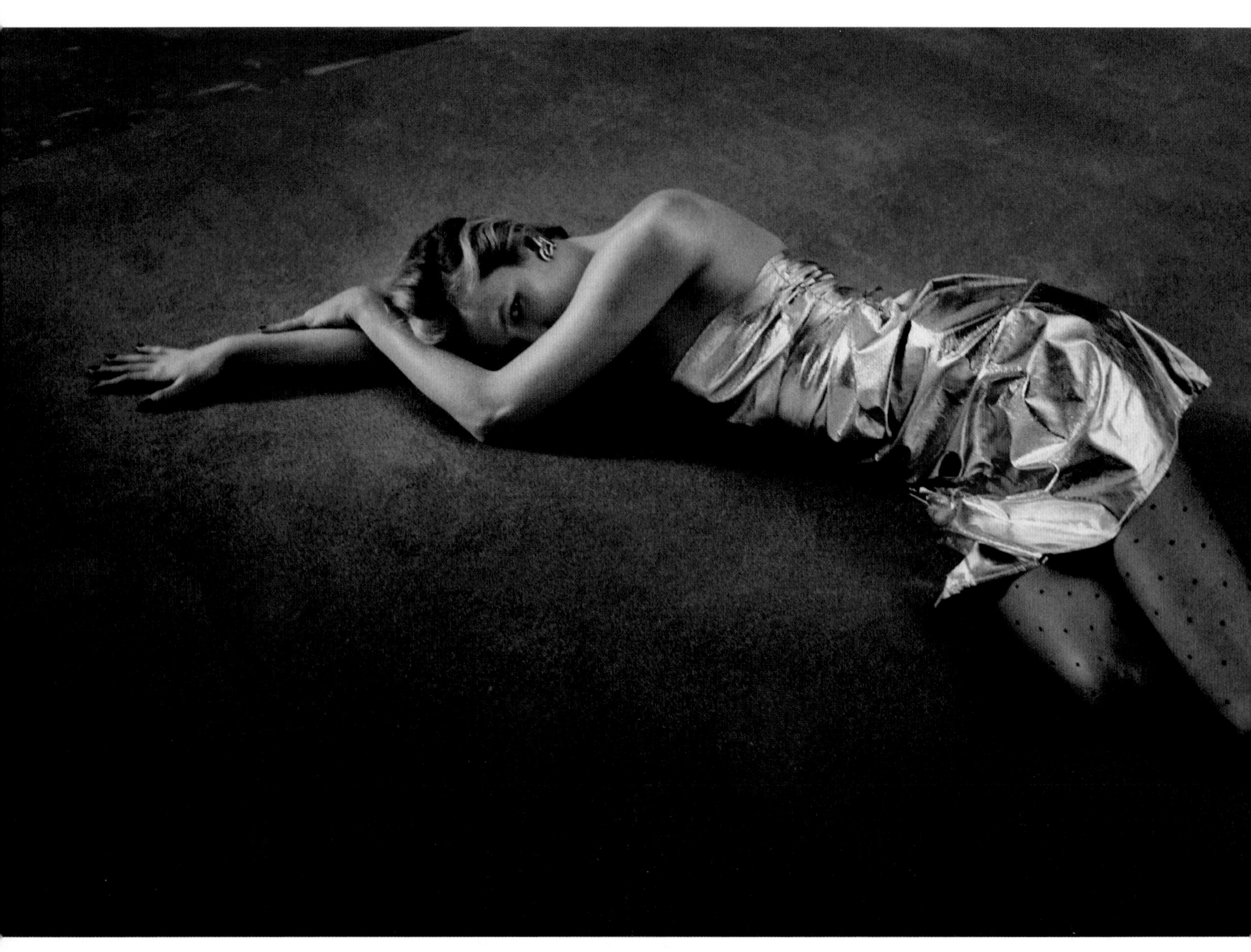

Karlie wears metallic minidress by DONDUP; *vintage heart earrings by* YVES SAINT LAURENT *from* STAZIA LOREN; *point d'esprit tights by* GERBE

Binx wears viscose dress by SPORTMAX; *white eco-down leather belt by* ELISABETTA FRANCHI; *pearl necklace by* UNDERCOVER; *tights by* JONATHAN ASTON; *white kitten-heel shoes by* AGL

Frida wears pink silk embroidered dress by VALENTINO

Cami wears gardenia light tweed oversized cardigan jacket with jewelled buttons by GUCCI; *large boater with petersham band by* PHILIP TREACY; *multi-pearl necklace by* UNDERCOVER; *shoes (just seen) by* BALLY

Cami wears striped loop-collared silk shirt by PAUL SMITH; *techno cotton Spencer jacket by* BEATRICE B; *knickers (just seen) by* FIFI CHACHNIL

Julia wears black, white and rust-coloured bikini and large black enamelled earrings all by MISSONI; *silk trench coat by* ERIKA CAVALLINI; *brown leather hat by* STEPHEN JONES FOR CHRISTOPHER KANE; *stockings by* CALZEDONIA; *beige and white fringed crocodile sandals by* SANTONI

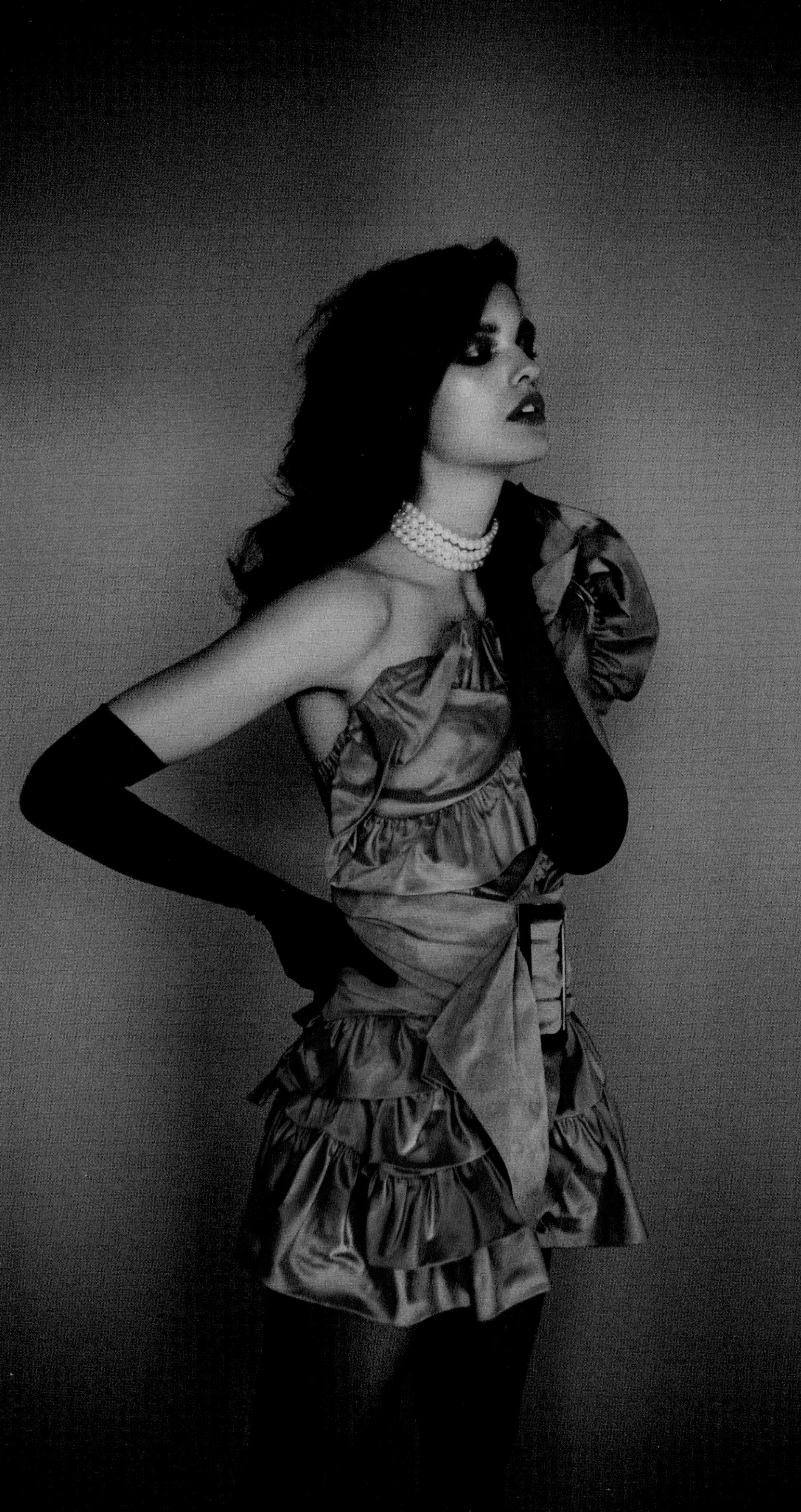

Julia wears silk Tirreno Sol dress by ANDREAS KRONTHALER FOR VIVIENNE WESTWOOD; *purple silk large wrap gold-buckle belt by* PHILOSOPHY DI LORENZO SERAFINI; *purple satin Helen gloves by* CORNELIA JAMES; *pearl choker by* KENNETH JAY LANE; *tights by* WOLFORD

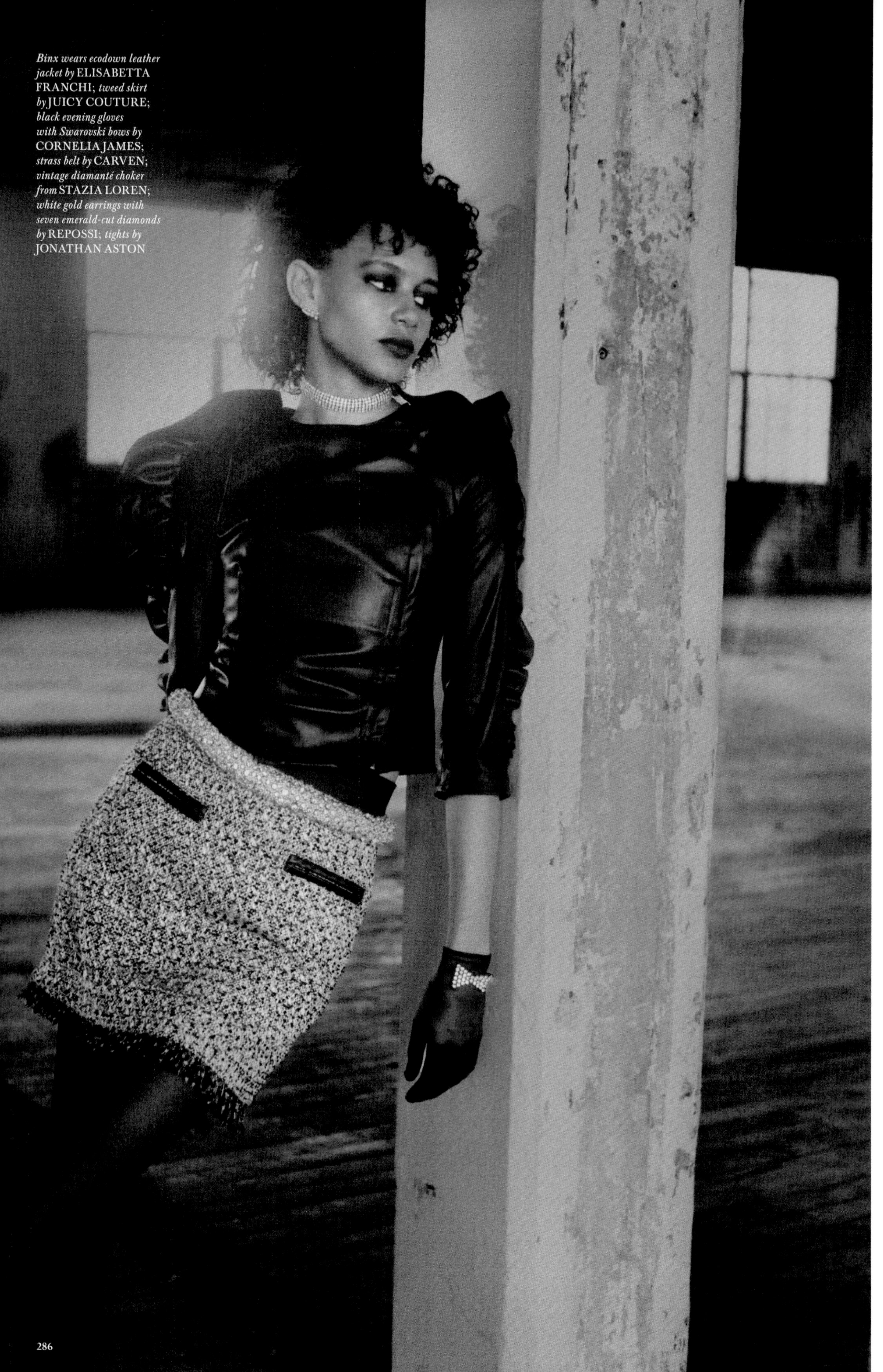

Binx wears ecodown leather jacket by ELISABETTA FRANCHI; *tweed skirt by* JUICY COUTURE; *black evening gloves with Swarovski bows by* CORNELIA JAMES; *strass belt by* CARVEN; *vintage diamanté choker from* STAZIA LOREN; *white gold earrings with seven emerald-cut diamonds by* REPOSSI; *tights by* JONATHAN ASTON

Julia wears red and blue leopard-print top and pleated skirt both by PROENZA SCHOULER; *navy tulle long-sleeved Mia dress (worn beneath) by* EMMA CHARLES; *Honeycomb earrings by* KENNETH JAY LANE

Frida wears black knickers by FIFI CHACHNIL; *red suede Romy 100 shoes by* JIMMY CHOO; *contrast-seam stockings by* JONATHAN ASTON

Hair CECILIA ROMERO Make-up LISA HOUGHTON Manicure MAKI SAKAMOTO Set design PHILIPP HAEMMERLE Production SOCIETY MGMT Retouching KAPSURE Models BINX WALTON, CAMI MORRONE, FRIDA AASEN, JULIA NOBIS, JULIA VAN OS, KARLIE KLOSS Photographic assistance JASON GEERING, JOSHUA ELAN Digital technician BAIN STEVENS Fashion assistance OGUN GORTAN, LEN BURTON, AMANDA DAY Hair assistance RACHEL HOPKINS Make-up assistance TIFFANY PATTON Thanks to SUNSET STUDIOS

Maurizio Cattelan
in

Agent Provocateur
agentprovocateur.com

spring summer 2017
Milan - Montenapoleone
London - Brompton Road
New York - Madison Avenue
Paris - Fauborg St.Honoré

PINKO
pinko.com

THE CROWN

While working on his first season devoted entirely to couture, Giles Deacon has produced a book documenting his label's 13 years of exquisite dresses

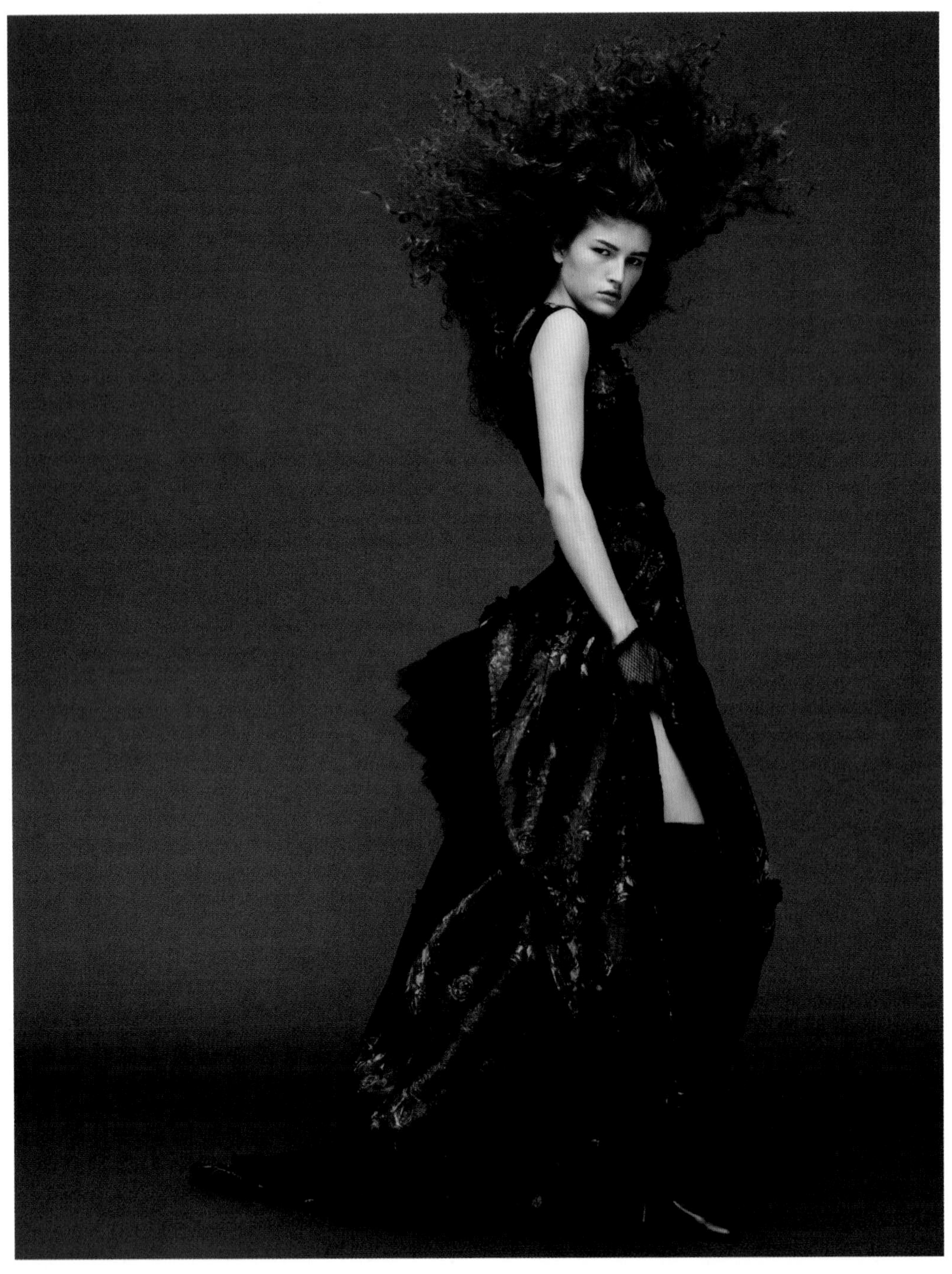

Photographer SØLVE SUNDSBØ Fashion Editor KATIE GRAND
Writer EDIE CAMPBELL

Last year Giles Deacon quietly suspended his ready-to-wear line to focus his attention on couture. Now his dresses are made to measure to the client's specifications and shipped out by helicopter from Battersea heliport. Sometimes his customers buy couture for specific events. 'But sometimes they just buy things to wear at home,' says Giles. 'Just to have dinner with their family of an evening.' Giles has also been working on a book that celebrates his work with two of his longest-serving collaborators: photographer Sølve Sundsbø and stylist Katie Grand. He says he didn't want it to be just a regular coffee-table monograph. 'It's not chronological, and it's about collaboration. It starts off with the Gisele pictures which were taken 13 years ago, and then you've got these super-technological whatchamacallits with all the digital manipulation stuff, and then covers of *The Face* with Liberty Ross. I hope it looks like a beautiful art book. I think it looks super.' *Giles, Sølve and Katie is published in February 2017*

Molly wears printed burnt Roase satin gazar gown with embroidered silk flowers by GILES DEACON COUTURE; *knee-high leather boots by* JIMMY CHOO; *black silk lace gloves by* CORNELIA JAMES

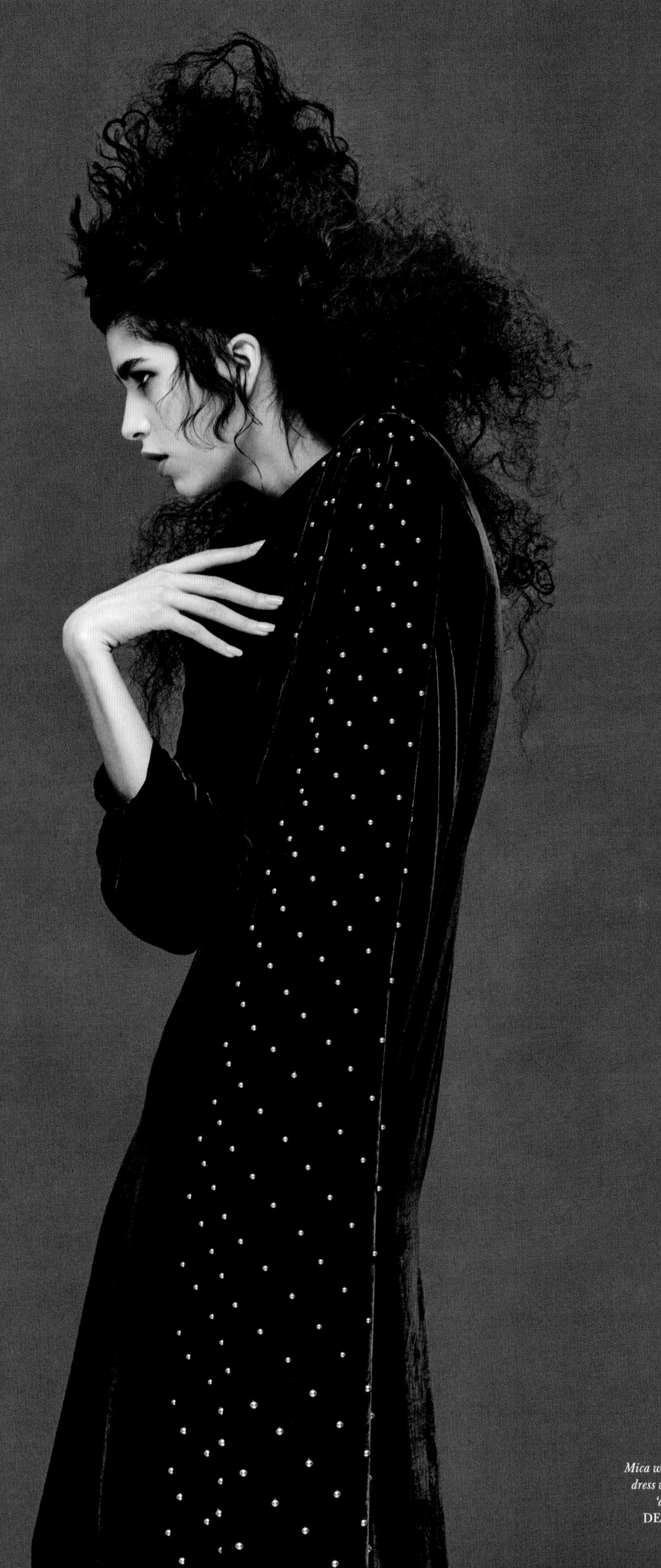

Mica wears dark purple velvet dress with embroidered pearl 'drapes' sash by GILES DEACON COUTURE

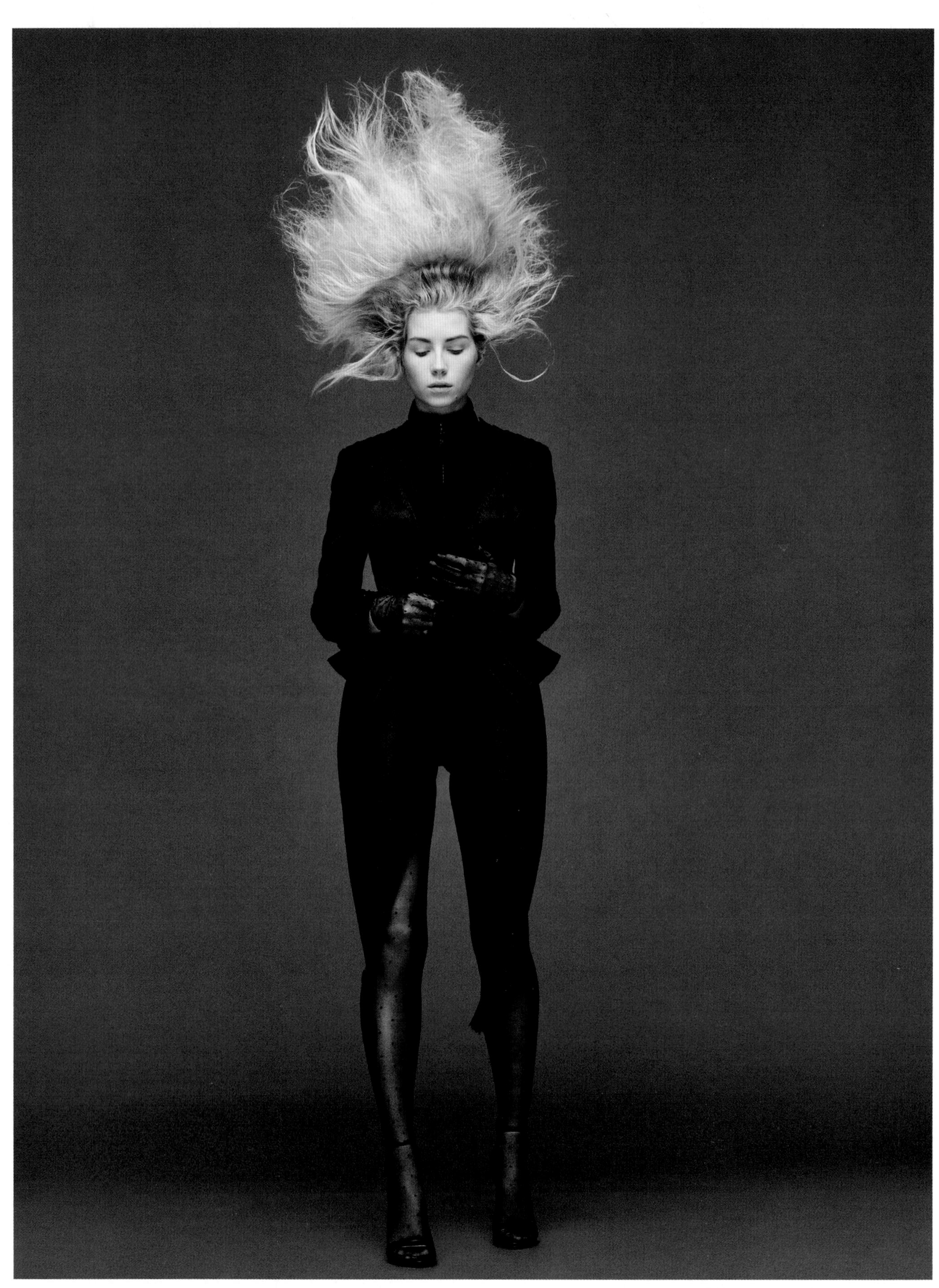

Lottie wears embroidered silk duchess Harlequin jacket by GILES DEACON COUTURE; *black silk lace gloves by* CORNELIA JAMES; *black point d'esprit tights by* GERBE; *black strap high-heeled shoes by* JIMMY CHOO

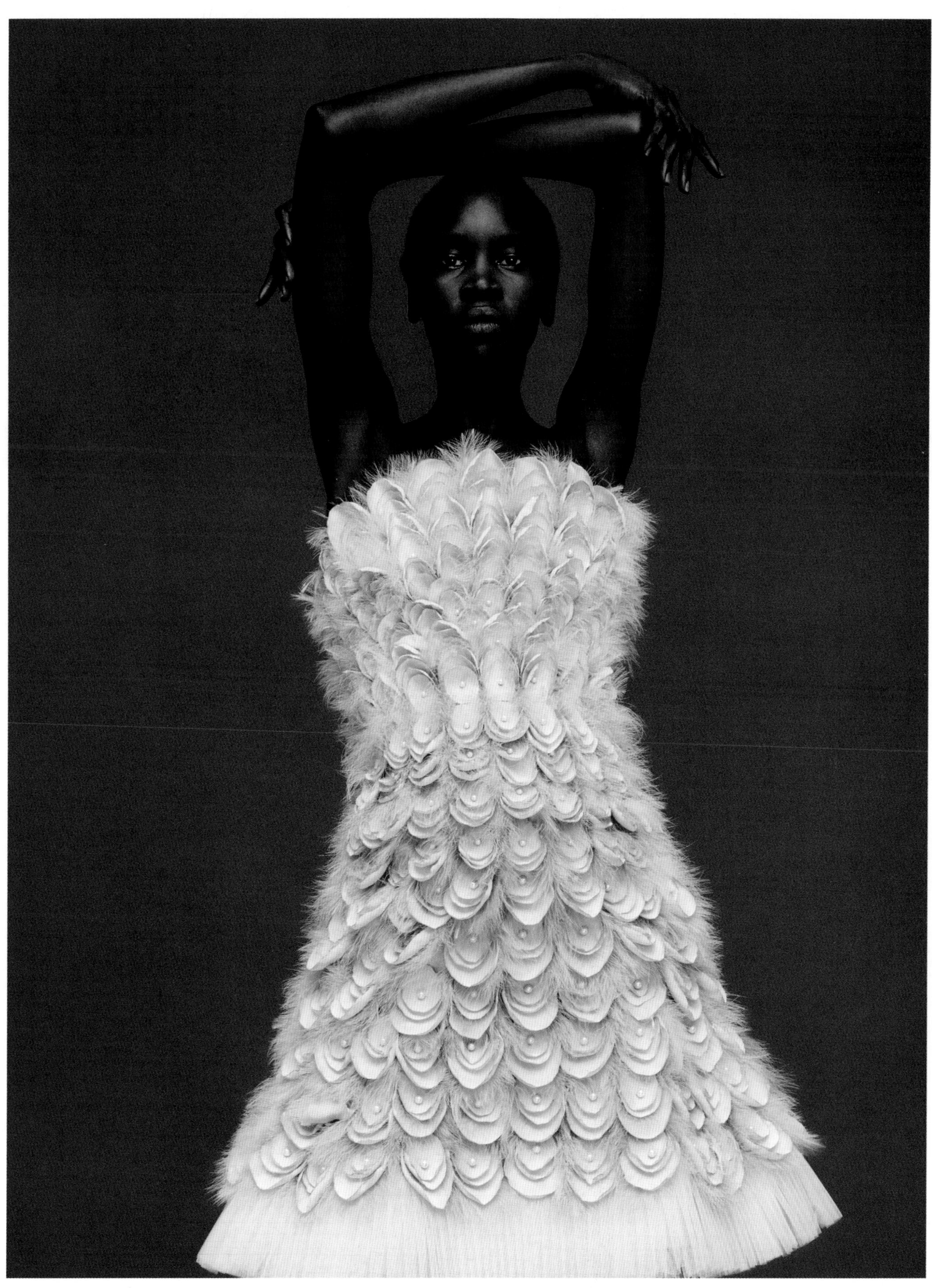

Alek wears pale pink silk layered petal and feather embroidered corset dress with pearl ornamentation by GILES DEACON COUTURE

Lily wears printed silk duchess draped gown with embroidered silk duchess corset by GILES DEACON COUTURE; *black lace gloves by* CORNELIA JAMES

Hair SYD HAYES Make-up MIRANDA JOYCE Manicure CHISATO YAMAMOTO Production PAULA EKENGER, SALLY DAWSON Retouching by DIGITAL LIGHT LTD Models ALEK WEK, LILY DONALDSON, LOTTIE MOSS, MICA ARGANARAZ, MOLLY SMITH Photographic assistance SIMON McGUIGAN, SAM HENDEL Digital technician ANNA HENDRY Fashion assistance OLIVER VOLQUARDSEN Hair assistance PAULA McCASH Make-up assistance HANNAH MAESTRANZI, VASS THEOTOKIS

Mica wears printed silk satin gazar gown by GILES DEACON COUTURE; *pale blue gloves by* DENTS

Spring
Summer
2017
BRITISH
GQ Style
GENTLEMEN'S QUARTERLY
On sale Thursday 16 March
Available in print and on your phone and tablet from the App Store & Google Play

L SPONSOF
WWW.TONIANDGUY.COM
F : TONIANDGUYWORLD
T : TONIANDGUYWORLD
I : TONIANDGUYWORLD
YT : TONIANDGUYWORLD
S : TONIANDGUYWORLD

Jena wears charcoal grey and white knitted dress, brown knitted long-sleeved top (just seen) and white leather heeled sandals all by MISSONI; *latte lambskin Lady Dior bag with large strap and gold adornments by* CHRISTIAN DIOR; *sheer gloves by* CORNELIA JAMES; *sheer tights by* FALKE

The Night of

Caught at the crime scene under the accusing glare of street lights, a line-up of the most wanted heels and handbags for spring

Photographer
DAVID HUGHES

Fashion Editor
VICTORIA YOUNG

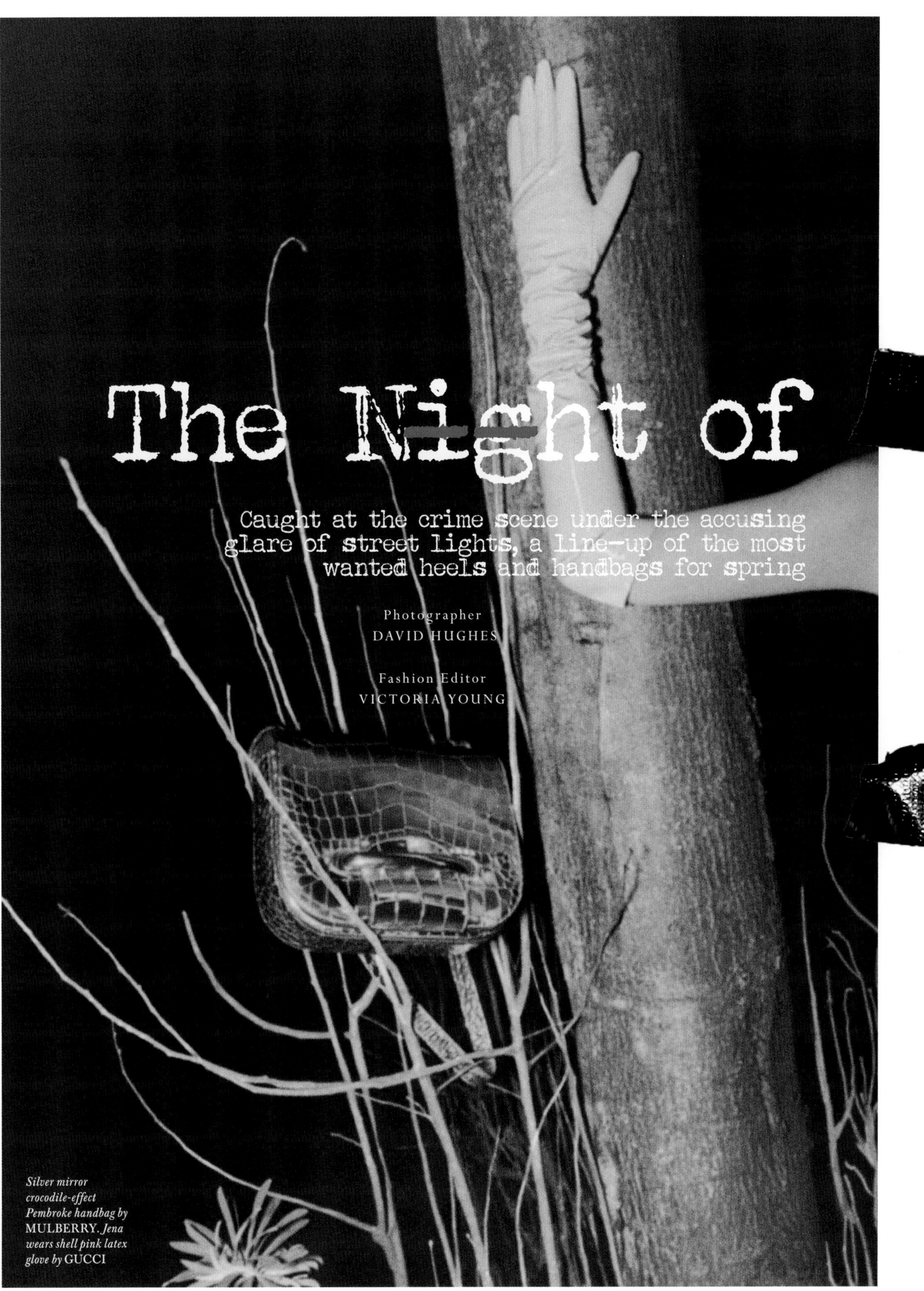

Silver mirror crocodile-effect Pembroke handbag by MULBERRY. *Jena wears shell pink latex glove by* GUCCI

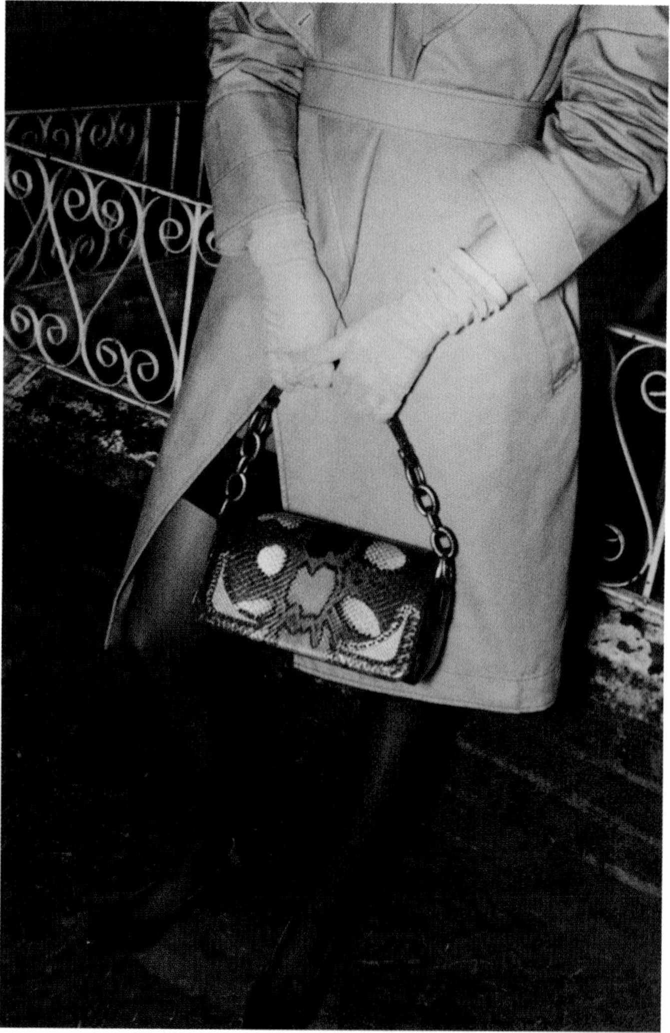

Left: Miss Tommy micro trunk bag by TOMMY HILFIGER

Right: Elsa wears beige trench coat by DKNY; *multicoloured python and goat leather Amarillo bag by* BOTTEGA VENETA; *black calf leather slingback kitten-heel shoes by* AGL; *sheer gloves by* CORNELIA JAMES; *black sheer stockings by* WOLFORD

Elsa wears black and multicoloured polka-dot chiffon silk dress, multicoloured striped jersey slip dress (worn beneath), black crocodile-effect calf leather kitten-heel shoes and yellow knitted wool socks all by GIVENCHY BY RICCARDO TISCI; *orange leather mini rucksack by* RALPH LAUREN COLLECTION

Elsa wears optic white sheer jersey dress by CÉLINE; *Mysore goatskin leather Octogone handbag by* HERMÈS; *suede Followup sandals by* STUART WEITZMAN; *stockings by* FALKE

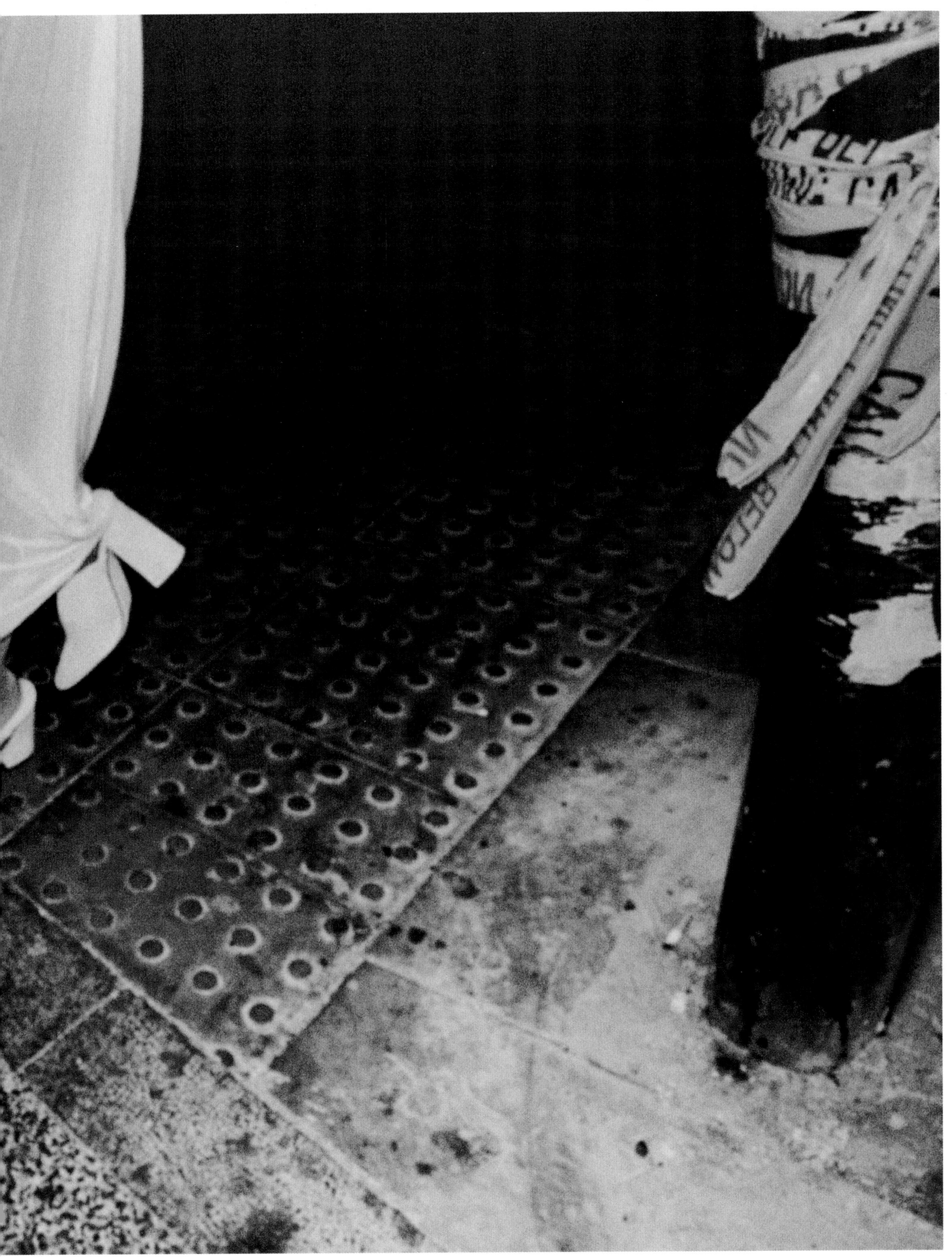

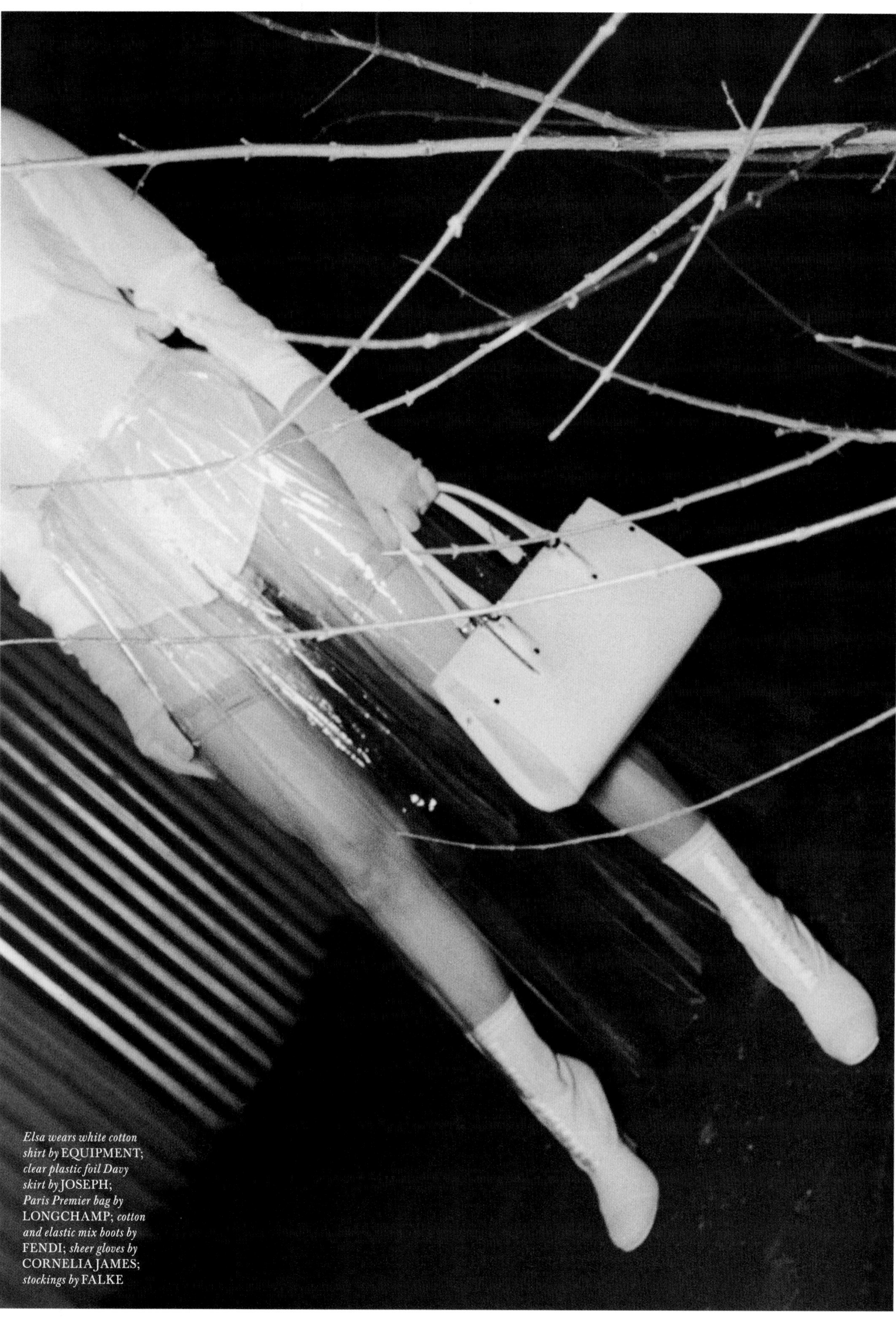

Elsa wears white cotton shirt by EQUIPMENT; *clear plastic foil Davy skirt by* JOSEPH; *Paris Premier bag by* LONGCHAMP; *cotton and elastic mix boots by* FENDI; *sheer gloves by* CORNELIA JAMES; *stockings by* FALKE

Left: black calf leather clog with wooden wedge sole by MONCLER

Right: silver metallic Angie shoes by GIUSEPPE ZANOTTI

Jena (left) wears cropped white trousers and white quilted cotton jacket (just seen) both by CHRISTIAN DIOR; *silver nappa Palace 100 shoes by* MULBERRY; *sheer gloves by* CORNELIA JAMES; *stockings by* FALKE. *Elsa wears beige cotton twill trench coat by* MARNI; *gold lamé dress by* KENZO; *small steam silk calf Bathurst satchel bag by* ANYA HINDMARCH; *red leather shoes by* RAG & BONE

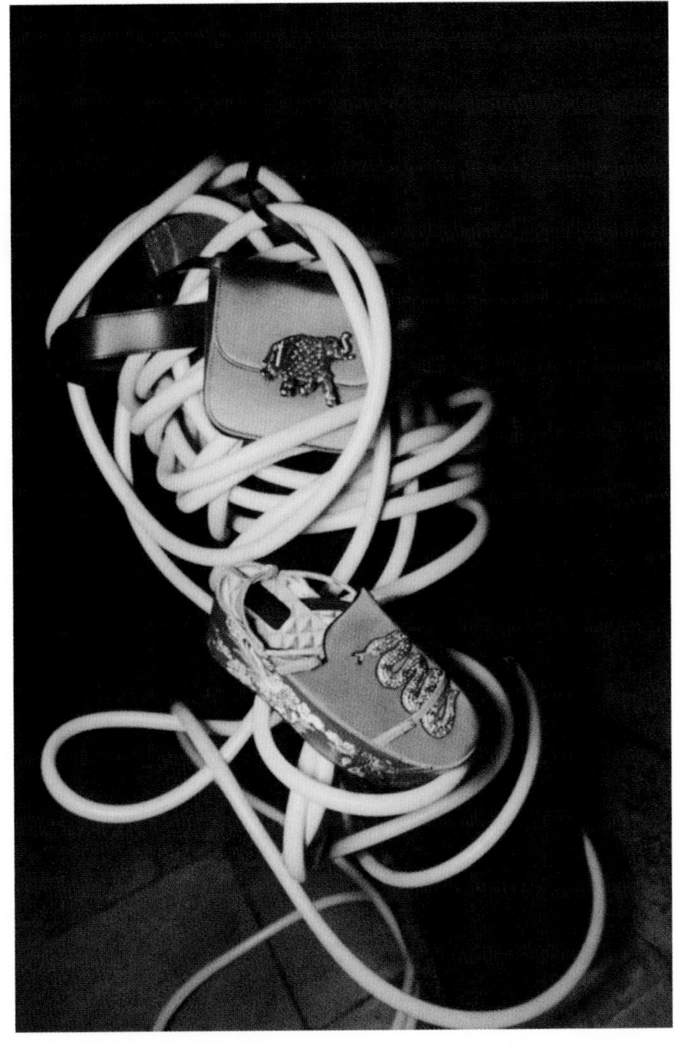

Left: frayed wool bag by BYBLOS

Right, from top: satin bag with calfskin detachable shoulder strap and metal elephant detail by EMPORIO ARMANI; *red velvet Tibet platform mule with crystal snake appliqué and yellow Tokyo-print wedge by* GUCCI

Jena (left) wears pink silk dress by VALENTINO; *gold and black leather Half Moon bag with gold chain by* LANVIN. *Elsa wears red wool jacket and silk dress both by* FORTE FORTE; *red velvet Mini DD bag and black velvet stiletto-heel boots with red velvet laces all by* DSQUARED; *sheer gloves by* CORNELIA JAMES; *stockings by* FALKE

Elsa wears red cotton and silk mix gown dress by MOSCHINO; *leather crocodile-effect clutch bag and red belt both by* FRENCH CONNECTION

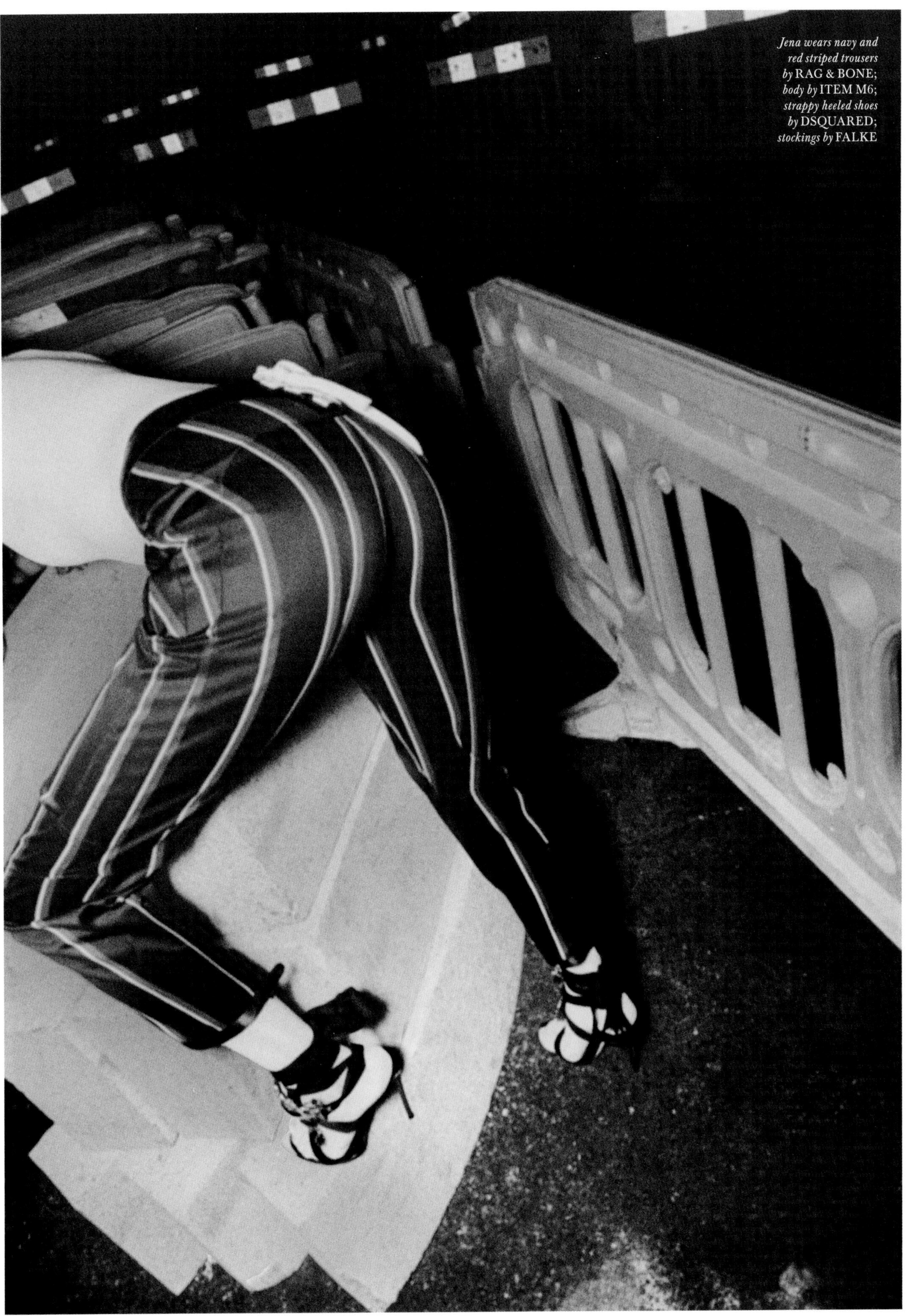

Jena wears navy and red striped trousers by RAG & BONE; *body by* ITEM M6; *strappy heeled shoes by* DSQUARED; *stockings by* FALKE

Manicure KATE CUTLER (Elsa), Trish Lomax (Jena and double shots) Set design ANNA BURNS Production MAP Retouching TABLET RETOUCH Models ELSA BRISINGER, JENA GOLDSACK Digital operators ROB JARVIS, BRUNO CONRAD at RAW DIGITAL Photographic assistance ANDY MOORES, SAM WILSON Fashion assistance FAINCHE BURKE

mylkchocolate
Photo
#LOVEME17 My name is Joyce Romero
love fashion/design and modeling.
#LOVEME17 @thelovemagazine
@KendallJenner @kegrand
ara from Romania.I love
ging,fashion and photography.
julianmackay
xtxtxox
olegkasynets
397 likes
olegkasynets My name is Oleg and I
am 20 years old. I am originally from
Ukraine but am now living in Toronto.
People call me a FIREHEAD because
of my fiery red hair and dynamic
personality. I love choreographing,
performing and teaching dance to my
LOVE's casting call!!!

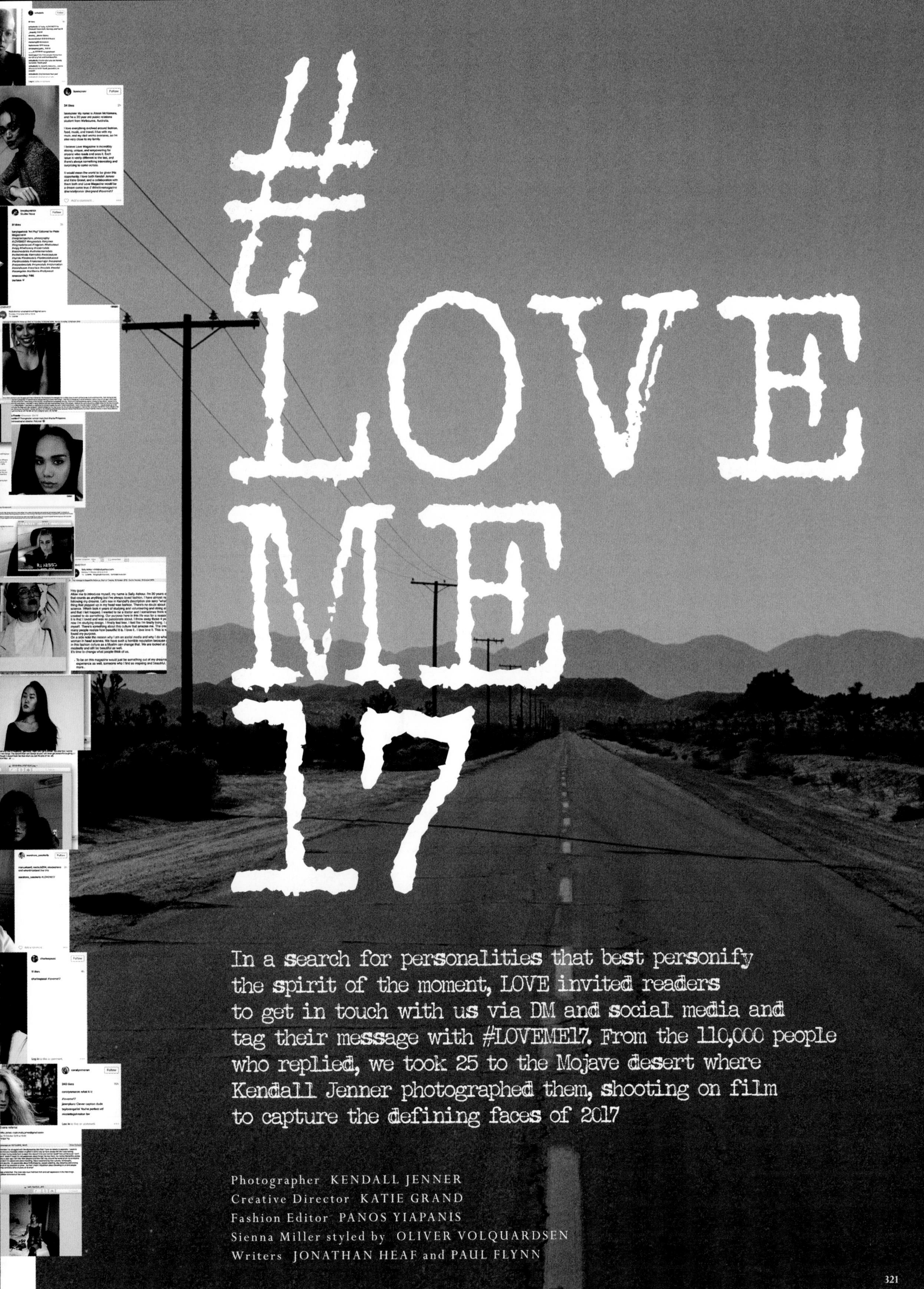

#LOVE ME 17

In a search for personalities that best personify the spirit of the moment, LOVE invited readers to get in touch with us via DM and social media and tag their message with #LOVEME17. From the 110,000 people who replied, we took 25 to the Mojave desert where Kendall Jenner photographed them, shooting on film to capture the defining faces of 2017

Photographer KENDALL JENNER
Creative Director KATIE GRAND
Fashion Editor PANOS YIAPANIS
Sienna Miller styled by OLIVER VOLQUARDSEN
Writers JONATHAN HEAF and PAUL FLYNN

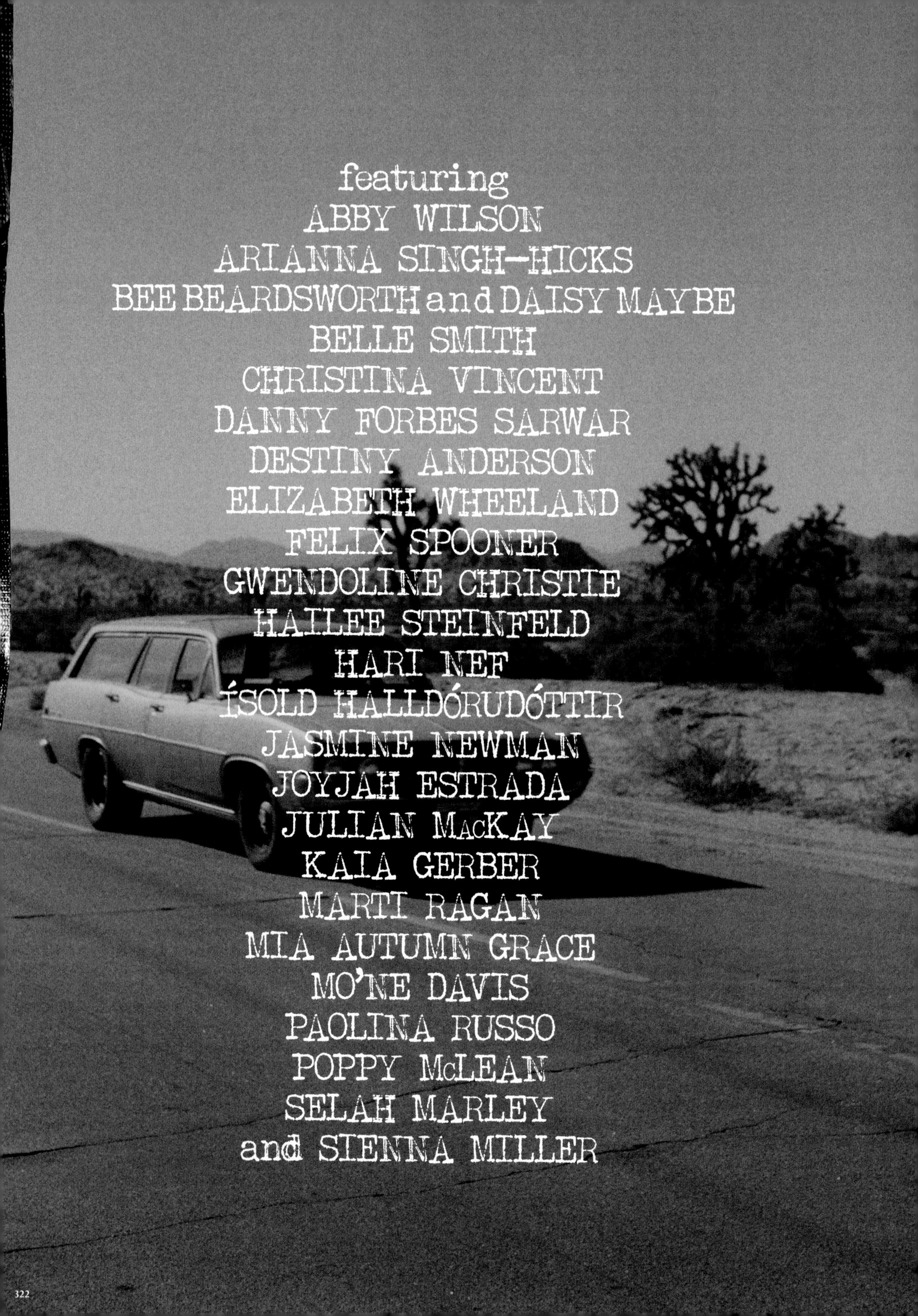

featuring
ABBY WILSON
ARIANNA SINGH-HICKS
BEE BEARDSWORTH and DAISY MAYBE
BELLE SMITH
CHRISTINA VINCENT
DANNY FORBES SARWAR
DESTINY ANDERSON
ELIZABETH WHEELAND
FELIX SPOONER
GWENDOLINE CHRISTIE
HAILEE STEINFELD
HARI NEF
ÍSOLD HALLDÓRUDÓTTIR
JASMINE NEWMAN
JOYJAH ESTRADA
JULIAN MacKAY
KAIA GERBER
MARTI RAGAN
MIA AUTUMN GRACE
MO'NE DAVIS
PAOLINA RUSSO
POPPY McLEAN
SELAH MARLEY
and SIENNA MILLER

Despite the sharp, morning sun creeping over the San Gabriel Mountains turning the earth sepia, the desert is still cold enough to make your brain ache. Below the rocky ridges and nooks that hide rattle snakes and coyotes, the plains of Saddleback Bute State Park resemble a lunar surface, a view that Buzz Aldrin might describe as 'a beautiful desolation'. We're about two hours north of Hollywood's raw juice bars and All-Star Bus Tours, although we may as well be decades; it's a cowboy landscape of long highways and empty plains.

The only earthly indicators are the odd Joshua tree sprouting up through the dust, and every hour or so, an unmanned drone hums across a big cinematic sky, sinister traffic from a nearby military base. Inside a run-down petrol station café – it's a film set; nothing here works, especially not the heating, as we're all finding out – Kendall Jenner is bouncing from one booted foot to the other in an attempt to keep the blood flowing through her long, lithe limbs. Her shoulders are raised and tight and she has her sweater sleeves – a vintage find, 'or at least it smells like a vintage find' – pulled down around her fingers. She hasn't a scrap of make-up on, her raven hair is pulled back into a short ponytail and her socks are tucked into her tight jeans like someone who knows she's about to be on her feet all day.

'Hey everybody!' The crowd of optimistic teenagers, twentysomethings, wannabe film stars, gonnabe supermodels, InstaGirls, rudeboys, singer-songwriters, baseball players, creative chameleons, DJs, artists and – sure, why not? – icons-in-waiting answer like a room full of diligent students: '*Hiiiiiii...*' – a cute call-and-response that gets some of the crowd giggling into their hot coffee. As the talented allsorts chew on their rolled oats and wonder 'What next?', the woman who, for only the second time in her professional life, will be behind the camera calling the shots, rather than in front of the lens posing for them, grabs a paper plate and raids the fruit tray. We're here to work, sure, but first fuel.

Everyone here knows who Kendall Jenner is. And the television-star-turned-fashion-model knows more about each of the 25 finalists of the #LOVEME17 project than they are probably aware. In the months and weeks leading up to this cool day in the desert – in close cahoots with the magazine, of course – Kendall has been sieving through the 60,000 or so video entries, looking for something, or someone, above and beyond the extraordinary. Hoping to come across an icon might be considered a little precocious, or at least a little ambitious. But talking to a handful of the talent sat shivering here it's clear that millennial creativity is ripe and bursting out of social media like lava.

'I think we want to shine a light on unseen originality,' explains Kendall when we squeeze into a booth together to talk about #LOVEME17, a rare moment of tranquility over the next 48 hours. Is Kendall nervous at all about the shoot? 'Not nervous. Maybe I was three days ago; some butterflies, you know? I mean, listen, this is only my second-ever professional shoot for a magazine. I shot Kaia [Gerber] for the last issue, but that was literally her and me, and my manager acting as my photo assistant. Not the same deal. Here we have over 20 subjects, a huge set, two full days of shooting and a crew of dozens. There are two trailers of clothes. We have a Winnebago for make-up. I feel like Katie really threw me right in at the deep end here. But it's awesome. I like pressure.'

So does Kendall have a game plan? 'You know, I don't! I have some ideas, sure. I was on Tumblr all day yesterday looking through pictures for inspiration. You can plan but you never know until the person is in front of you.' And if she senses the vibe isn't quite right? 'I think you need to take a step back. It's like when you're trying on a dress for a night out – if you keep looking at the same outfit time and time again in the same mirror, you won't get anywhere. You need to step away from it, give it a moment and then come back to the problem.' For someone who seems to want to achieve pretty much everything by the time she's 25, Kendall seems remarkably zen about today's undertaking. If there's any sense that she feels the world's lens on her every move, her every career flinch – which it is – then she doesn't show it one jot.

The sceptic is always going to raise an eyebrow when they hear a model wants to do anything else with her career other than stand around under bright lights and throw a shoulder to the lens. This is because we carry the prejudice around with us that models are lacking the grey matter to apply themselves to anything more complex than a pout. This is, of course, shameful. Some people also think all that models are interested in is boosting the followers on their various social feeds, and cold, hard cash. This is, of course, utter rubbish. 'I've always had the photography bug,' admits Kendall when I ask her what drew her to taking pictures rather than any other creative output. 'When I was a kid I was always asking my mum for a new camera. When she eventually gave in, I'd grab my friends and we'd go into the back yard and shoot each other. It was all very amateurish and make-believe but I could sense how much I liked it. When I was in high school I took photography classes and actually went to photography school for a while.'

So what happened? 'Modelling. Suddenly I was being offered all these opportunities at the other end of the camera. I couldn't really turn it down.' That said, Kendall never stopped learning; the fact that she was now finding herself the focus of some of the most gifted fashion photographers in the world wasn't going to be an opportunity she was going to squander. 'I wouldn't let on that I was into it, but I would quietly listen and ask the odd question about lighting and stuff. This sounds like I'm being cocky, but Mario [Testino] always said he thought I had a good eye – and when someone like Mario is telling you that, you need to sit up and take notice. He'd look at my Instagram feed and be really complimentary, which is basically insane.'

By the end of 2015, however, Kendall knew she had to scratch that creative itch. 'Photography has always been there for me in the background. But a year ago I went and got my first film camera and actually started taking it seriously. I love taking pictures of my friends, or just a couple I see on the street. I won't ask, I'll just catch them in the moment.' Did Kendall take any tuition? Did Bruce Weber give her some homework? Or did Mert and Marcus set her some practical tasks? 'No, not quite... Have you ever seen *Hannah Montana*?'

Why – did Miley Cyrus teach her how to use a Leica? 'No, but the kid who played Rico did! His name is actually Moisés Arias and I've known him for six or seven years. Incredibly talented; his imagery, not just stills, is breathtaking. He's the person I went to when I got my first film camera, a Pentax K1000 with a 50mm lens. We just spent two days in LA running around experimenting. When I show him my photography now and he likes an image he freaks out. "Kenye!" – he calls me Kenye – "I fucking love it!" It makes me happy when he freaks out.'

Seeing Kendall work, picking her points around the desert set, working the angles, judging the light and shade, interchanging between a Leica, a Pentax and her new Contax, you'd hardly think she'd only be taking pictures for 12 months. Shooting film is also no tea party, especially if, like KJ, you're set on developing the film yourself in your own dark room. Of course, diligence aside, she's something of a presence.

Remember, one week after this shoot she will be strutting down a runway for Victoria's Secret looking like the physical manifestation of a sex-themed roller coaster. Still, on set she's incredibly calm and quiet. Not for Kendall any of the clichéd fashion photographer 'oohs' and 'ahs', oh no. This photographer lets the subjects find their own pace, position and pout. Well, at least until they are in need of a little steer. 'It helps that I've been in front of the camera so much,' Kendall admits. 'I can tell them little tricks: "Keep your chin up" always seems to work.'

Kendall is also the first photographer to shoot the Burberry February 2017 Collection, which won't be presented at London Fashion Week for another four months. 'Championing the future generation of creative talent is something I'm very passionate about,' Burberry chief creative and chief executive officer Christopher Bailey will later comment on Kendall's shoot, 'and celebrating creativity in all its guises has never felt as important as it does today.'

Word drifted in to camp yesterday that Kendall had taken a sabbatical from her Instagram feed. In fact it wasn't so much a rumour as headline news on CNN since the afternoon. Much of social media was in mourning because of it, apparently. Although she'll be back on Instagram tomorrow – 'Everyone should detox from their feeds once in a while' – it does make one wonder: is she getting more protective over what visual imagery she puts out into the world now that she is turning pro? 'Well, I can see how you might get to that conclusion, and maybe I need to pay more attention. I think I am going to put more of my work up there, more of my taste rather than just a throw something out there.'

I wonder how Kendall feels about turning from being the hunted to the hunter. A person who has been preyed on and chased down by men with large cameras is now training the lens on someone herself. Does it feel weird? 'Well, I'm not a paparazzi. Actually, one of my favourite photos I ever took was when we were in Paris. The paparazzi where going for it, chasing us on mopeds. One of them pulled out in front of us, went ahead and then pulled into an alley and waited for us. As we passed them I snapped a quick shot, so I have this great image of a pap with his hand covering his face. I thought, "Yeah, fuck you. It doesn't feel so great now, does it?!"

Just as so many of the young #LOVEME17 entrants are fans of Kendall's, who is she a fan of in the photography world? 'I mean, you don't get much better than Herb Ritts.' And contemporary photographers? 'Theo Wenner. He actually shot my recent 21st birthday party. There was no way I was going to take any pictures, 'cause I was so drunk. I can be honest about that now. Theo took this great shot of Kim [Kardashian], at the Beverly Hills Hotel, some of my favourite pictures of her. I love Theo's moods; no make-up, Kim was just wearing some hotel PJs... It's authentic. I'm the same. I'm not into pushing the print through loads of Photoshop or anything. I don't mess with the light. I just shoot, print and then that's what you get. Cindy Crawford once told me to shoot film as it saves so much time. With film you won't have crowds of people going over each image on a computer screen through the day.'

So which icons would Kendall like to shoot? 'I mean, obviously Angelina Jolie, although I'm not sure how much of this stuff she does any more, she's very low-key nowadays – but let's put it out there... If I could go back in time I'd like to do Marilyn Monroe or Audrey Hepburn. David Bowie and River Phoenix – he was so fucking cool and just beautiful.'

And with that, word reaches us from the trailer that the next #LOVEME17 subject is ready for their close-up. KJ sticks her phone in her back pocket and slings her camera over her right shoulder, heading out into the desert. The sun is higher now and the mercury is rising. Kenye squints east, her palm flat against her brow, as she looks to find the right light. *Jonathan Heaf*

Mia Autumn Grace Student

Mia Franco went to sleep early at home in Phoenix, Arizona on Tuesday 8 November 2016, the night that Donald Trump became President Elect of the United States of America. 'I was getting really stressed,' she says, 'so I went to bed. For some reason I just knew what was going to happen.' Mia is just 15 years old. She'd talked with her family about what the implications of a Trump presidency might mean for girls her age; how choosing a man who made electable the clear language of disrespect over inclusivity might impact over half the population of the most powerful nation in the world. Even hearing the words 'Donald Trump', Mia says, 'makes me anxious and angry and a little bit upset. Especially being a girl, about to be a woman. It really makes me want to do a lot of things to change stuff. I talk through a lot of this stuff with my mom because she's very politically active right now.'

Mia has five sisters and one brother. The Francos consist of Meghan (26), Jenna (22), Emily (20), Sarah (17 – 'we're like twins'), Collin (11) and Keira (eight – 'she's spoilt because she's the littlest'). All the Franco kids have been home-schooled by mum, Barb. They are resourceful, funny and a testament to the power of a woman who does things her way to bring the best out in her kids, whatever societal impediments might be thrown their way. Mia describes herself as an introvert but acquits herself marvellously in conversation, talking with confident, bright certainty.

Mia and her sister Sarah are teaching one another Japanese right now. They swap notes in the language when their little brother and sister irritate them. Mia is obsessed with the world of Harry Potter. She doesn't have posters on her bedroom wall, but she does have a pile of magazines featuring Cara Delevingne and Kendall Jenner 'in a special place in my room that I don't let anyone else touch'. She began her collection in earnest in 2015. 'I was never

Mia wears custom-made wool argyle jumper with ruffles by PANOS YIAPANIS'S STUDIO

MIA /
'Hearing the words "Donald Trump" make me anxious and angry and a little bit upset'

Mia wears custom-made wool argyle jumper with ruffles by PANOS YIAPANIS'S STUDIO

'I was very, very impressed with Mia. She'd never been shot before by anyone but her big sister back home in Arizona and she is a total natural. Now she's on the cover of a major magazine. The photos of her are stunning. She was so mature in front of the camera you'd forget and then she started talking and you're like, my God, you are 15 years old. She was comfortable even with a lot of people around her. She's got a lot of confidence and what's so super-cute about her is that she doesn't even know she has that confidence yet'

Mia wears custom-made wool argyle jumper with ruffles by PANOS YIAPANIS'S STUDIO

Mia wears white cotton-blend lace T-shirt and white cashmere cable-knit jumper both by BURBERRY; *vintage black* BODYMAP *leggings from* PANOS YIAPANIS'S ARCHIVE

All BURBERRY *items throughout are taken from* THE BURBERRY FEBRUARY 2017 COLLECTION

Ísold wears navy wool coat by BALENCIAGA

ÍSOLD /
'I do it all: paint, take pictures, film. I want to travel the world making art. That's the dream'

interested in fashion before. I drool over those magazines. They are a big statement in fashion to me.' She keeps a notepad in her bedroom with the places she'd like to go when she gets to leave home and travel. Her top three are currently Japan, Italy and England. Her favourite song this season is Coldplay's 'Hymn for the Weekend'. She has a special recipe she cooks at home of her own invention. 'You break up a bunch of lettuce, put quinoa and rice on top and then put some ketchup and sriracha on it,' she says, imitating the manhandling assemblage of her concoction as she speaks. Mia is the very definition of American innocence. She could have been beamed in just as easily from a Henry James novel as a high-school rites-of-passage movie.

Mia woke on the morning of 9 November to find 56 messages on a family text-chat with her siblings, sharing the deflating news of the Trump victory. In her head, Mia's happy place is the house she was born into, in rural Pennsylvania, one she left at five when dad's work as CFO of Northwestern Medical Group meant relocation. 'We used to go down to creeks all the time and go into the woods, and in wintertime we'd play in the snow and go sledding. We had this giant ditch outside our house and I was terrified of it.'

Donald Trump represents a different kind of fear at the outset of Mia's adult life. She is trying to keep a positive spin on all this. 'Yeah, I mean, if you look at what happened with the 18- to 25-year-old early voters, there is hope for the future,' she says, pointing out that it is her generation's job to interrupt the ludicrous blip in American political history, a line in the sand for extreme capitalism when bling beats brain. 'So, yes, it gives you hope.'

That morning, Mia's mum drew back the curtain that separates Mia's bedroom from the rest of the family homestead and saw her daughter sitting on the edge of her bed, crying. 'She sat on my bed and she was like, "Do you want to talk about it?" And I was like, "No."' Mia had other preoccupations to deal with. To distract herself from the political storm ahead, she checked her email, Snapchat and Instagram, where she goes by the name of Mia Autumn Grace. To her absolute delight and amazement, on that very morning she'd been picked for #LOVEME17. For her audition video she had performed the cancan against her blank dining-room wall. 'I was just, oh my gosh, this is going to be the most terrible day of my life,' she says, 'and I went on my email and I saw this message asking if I'd like to come and be photographed. My stomach dropped so hard and I got out of my bed and I was just crying and crying. My mom was like, "Stop reading the news, you don't need to worry about it right now." I said, "It's not the news, it's my email! I got chosen! I get to go to LA!" This is actually the best day of my life.'

And the world still turns. At 15, each cloud, however stormy, has to come with its own individual silver lining. It's the law. 'Isn't it?' nods Mia Franco, incandescence and joy beaming all over her face. *Paul Flynn*
IG: @miaautumngrace

Ísold Halldórudóttir Filmmaker

How do we find ourselves in unexpected places? Ísold Halldórudóttir, a young filmmaker, traveller and artist from Iceland, isn't sure she has the answers. 'I have no real idea how I got here,' she giggles, her smile hiding beneath it a bellyful of butterflies.

Ísold is nervous, partly as she hasn't previously experienced anything quite like this shoot in the desert – it's very relaxed, but it's still something of a circus for an outsider – and partly because being pushed into the spotlight has, in some way, raised a mirror to her own life and future ambitions. Not only is she being photographed by Kendall Jenner, she has also been asked by LOVE to make several films that will be published online in tandem with this very special issue.

'I was at work when I found out I'd been picked by the magazine,' she says. 'I work in a book store called Eymundsson, in Reykjavik. I had uploaded a few of my videos to Instagram and I kept checking for an email or tag or *something* – a sign, give me a sign! This became a daily routine. An hourly routine. When I found out that I was coming to America, to Los Angeles, my jaw hit the floor. Nothing like this has ever happened to me. In some ways, it makes me happy to share this platform with so many other creative people. It confirms that my love for art isn't perhaps as misplaced as I worried it might be. This is who I am.'

Ísold may not have all the answers yet, but she's looking to artists such as Yoko Ono to light the way. 'I love her work. The piece where she has people cutting up her clothes – so brilliant. The idea that you can be powerful while also being peaceful, this I find appealing. The world, at times, can be disrespectful and pessimistic: I want to be optimistic. But I want also to challenge. I think sometimes being an artist is about being selfish; following your voice, even if others disagree. Making art is harder than some people think.'

For Ísold, art runs in the family. Her mother is a photographer, her dad is a musician and her grandfather is a painter. She understands the illuminating power of visual creation; how it can transform perspective, reinvent preconceptions of beauty. 'I do it all. Paint, take pictures, film. I just want to create. I was born and raised in Iceland but we moved to Denmark for a bit and I felt unwelcomed by the education system there. I didn't think I was getting anywhere at college and I was being bullied, so I dropped out. I made my mind up that I wanted to work my ass off, buy a Land Rover Defender and then travel the world, making art as I go. That is the dream. Maybe this is the first step.' *JH*
IG: @7520c

Joyjah Estrada Online influencer

Joyjah Estrada is #LOVEME17's very own Cinderella, and like her cartoon counterpart she very nearly didn't make it to the ball. 'I heard LOVE wanted me for the shoot; it was an incredible moment for me, and for my country…'

That bit about her country rooting for her? That's not Joyah being sycophantic. Or parading some flimsy ego around like a teenager with a copy of *On the Road* tucked into their jacket. Joyjah lives in Belize, a pin of a country on the eastern coast of Central America with a population just slightly larger than Cardiff's. To say Joyjah is known in Belize is to say cinephiles know Robert De Niro – it's a given. She's everywhere and knows everyone. As a beauty 'influencer' on Instagram – 140,000 followers and counting – she's one of the first stars of the new digitally savvy cosmetics industry in her country. So when Joyjah says they, her fans, were rooting for her, they were rooting for her.

'But then we had a a bit of a problem with the visas.' Of course, getting on a plane nowadays can be complicated. And entering the United States of America since Donald Trump went from being WTF to PEOTUS can be even trickier, especially from a country like Belize – and especially if you don't have the correct paperwork. 'Basically, time was very tight. I needed a visa and an appointment to get a visa within two days. It was looking almost impossible. Then a friend suggested I reach out to the prime minister's wife to see if she could help.' Who knows what kind of swing Melania

#LOVEME17 submission film screenshot by ÍSOLD HALLDÓRUDÓTTIR

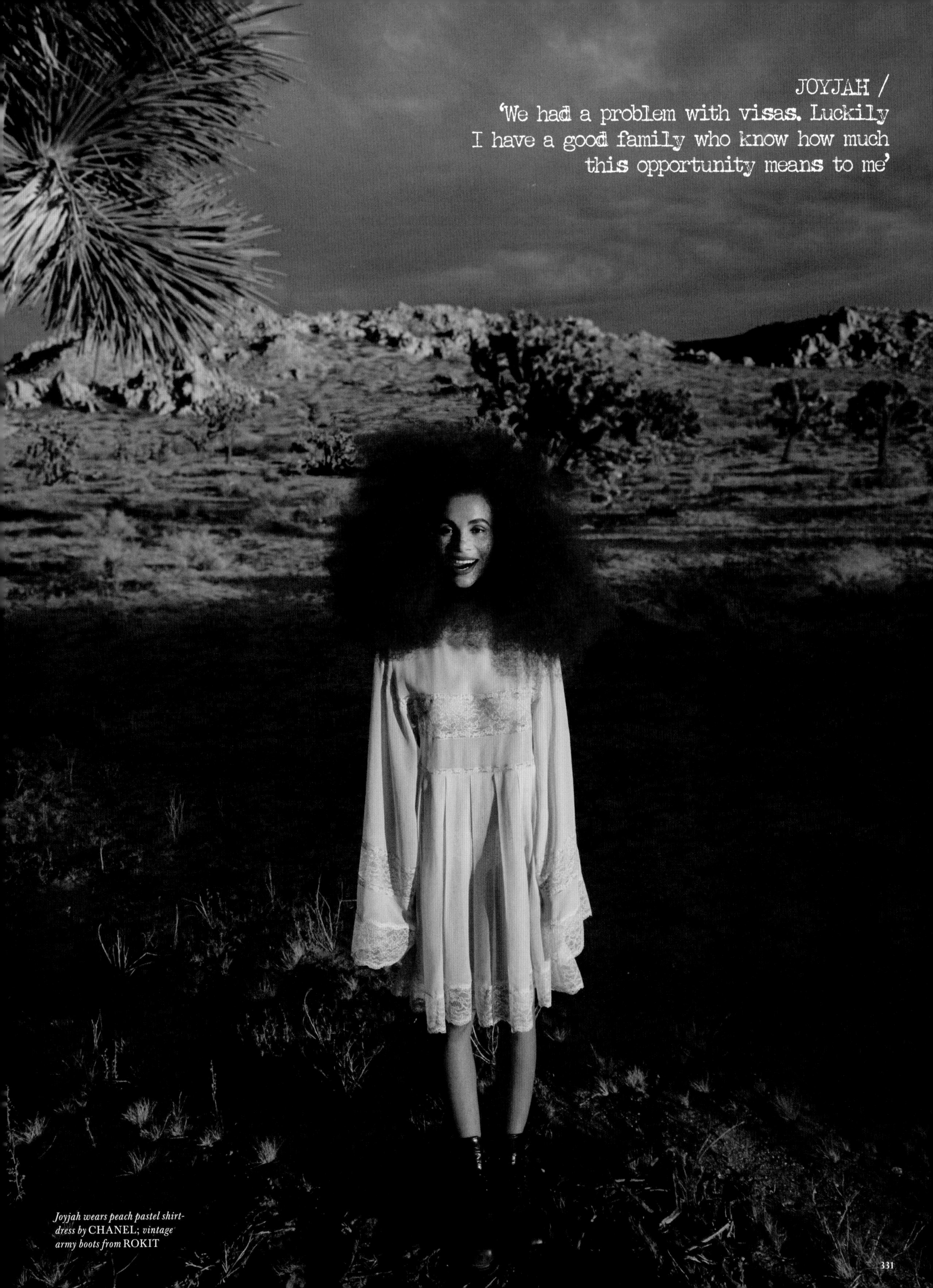

JOYJAH /
'We had a problem with visas. Luckily I have a good family who know how much this opportunity means to me'

Joyjah wears peach pastel shirt-dress by CHANEL; *vintage army boots from* ROKIT

Joyjah wears embroidered velvet dress by MARC JACOBS

'I loved how committed Joyjah was to the project. She flew in from Belize, had all these visa problems and then was a dream to shoot. She has that amazing face, all those freckles, and she seemed so genuinely excited to be there. She got the best time of day, the golden hour just as the sun was setting, and she brought along a Kylie Lip Care, which is my little sister's line. She was really, really sweet'
— Kendall Jenner

BELLE /
'Meeting Kendall Jenner was similar to meeting the Mona Lisa – you see her everywhere'

Belle wears vintage Aran-knit jumper from BEYOND RETRO; *black leather zip-around hot pants by* VETEMENTS X SCHOTT; *black leather overalls by* RAF SIMONS; *vintage blue pinstripe cotton shirt (worn beneath) by* POLO RALPH LAUREN; *white cotton poplin and lace dress with broderie anglaise trim (just seen) by* BURBERRY; *vintage eyelet belt from* PANOS YIAPANIS'S ARCHIVE; *grey wool socks by* HUE; *vintage tan leather boots from* BRICK LANE VINTAGE

Belle wears white cotton poplin and lace dress with broderie anglaise trim by BURBERRY; *rings Belle's own*

'I found myself welling up with tears, cradled by Gwendoline Christie while admiring the genius of Panos Yiapanis'

Belle wears white cotton poplin and lace dress with broderie anglaise trim by BURBERRY; *black leather overalls by* RAF SIMONS; *vintage eyelet belt from* PANOS YIAPANIS'S ARCHIVE; *rings Belle's own*

Belle wears white cotton poplin and lace dress with broderie anglaise trim by BURBERRY; *black leather overalls by* RAF SIMONS; *vintage eyelet belt from* PANOS YIAPANIS'S ARCHIVE; *grey wool socks by* HUE; *vintage army boots from* ROKIT; *rings Belle's own*

Trump is going to have on broader issues in the States, but it seems that the First Lady of Belize, Kim Simplis Barrow, has got her fingers in all the right pies. 'Kim managed to get me an appointment and I got the visa. Everything seemed fine to book my flights to LA for the shoot with Kendall.'

But hold the bubbles: of course, it wasn't that simple. 'The visa office spelled my name wrong! Just one letter. My name is Joyjah A Estrada and it was issued as "Joyjah *O* Estrada". It meant I couldn't risk booking my flights. I had to go back to the embassy. But there wasn't enough time to get my visa and also make it to the airport. Thankfully, I have a good family that knows how much this opportunity means to me.' Eventually Joyjah got on that plane and raced to the cold LA desert, being the last one of the talented contributors to be shot by Kendall on the final day.

In fact, timing had it that Joyjah caught that perfect light, the last 20 minutes before the sun dips behind the mountains, when everything you see turns to gold. If anyone illuminates the youthful spirt of what the #LOVEME17 project is really all about, then it's Joyjah – someone with an innate talent who will go to almost any length to ensure their work is seen, even in the face of so much restrictive red tape. There's a hunger to go further. To reach beyond their social feeds. To ensure their voice is heard, their film is made, or their creative conjuring is witnessed by the wider world. 'To be here completes a circle for me,' Joyjah states, clearly a little emotional. 'I was bullied as a kid, a mixed-race kid in a mostly black community. I used to go home crying, asking my mum if I could somehow get my freckles removed. And now this.' *PF*
IG: @joyjah

Belle Smith Artist

'The moment I saw LOVE magazine's announcement, my heart stopped and sank to my feet. All I could think about were my dreams, dreams that have been a part of my life for years.

'As a 19-year-old artist, filmmaker, model and aspiring actress, I have starred in, directed, filmed and edited my own films for four years. I used YouTube as a creative portfolio as well as an outlet that allowed my art to have an audience. As a second-year film student, I wanted nothing more than to take a leap into the world of art in a role that allowed me to use my multifaceted interests and talents in the arts. I am a constructor of things, magical realities. At the age of three, the movie *Beauty and The Beast* shaped me, including my name (my given name is Victoria). At 15, Tim Burton and Johnny Depp inspired me to focus my artistic talents on filmmaking. The worlds, the stories and the people they create bring me the utmost joy as well as emotional and artistic stimulation. Karl Lagerfeld was the man who dazzled me into the fine art of fashion, and Alessandro Michele inspired me to take risks with my creativity. Steve Jobs and Arthur Schopenhauer reminded me of the power that design and aesthetics have over our world. Beauty is important, contrary to what many think, and it is everywhere. Charlie Chaplin, Marlon Brando, Winona Ryder and Heath Ledger have inspired me to take on the art form that intimidates me the most: acting, the art that channels life the closest.

'I was chosen to be one of the 25 people to be flown out to Los Angeles for Katie Grand's brave and genius Willy Wonka quest alongside Kendall Jenner. The night before I left, my dad reminded me of the last time I was in LA. Three years ago, I spent my entire spring break curating a short experimental film that was entirely inspired by LOVE. My creative drive and energy was provided to me by LOVE. It is a fashion magazine like no other. LOVE didn't treat me as a consumer, it treated me like the artist. LOVE filled me with the thrill of inspiration and the idea of creative choice, something I can confidently say I *live* for.

'On the first day, I walked out of a car to meet Katie Grand. The person responsible for the beauty that shaped so much of my world was standing directly in front of me. This was a moment so beautiful, so magical, I will never forget it. My eyes filled with tears and I couldn't help but give her the enormous hug she deserved. Meeting Kendall Jenner was similar to meeting the Mona Lisa – you see her everywhere. From creative brainstorming together, to hopping fences and making shadow puppets in the sand, it was an absolute pleasure.

'If I'd been told what was ahead of me at that moment, I would have lost it. That evening I was invited back for the second day to shoot moving images, where I was lucky enough to not only film behind the scenes but direct my own visuals as well. Upon wrapping, I found myself welling up with tears over and over again, somehow managing to find myself cradled by Gwendoline Christie while simultaneously admiring the genius of Panos Yiapanis. Later that night I received an email from Katie, inviting me to do another moving image in London.

'Over the past year, I remember thinking about the most perfect career path and LOVE always came to mind first. It is one of the goals I had set for my life, but a goal that I doubted would ever happen. LOVE was a place of such beauty and risk that I so strongly resonated with and adored. Its dominance in media was captivating, its digital content *never* failed to hit the most cool mark and its *insane* print was a true work of art. LOVE is where fashion fully embodies art. Throughout the shoot, I truly couldn't stop smiling at the people around me. Watching everyone's beautiful energy and childlike enthusiasm, I couldn't take my eyes off anyone, and I couldn't have felt more at home and myself. People were making creative decisions left and right and not having to justify why they were doing something, because if it worked, it worked. I needed to see it in the works, in a professional setting to know I had been doing something right all these years. School has always been bitterly against the hypercreative, so I have never felt more reassured. I had always felt that about LOVE: it was almost like a safe place for me, a place where creativity *truly* ran free. Katie invited me to work on moving image at Miu Miu. I cried. And cried.

'A day later, Katie asked me if I'd like to join the LOVE team, starting with filming Tim Walker as he shot this issue's Margiela story. There isn't a single other group of people or place that I would rather be a part of. I will never be able to thank you enough, Katie Grand. I cannot believe it is you who has believed in me. The most picturesque scenario – it almost feels like it was written by myself.' *Belle Smith*
IG: @belleleighsmith

Selah Marley Physics student and singer

Selah Marley received her Christian name biblically. 'It's in Psalms and it means to reflect, to meditate, to stop and think,' she explains. 'It suits me a lot. A little too much, actually. I can be a very serious over-thinker.' She rummages through her tote to find two books she's currently devouring. The first is *The Bhagavad Gita*, the second *Parallel Universes: The Search For Other Worlds* by Fred Alan Wolf. Selah is studying in her freshman year at New York University. 'I never really wanted to go to college. NYU was the only place I applied to and I got in – so, "Yeah, I'll go."' Her educational speciality is the connection between science and spirituality. 'I can create my own major, so that enticed me. But school for me? I don't know. I'm just not into the whole institutional side of things, I just want to be free. It's like a box and it kind of limits you.'

While at NYU, Selah is developing fresh angles on quantum physics and astrophysics in relation to God. 'This idea of space-time and existing outside of space-time. Quantum physics basically brings in the idea of an observer,' she says, flicking through the copious notes she's scribbled in *Parallel Universes*, 'because as humans we can only look at one thing at once. That's one moment, this is the next. I've been trying to battle that in my head. I think that's the thing about humans. We can only do one thing at a time. Versus the Most High, who is all that is.' In three years' time she should have squared the circle to at least her partial satisfaction. 'It's intense and that's why I complain sometimes. I pick classes because of what I want to say.'

Selah is still only 19. 'I can open books,' she continues, 'and go, OK, this is science and spirituality and that's what I want to talk about. But I don't always like how it always has to go to someone else.' Cross-referencing is a problem when you have a vivid and inquisitive mind: 'I wish I could create my own areas, and I feel like school doesn't necessarily allow that. It's more, "So what does Steven Mitchell say?" I'm like, "Woah, Steven Mitchell says this but Selah says *this*!" Sometimes, they don't believe: they want to expose you. And I appreciate that. But I feel like they should believe in us, in the youth.'

Selah wears black off-the-shoulder dress by YOHJI YAMAMOTO; *leather oversized flat Perfecto jacket by* VETEMENTS X SCHOTT; *vintage army boots from* ROKIT

Selah wears black shirt and black shorts with side stripes both by VERA WANG; *vintage army boots from* ROKIT

SELAH /
'You'd be surprised at what young people know – especially in the information age, when we have everything at our fingertips'

Selah was named well. She defies all expectations of celebrity offspring and is a great testament to her hallowed bloodline, one that includes the generation-defining figureheads of grandfather Bob Marley and mother Lauryn Hill. 'That's two tremendous legacies to live up to and I've always had that pressure.' When she's not considering the academic implications of an omniscient being on science, Selah makes music of her own. In *The Miseducation Of...* (an irony, given Selah's current studies), her mother was responsible for crafting a stone-cold classic, one of the greatest albums of all time. 'Yeah, no pressure,' she laughs. 'It used to kind of hold me back, because I felt like – and still do – that those are big shoes to fill and huge footsteps to follow. But I've learned that it's not really about that. It's about how you express yourself and how it flows for you.'

Selah has a very clear idea of what it means to be a young black woman in America today. 'It means a lot. Being a young black woman in America is a box within itself, just because people expect you to be a certain way. However, I do feel like we are granted way more freedom than we used to be, and I feel positive. I like to challenge people and make them think. I've had so many awesome, awesome talks with young black youth, in random places – in parks, even. We'll just start talking about insane things. Sometimes it's spiritual, sometimes it's philosophical and sometimes it's about the government. You'd be surprised what young people talk about and know. Especially in the information age, when we have everything at our fingertips. How could you not? Curiosity is the thing.'

Selah currently has only one song on her Soundcloud. She has learned to remove the hypercritical voice inside her, which speaks of legacy and finding her own connection between the spirituality and the science of creation. 'It's not even about it being good,' she says of her music, 'because when you're really making art, and it's in tune with yourself, then it doesn't matter what anyone else thinks. This is my work and my art, and I love it.' *PF*
IG: @selahmarley

Hari Nef Benchmark millennial

In a world riveted by the changing patterns and possibilities of gender, sexuality, self-invention and acceptance, model/actress/benchmark millennial Hari Nef has become the Chloë Sevigny de nos jours. Stepping off set and sitting in a car lot in the desert, a bloody scratch on her knee, blazing sun in her eyes, she's every inch the divining rod for the margins of her generation, the one who escaped the underground, keeping close to its core values in order to change a bit of the mainstream.

How was being shot by Kendall? 'I love shooting with male photographers, but at the same time I feel like I'm "modelling" for them a little bit. With female photographers, with Kendall, I didn't feel much pressure at all. I feel like they understand what it is to be looked at so I feel comfortable being looked at by them. It was actually really pleasant. She was intuitive.'

Do you watch Keeping Up with the Kardashians? 'I've never really watched it. I've seen little glimpses.'

Does that world interest you? 'I don't watch it, but I have Twitter and Instagram, and I'm a model. She's the most famous model in history. I don't want to narrativise her or her practice, but with her embarking on this new journey as a photographer, I'm sure there's a vulnerability there. This, to my knowledge, is her second photography job. That would frighten me. I don't know what she's feeling right now, but the fact that she is doing it and approaching her role in this industry with a sense of play, I think that's cool.'

Are you learning to see yourself through the objective gaze? 'Of course – It's a part of what I do. Everything I do comes down to my body at the end of the day. You have to choose your collaborators really carefully, because whenever you enter into something collaborative, you're surrendering yourself, your body, your vision, to the vision of others.'

Do you think there's a specific job for you in life? 'Yeah. I had my palm read once. The reader looked at my palm, their eyes widened and they said: "Ancient, unintelligible voices have been whispering in your ear your whole life. They have been talking to you, and it is going to be your life's mission to translate those voices." I come from the first American generation in history that constantly evaluates its happiness. It's not even something my generation were taught, it's something we intuited. Our parents weren't like that. They got on with it: this is the way it is, suck it up. This constant evaluation of our happiness, while selfish in ways, is starting to uncover and blow the dust off embedded things, whether physical, conceptual, discursive, theoretical or anything in between that feel like they block us from happiness. I'm definitely guilty of being a part of a millennial generation that wants to be happy all the time.'

What is happiness? 'I was told it was love and stability and prosperity and respect and support, and I think that's all true, but I also think happiness is not something you can hold in your hand, point to and identify. It's a vector. It's progress.'

Is happiness the same as contentment? 'Contentment is just not something I let myself feel a lot. Personally, I'm so goal-oriented. I've always got the carrot in front of me. It's an obsession but it's an obsession that I know doesn't serve me. It's so predicated on success or failure and it's difficult for me to give myself a break. If you ever see somebody give me a compliment, my whole face tenses up, I say something silly out of the side of my mouth, I roll my eyes or stick my tongue out. I say something self-deprecating.'

Do you come from insanely ambitious parents? 'I come from a mother with very high standards. I would come home with a straight-A report card and I would be like, "Mom, look," and she would just be like, "I expect that from you." It wasn't like a Tennessee Williams thing where there was no love and support, because there was, and if you're going to put in that little prickly part then you also have to talk about how my mom is my biggest fan.'

Is achievement an easier goal than love? 'Yes. Because achievement you control. Love has other people implicated. And I always hated group projects.'

Whenever I think about ultimate ambition, I think of Nicole Kidman winning her Oscar. 'I think about myself winning an Oscar every day *(laughs)*. Maybe your Nicole Kidman was my Anne Hathaway. She looked at her Oscar, she looked at everyone else and she goes, "It came true. I did it." Everybody was being so awful to her during that Oscar season because they found her so unlikeable, but I was so into Anne Hathaway at that point. She clearly wanted it, clearly didn't care about wanting it and clearly didn't care about other people seeing her wanting it. I watched her in *Les Mis* and I not only saw her performance, I saw her waking up that day, hydrated, skin perfect, rail-thin and hair buzzed for the role. I saw her looking in the mirror and saying to herself, "I am going to win an Oscar today." I watched someone who wanted something and got it.'

Have you rehearsed your Oscar speech? 'No, of course not. Well, I mean I'll probably thank everyone on my team and then say a bunch of statistics and then just leave.'

That's not true, is it? 'You have to understand that I don't want to want that as much as I do, but I won't beat myself up for wanting it. I'm just trying to figure out how to set myself up so that if it doesn't happen and things don't go that way I will be OK. I don't want to live in regret and in disappointment. I'm really trying to go easy on myself.'

Take me back to a conversation earlier, when I said I loved your New Yorker *feature and you said, 'It's the only piece of press I need.'* 'It was a quip. I don't think that's true, necessarily. That was something that my publicist said that I was facetiously repeating. There are definitely people that don't read *The New Yorker* who I want to reach.'

Was your mother proud of that? 'Oh, I didn't grow up in a *New Yorker* house. I grew up in an *Us Weekly* house.'

Would your mom be more interested by your being shot by Kendall? 'Absolutely. I love to talk to my mom about my fashion bookings, because she's very tuned in to fashion and pop culture but not in an insider way. So it's cool to see what's reached her and what hasn't.' *PF*
IG: @harinef

HARI /
'With female photographers, I feel like they understand what it is to be looked at, so I feel comfortable being looked at by them'

Hari wears tailored jacket by BURBERRY MENSWEAR; *ivory vintage blouse from* SILK & ROPE

Hari wears black sweathsirt (worn inside out) by GIVENCHY BY RICCARDO TISCI

'Hari was so cool. We'd never met before. She turned it on and you could tell that she loves being in front of the camera – it comes naturally to her. I'd not thought about what she said about being shot by a young woman before but it is so true. I don't think I've ever been shot by a woman around my age before, and I guess that would be more comforting for me, too. Of course, she got a little injury on her knee but she just laughed it off. She was a champ, for sure. Hari is just so freaking cool'

– Kendall Jenner

Sienna wears white cotton poplin and lace dress with broderie anglaise trim by BURBERRY; *A Great Unknown ivory cape attributed to Callot Soeurs c1949 from* WILLIAM VINTAGE; *vintage cotton slip from* MODES AND MORE

SIENNA /
'I feel like I've got to a place where I'm really content. Because that's the focus: my work'

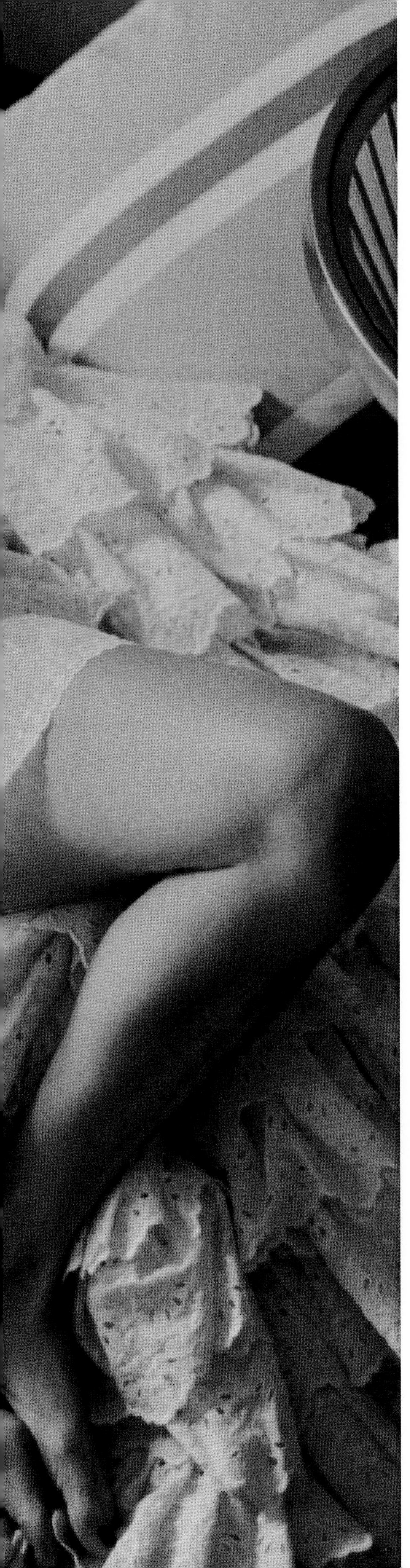

Sienna Miller Actor

Sienna Miller's trademark, according to her IMDB page, is that she 'often plays chain-smoking, drug-addicted and emotionally drained characters'. The actress looks mock-aghast when informed of the accreditation when we meet for an early lunch in a West Village corner bistro. 'As in the interesting people?' she laughs. 'Yes. Why would I not? If you can watch a wife who's emotionally drained and drug-addicted, it's much more interesting, isn't it?' She pauses for a moment to consider her roles from her past. 'That's not true anyway, is it? I'm trying to think now. I've definitely played a few junkies. But *she*'s not.' Sienna bowed over Christmas in the Ben Affleck-directed, Prohibition-era gangster epic as one of the molls in *Live by Night*. 'Oh, she is at the end, yes,' she corrects herself. 'At least, she was in my mind. She doesn't have a choice. She comes from hell, basically. Her father's a pimp and her uncle's a murderer.'

Sienna first met Ben Affleck when she was 20, on her first trip to Los Angeles for her first big Hollywood audition. He's one of a coterie of Hollywood players she's amassed onside over 15 years in the business. 'I screen-tested for a film that Uma Thurman ended up doing,' she says. 'But Ben really fought for me to get it.' It was to play the romantic lead in John Woo's $60million sci-fi drama, *Paycheck*. 'He's the best,' she says of Affleck. 'I've known him on and off, we're with the same agency and he's always been a supporter. His films are big and they're crowd-pleasing and they're intelligent. He's the real deal and the loveliest man.'

As she hit 35, three days after *Live by Night's* commercial release, Sienna's story is not so much an overnight perception-turnaround as a stealth initiative in our understanding of who she is and where her talent resides. Few British actors have had to put in quite so much legwork to get their gifts noticed over the gossip. Sienna appeared, like some English rose from an F Scott Fitzgerald novel transposed into a collection of bespoke-kitchen afterhours in Primrose Hill, just as the Nineties domestic party circuit hit middle age and began taking the requisite medication for its starry hangover. Now she has a daughter, Marlowe, who has started school in Manhattan, and a house not far from our lunch date which she rents from the fantastic ex-pat British restaurateur Keith McNally.

'I said it'd be a year,' she says of relocating to New York, 'but I feel it'll be longer. I rented this amazing house that I can't afford for long. I thought, I'll have an amazing year and chuck a load of cash at it, so it's only downhill from here. I'm not living a realistic life. But I love it.' Marlowe's school, she says, is amazing. 'It's so progressive. On the first day they gave us a leaflet saying "how to raise an activist". It's so me, it's perfect. Whereas in London it's a bit more formal and I got freaked out and I just spent my life saying "sorry" the whole time. And I don't want my kid to be around that.' In 2017, with *Live by Night* buzzing, the Brad Pitt-produced *The Lost City of Z* due out on 24 February, and a tick-list of gently progressive supporting roles in rangy material, from the high dramatic (*Foxcatcher*) to the brutalist exotic (*High-Rise*), Ms Miller feels, finally, like the film star she was supposed to be from the outset.

She has starred on Broadway as Sally Bowles in Sam Mendes' sensational *Cabaret* revival – she was out with her co-star, one-man charisma machine Alan Cumming, last night at Joe's Pub – and will this summer star as another thespian femme fatale, Maggie in *Cat on a Hot Tin Roof* in a West End revival of Tennessee Williams' classic. 'I feel like I've got to a place where I'm really content. Because that's the focus, my work. I don't think I've ever had that, and it was a real struggle when I was younger. I never felt like I was taken seriously and I felt like I was constantly battling preconceptions.'

She's delightfully sanguine about her topsy-turvy tale of fame. 'It wasn't premeditated,' she says of the notoriety she earned during the party years. 'I was just young and thrown into something I couldn't deal with. It was literally overnight.' Like countless people before her, she thought she could invent her own rules when it came to how that would play out with the press. 'My reaction was not to conform and behave. I probably could've had all that I'm experiencing now if I'd been savvy and smarter. But I just wanted to have fun and not taper my behaviour in any way, and it was hurtful, somehow, to my career, my reaction to that kind of fame. I wasn't focused in the way that I am now. I'm also a lot more boring. I was all about having fun then. I grew up in the Nineties watching everyone getting away with what they got away with. I was like, oh, the Gallaghers [did it], fuck it. Then everyone suddenly got a bit more puritanical.'

Marlowe, she says, was not named after *Dr Faustus* author Christopher. It was a name she first heard when Jude Law's sister Natasha chose it for her son. Sienna likes boys' names for girls. So that was that. She can see Marlowe, who is four, as a teenager already. 'I'm in trouble, and it's my fault. My gene pool is strong in there.' She laughs. 'We'll see. She knows what she wants and she knows how to get it. She's my only child, you know?' She thinks that in regard to her own mother, who was Bowie's PA for much of the Seventies, she is rating well. 'You hope that you will be better, because that's the point. And then Marlowe will be better than me. Parenting is different now than it was then.'

Sienna wears white layered lace shift dress by BURBERRY; *vintage collar from* ALFIES; *vintage silk shawl (draped in lap) from* CENCI

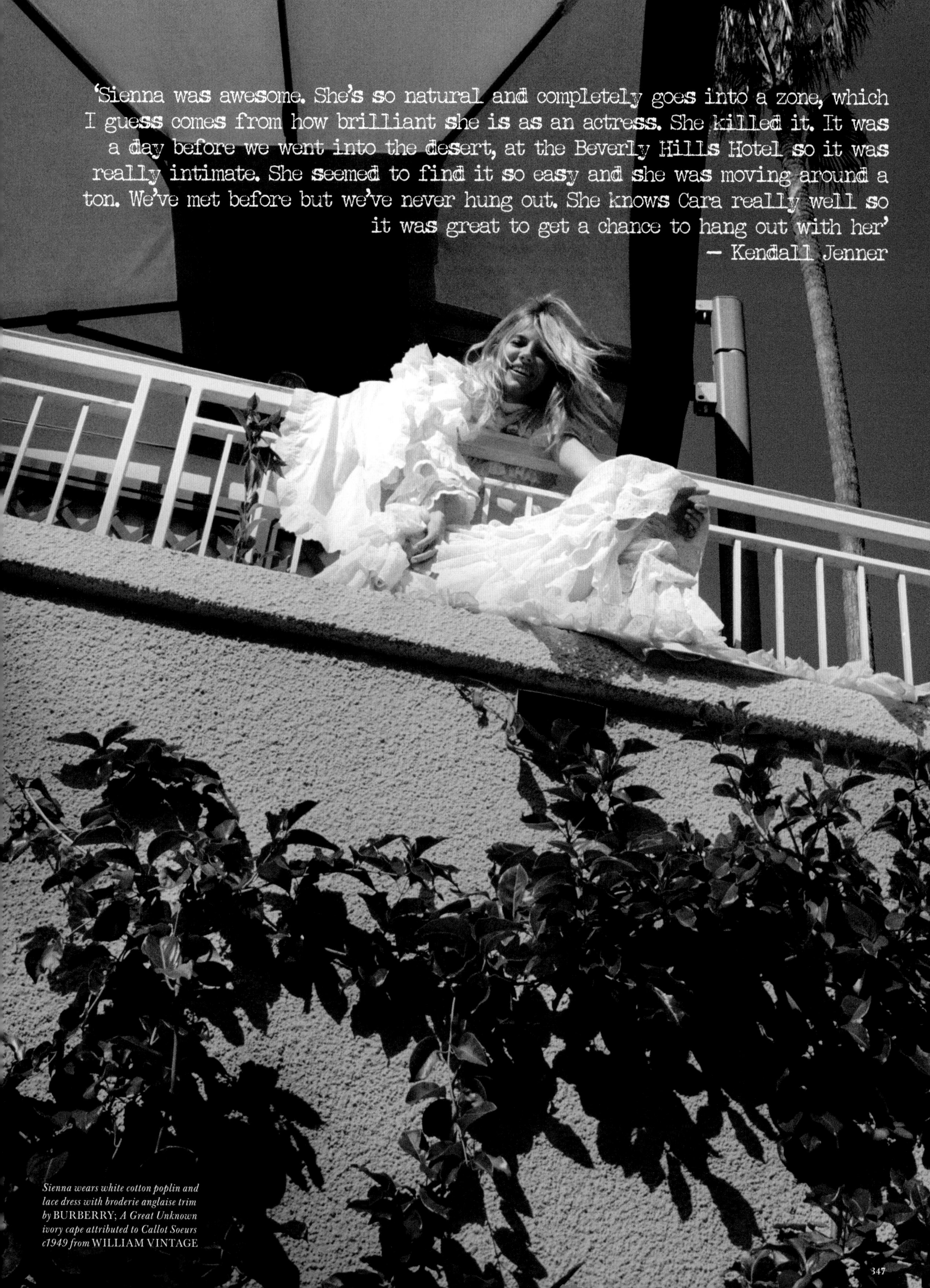

'Sienna was awesome. She's so natural and completely goes into a zone, which I guess comes from how brilliant she is as an actress. She killed it. It was a day before we went into the desert, at the Beverly Hills Hotel so it was really intimate. She seemed to find it so easy and she was moving around a ton. We've met before but we've never hung out. She knows Cara really well so it was great to get a chance to hang out with her'
– Kendall Jenner

Sienna wears white cotton poplin and lace dress with broderie anglaise trim by BURBERRY; *A Great Unknown ivory cape attributed to Callot Soeurs c1949 from* WILLIAM VINTAGE

SIENNA /
'I don't give a shit now. Anyone can say anything and it doesn't bother me'

Her pregnancy she describes as a drama of three acts. 'I was puking for the first three months, really happy for the next three and a whale for the last three.' Marlowe's foot got stuck under her ribcage toward the end, 'Which happens, and she was kicking all the time. I was one of those really ugly pregnant people. My lips blew up like balloons, I was double-chinned and the photos of me after giving birth are the worst things I've ever seen. Sometimes we get them out and literally cry with laughter. Some people glow; I was a monster by the end. But I loved it. I would do it again and again. It's pretty magical, growing a human.'

The birth, she says, was 'hell. Twenty-seven hours. It ended in an emergency C-section.' She intended to have a water birth, in the same pool at the Portland Hospital in which Keira Knightley, among others, has given birth. 'That was the plan. Ten days after her due date when I was wandering around in a bra, Poppy Delevingne came to see me and brought me vegan cupcakes and I nearly killed her. She said I was just sitting there in my bra and my huge lips, staring. [Marlowe] wouldn't come out, so she got induced. Then I went into labour and the induction kicked in. And she was back to front and it went all wrong.' All she can remember for the first 12 hours is wallowing in the pool with a man coming back with more and more gas and air. When she went into surgery, she remembers looking over and seeing Marlowe's father, the actor Tom Sturridge, turning white in his scrubs. 'It got really dramatic. No one needed to see me in that state.' Her sister Savannah was there, too.

'A guy was like, "Start pushing,"' she continues, 'and by that point I couldn't feel anything and my legs were like elephant trunks because I was so filled with drugs – I might show you a piccy one day. Their faces!' The irony that the most drugs Sienna Miller is ever likely to take in the NW1 postcode was in a private hospital is not lost on the star. 'They pumped me full. I didn't know what I had. It was bad.' A friend recently described her caesarean to me as like having someone doing the washing up in your stomach. 'That's totally what it was like!' says Sienna, practically convulsing over her asparagus risotto. 'Oh. My. God. Tom said it was like watching that game, Operation.'

Sienna has yet to traumatise Marlowe with the tales of her troublesome gestation and entry to the world. She says she nagged her mother to tell the stories of her own birth, only to find out 'I had the chord wrapped around my neck and I flatlined'. It turns out that the all-new, boring Sienna, with her upscale brownstone walk-up and her fantastic new artistic portfolio, is not quite the dullard she sells. She's still as funny, charming and likely to say exactly what she wants as before. She says she's trying to teach Marlowe about a new album every week. Her four-year-old adores *Pet Sounds*. Last night it was The Smiths. 'So she was sitting in the bath, singing, "I know I'm un-love-a-ble."'

On being shot by Kendall Jenner for the #LOVEME17 profiles, Sienna only has warm words. 'I trust the magazine and I trust Katie and I thought the photos Kendall took of Kaia [Gerber, for LOVE issue 16] were beautiful.' So she entered the experiment. 'I was so impressed with her as a photographer. She's definitely got an aesthetic. She was really professional, took it very seriously and understood everything involved. It did what the magazine does in terms of embracing new people and giving them opportunities.'

Unlike Kendall, Sienna only has a private Instagram account. She's being encouraged by her representatives to go public. Is she worried it might open a similar floodgate to before, when every detail of her private life, every soiree into the night and trip home in the morning was pored over, blurring the focus on her clear and present acting talent? 'No,' she responds flatly. 'Also, I don't care now. It doesn't affect me. It affected me then, which somehow perpetuated it. But I don't give a shit now. Anyone can say anything and it doesn't bother me. And I'm secure in my ability to do my job. And anything else that's extraneous I don't care about. I think I just became a mother and I just grew up.' *PF*

Paolina Russo Fashion student

Paolina Russo is 21. 'Freshly 21,' she clarifies. When she was 16, Paolina made her first trip away from Markham, the boring Toronto suburb she grew up in. She booked herself a ticket to London. To mark the occasion, she bleached her hair for the first time. When she walked in the room, her mother, an émigré from the Philippines who'd committed to her own fair share of DIY fashion as a teenager, looked horrified. 'I came home and my mom was like, "What the fuck?"' she says. 'From that moment I was hooked.'

Paolina's mum has settled into her amazing creative daughter's vibrant look now, one that is in thrall to the voguish European habit for extreme technicolour eye make-up and dip-dyed hair that changes shade with the regularity of TV channels. 'My mom was exactly the same as me as a teenager,' explains Paolina. 'I think I get it from her, 100 per cent. When I was a young teenager she would tell me about all the stories of her growing up. She was a club kid. She'd dye her hair all the time, turn curtains into clothes. I was like, that's what I want to do, it sounds so cool.' Paolina put her inspirational ideas into practice and by 16 was wearing a fully crafted wardrobe, pieced together from cheap thrift finds, hand-me-downs from both her mother and grandmother, and pieces she'd nipped and tucked to her own specifications. 'I think she was so freaked out because she saw herself in me. Oh no. I think she was afraid of me turning into her, because she knew how she was. History repeats itself.' The only designer item of clothing Paolina owns is a pair of Miu Miu shoes she picked up for $40 on eBay. 'That's enough for me.'

For Markham, Paolina's look was a lot ('maybe a touch too much') but she cast her geographic net wider, taking the art foundation course at Central St Martins and finding her natural home on the fashion BA. Paolina is currently in her third year and interning at Margiela in Paris, which she loves. 'A lot of the stuff that I do is really hands-on. I like to make things and be really physical with it, which is exactly the kind of work I get to do at Margiela.' London, she says, was a baptism of fire. The first night out she had was at the legendary (now closed) spit-and-sawdust Hackney Road gay bar, The Joiners Arms. She saw the curious, bunker-like Dalston basement Vogue Fabrics at its peak. 'It was so good,' she says, 'Like, amazing. There really is nothing in Toronto like that.'

Paolina's night-time habits in exciting basement spaces, where a generation learned to loosen up about strict sexuality and gender divisions, have spilled into her private life with her boyfriend, a set-design student who will 'definitely' collaborate on Paolina's 2018 degree show. 'It's great to work with people that you really love, that you share an aesthetic with and that you can work really naturally with.' Of their meeting, she says, 'It's a really insane story. We lived together and he was gay. And we were just best friends. We always said it would be so amazing and that "I love you so much but it can't happen because you're gay". But we just ended up falling in love and we've been together for nine months now. We merged together so creatively and were so compatible in that way that it just felt so natural and didn't feel like, oh, this is my sexuality and this is who I am. He's just a person.'

Paolina's folks back home in Markham are fully abreast of her personal life. 'It's a strange concept for people to wrap their heads around, but it works. My mom and dad know the story, they know everything. They love it. It's amazing that they've been so supportive in everything I do. They don't question me.' Just like her wild and distinct preference for creating the wardrobe she wants to wear, the hair colour she chooses that day and the make-up she's nicked from a counter, Paolina has always seen people first, sexuality second. 'I've always felt like that. To come to London where other people do too has been really liberating.' *PF*

IG: @calurvillade

Sienna wears white cotton poplin and lace dress with broderie anglaise trim by BURBERRY; *A Great Unknown ivory cape attributed to Callot Soeurs c1949 from* WILLIAM VINTAGE

Paolina wears vintage patterned knit jumper from BEYOND RETRO; *white cotton-blend lace T-shirt (worn beneath) by* BURBERRY; *tweed skirt by* CHANEL; *fishnet tights from* HUE; *vintage army boots from* ROKIT; *necklaces Paolina's own*

Paolina wears orange and green striped rugby shirt by MARC JACOBS; *necklaces and earring all Paolina's own*

PAOLINA /
'I like to make things and be really physical with it, which is exactly the kind of work I get to do at Margiela'

Poppy wears black oversized shirt by VETEMENTS X COMME DES GARÇONS; *leather oversized flat Perfecto jacket by* VETEMENTS X SCHOTT

POPPY /
'Sometimes you've got to be adventurous and step outside what people tell you to do. It's OK to be different'

Poppy McLean Goth

In 2006, five-year-old schoolgirl Poppy McLean from Cleckheaton, Yorkshire, told her mum she wanted to be a Goth. Mum replied with a parentally good-natured 'don't be daft'. Poppy isn't even sure where she'd first heard the word. 'I was watching a programme on CBBC about vampires,' she recalls, 'and there was this girl called Ingrid who had black hair and a red lip – I think that's where it originated for me.' Now sporting a sleek black bob and red lippie reminiscent of Uma Thurman's in *Pulp Fiction,* inspired by Bring Me The Horizon singer Oli Sykes' ex-wife, Hannah Pixie Snowdon, Poppy is pleased with her resolve to defy Cleckheaton's local styling tropes and go her own way. 'I just think there's a lot of things going on in the world and everyone's being told how they should be. Sometimes you've got to be adventurous and step outside what people tell you to do. It's OK to be different.'

Poppy loves screamo: her mum's had to get used to it blaring through the floorboards. She cannot wait to get her first tattoos. She has two best friends. There's Jess, the only girl she speaks to at school. Jess is into trap and dresses like the other kids at school, but they share a morbid teen fascination for serial killers and Jess understands Poppy's resolve to soldier her own way through her teenage years, dancing to her choice of tune. 'She always says I'm that very quiet person who observes a lot. I'm very self-aware and notice everything that goes on. That creepy Goth kid that stands in the corner just watching you? I'm probably that at school.' Not speaking to the other kids doesn't bother Poppy. 'My school life and my personal life I like to keep very separate. I feel like – pardon my language – the people that give me shit at school don't deserve to know anything that happens or what I do out of school.'

Poppy's secret life is as a burgeoning author online. Her episodic tale *I Live For These Moments With You* is a fabulous, earnest reimagining of The Joker's story ('I love Jared Leto more than anything'), introducing him to a civilian love interest who eventually takes on his superpowers by osmosis. Poppy's word skills are A+. She tells the story beautifully and has a growing fanbase of her own now, who she talks directly to online, explaining the different plot diversions and why she made the decisions to take narratives the way she did. When *These Moments* reached 5,000 regular readers, her step-dad began understanding something of Poppy's decision to do life her way. He tried to find the tale online. 'He couldn't believe it, to be honest with you,' she says. When LOVE meets Poppy in the desert, she has 120,000 hooked on the story. She says it's not too racy. 'There are a few kissing scenes,' she explains. 'It's not quite *Fifty Shades of Grey*, nothing like that yet. Maybe in the future, when I'm over 16.'

There has been one brilliant accidental side-effect to Poppy's imaginative, clever and self-motivated life of storytelling online. You hear a lot about the trolls these days, don't you? But not so much about fantastic friendships being forged over the wire. In the wonderful panoply of new global communication streams, Poppy has a best friend from Detroit called Brianna. Before chatting online to Brianna, everything Poppy knew about the city was gleaned from Eminem's fictional biopic, *8 Mile*. And what does Brianna know of Cleckheaton? 'Probably nowt,' Poppy says. She'll find out after the shoot. Brianna and her mom have flown into Los Angeles to meet up for the first time while Poppy's in the country. In the 21st century, loneliness need not be an option. She's a smart lass, our Poppy. *PF*
@pixievonteese

Daisy Maybe and Bee Beardsworth Artists

Where is home?

Daisy: 'I'm from Hackney. Bee is from a farm...'

Bee: 'It's not a farm! I grew up in the Cotswolds. It's the countryside, Daisy. Although my father is a pilot so we lived all over: Cape Town, Tokyo, Sydney, Holland, now London. My parents still have a house near Tetbury.'

The Cotswolds? That's as trendy as Hackney nowadays.

Bee: 'Yeah, I know what you mean. "Trendy!" That's such a throwback word. It's cute. Maybe we should start a revival...'

Walking along the dusty desert highway with twentysomething best friends, artists, musicians, lovers and all-round creative confederates Daisy Millman and Gabrielle 'Bee' Beadsworth, it's easy to get seduced. Maybe it's the setting, maybe it's their chemistry, but if French director Xavier Dolan remade *Thelma and Louise* for Generation Snowflake, this pair of Brit hipster lovebirds would make pretty decent leads. As we stroll with one foot on the sun-cracked tarmac, the other on the gravel, the sun playing King Midas with skin and hair, the pair flirt with ideas, with language and with each other in a way only the young and free know how to.

The pair met at a house party in Dalston last year. (Well, of course they did.) 'It was the *after*-after-party, actually,' giggles Bee. 'It was the early hours of the morning and I was still up. Daisy came over to see a friend and had plans to go to yoga or something. I was in no state for yoga. I think I loved her immediately. She was with this other girl who was annoying and rude. She said something to Daisy and I was like, "Don't fucking speak to her like that."' Daisy finishes the tale, as is often the case in their conversations: 'In March a mutual friend had a performance-art thing and we all went to the pub afterwards. I went outside for a cigarette and we just started chatting. We were literally inseparable from that moment.' Bee concurs: 'I think Daisy is the only person I could actually live with that I don't want to kill that often.'

The house the've made together is a temple to their chaotic art endeavours. Although both aspirational polymaths, Bee is currently focusing on photography while Daisy is a singer-songwriter. 'We have my pictures everywhere, loads of fairy lights, lots of trinkets that we keep that remind us of nights out or trips. We also have a kitten called Gucci. And a ton of vinyl.' Their musical tastes range from predictable pop-cultural stalwarts such as Joy Division to heavier beats both contemporary (Skepta) and ancient (the Spitfire Boys). Amy Winehouse too has had a huge influence on not only their music education but also on how this generation feel public figures should behave. 'Fame can distort everything,' says Bee. 'From both sides, the public and the private side of the artists.'

Daisy: 'Some people feel celebrities are like gods. They're not, they're just human beings with superpowers.'

Bee: 'Well, except David Attenborough.'

David Attenborough?

Daisy: 'Watch out, she has a David Attenborough obsession. Look!' Daisy opens her coat to reveal a black T-shirt with Sir David's face, larger than a side of A5, staring out at us in neon. 'It's the only way I'll get her to snog me.'

Bee: 'Nature is my first love. Sorry, darling.'

Daisy: 'Yeah, well, nature can't take you for dinner – *darling.*' *JH*
IG: @beebeardsworth, @daisymaybefake

Felix Spooner Streetwear designer

One day, 19-year-old Felix Spooner would like his streetwear brand, Idle Assembly, to rival those of his heroes at Supreme, Palace and Gosha Rubchinskiy. 'I love the quality of their clothes, the subtle design. Hopefully I can make Idle Assembly as good as that.' The brand was named after his type of folk. 'People who are thought of as lazy because they don't want to do nine-to-five and conform to society.' Felix, whose business partner is coincidentally also called Felix (to add a further serendipitous twist: they're dating sisters), is one of those kids. In Wandsworth and Wiltshire, he grew up away from the sartorial elegance of London's past. His dad is a twilight entrepreneur who owns a corner of London's nightlife, including clubs Crazy Larry's and the Clapham Grand. He'd hide Felix, as a baby, under a table on nights out.

Felix flunked school from 14 on account of a prodigious weed habit. He likes drum and bass and trap and his favourite DJ is Motive, who he sometimes hears at Visions in Dalston. He has the most amazing, piercing ice-blue eyes and is signed to the model agency Anti. He gave up skateboarding at 15 on account of crashing into a cyclist on a rainy alleyway and tearing a ligament in his knee. His favourite films are strictly gangster. Really, he could not be any more 2017 menswear if he had a Palace triangle logo tattooed on his earlobe. OK, Felix. You can skateboard, you're into Supreme, you smoke weed, you like the nightlife and you've watched *The Godfather* multiple times. Tell me something that would surprise me about a scarily good-looking 19-year-old lad in London today? 'I watch *Friends* a lot. That's easy watching.'

Who's your favourite *Friend*?

'I'd say Joey.'

Do you think you and Joey could be the Chandler and Joey of streetwear?

'Maybe!' Felix looks temporarily elated at the idea, before bunking off for a snout. *PF*
IG: @felix___spooner

BEE AND DAISY /
Bee: 'Daisy is the only person I could actually live with that I don't want to kill that often'

Bee (left) wears black trench coat by BURBERRY; *black leather overalls by* RAF SIMONS. *Daisy wears tailored jacket by* BURBERRY MENSWEAR; *black leather overalls by* RAF SIMONS; *black sweatshirt from* PANOS YIAPANIS'S ARCHIVE

Daisy and Bee wear their own clothing and accessories

Felix wears hooded sweatshirt
by IDLE ASSEMBLY;
sunglasses Felix's own

Felix wears black wool blazer, black wool trousers and lace-trimmed underslip all by BALENCIAGA; *vintage army boots from* ROKIT

FELIX /
Felix flunked school thanks to a prodigious weed habit. He gave up skateboarding at 15 after crashing into a cyclist and tearing a ligament in his knee

Jasmine Newman High school student

Jasmine Newman first began customising her own clothes after casting her eye over *those* Vetements jeans in a magazine. Jasmine's a resourceful 16-year-old high-school student in Burbank, CA. Her dad is a manager at The Gap and her mum works on the counter at Macy's. Her favourite pop artists are Kanye, Drake and A$AP ('Given the choice? Kanye every time. He's a creative genius'). Jasmine takes full advantage of mom and pop's discount cards and her most recent acquisition was a wool-trim denim jacket on which she got a full $15 concession. She intends to practise on it the skilful needlepoint she's perfecting in her more advanced customisation endeavours. Today her brother, Tyler, who gave her a lift to the #LOVEME17 shoot in his beat-up car, has his name stitched early Daft Punk-style on to the back of his blouson by his sister.

Vetements is still out of Jasmine's price reach but it's nice to have something to aim for. One day she intends to go to fashion college in New York. In the meantime, if she can't afford the real thing, she figures, she'll have a go at adjusting hemlines and so on herself. 'It was about a year ago,' she says of her first endeavours in personalised couture. 'My clothes were getting boring and I had to change it up. It was first just ripping my own jeans and cutting the hems, then I started to do little lace-up designs on my shirts, then I started to do the sewing thing. I draw the clothing I'd like to create. It's mostly dresses right now.'

Jasmine's fashion heroes are Marc Jacobs and Dolce & Gabbana. She loves Kendall Jenner and was surprised by how earthy she is behind the camera: 'She's so great, she's so pretty and she's really nice.' In a sign of both the times and shifting youth patterns, she has never seen Kendall on *Keeping Up with the Kardashians*. She only knows her through her fashion life online, on billboards and in magazines. 'Yeah, just from following her on Instagram. I prefer Instagram and social media to TV.'

After the shoot, Jasmine will begin working her first Saturday shifts with her dad at the Downtown LA branch of Gap. She doesn't expect special treatment and extra coffee breaks. 'No, but it would be nice if he wants to.' *PF*
IG: @jasmineenew

Danny Forbes Sarwar Fashion hopeful

'I've always loved clothes,' says 17-year-old Danny Forbes Sarwar. 'I used to tell my mum and dad what I wanted to wear from the age of five.' Danny lives in Reus, a small town just outside Barcelona, and is studying for his baccalaureate. When he finishes, he intends to come to fashion school in London. The first outfit he remembers getting excited by was a dungarees-and-bandana combo he sported as a tot. 'My mum and my aunt liked putting different clothes on me and I really liked some of them. So I let them do it.'

His parents, Danny admits reluctantly, are cool people. They get it. Today in the desert, Danny is wearing a pair of torn denims handed down from his dad. 'He used to wear purple leggings underneath them,' he notes. His folks' fashion past is just piquing Danny's interest now. Mum grew up in Manchester through the glory years and Dad still likes to bust a look.

Danny instructed his family that he'd like to do his own clothes-shopping, thank you very much, at nine years of age. 'I've always loved shopping – but really intense shopping, getting anything from anywhere. Obviously my style has changed and still is changing; I think everybody's does, really. And while everyone's always known me for not being a hugely alternative person, I do have a very particular sense of what I want to look like. I don't go over the top, but I try to stand out.'

It's refreshing to hear that Danny's love of fashion has been welcomed at school, where the other kids have encouraged his style moves. 'I have honestly never had any kind of bullying,' he says. 'Seriously, I get respect, but then I don't think the cases of bullying in Spain are quite the same as they are in Britain. Everyone's had the odd comment, little jabs and jokes, but I've never been personally victimised.' Don't you just love the world sometimes?

Danny is very particular about his use of the word 'fan'. He mentions Björk ('she does things that are sort of wrong, but good for that'), an inherited love from his mum and dad, but cuts short of using the F-word. That is saved for Lana Del Rey, his absolute favourite. If Lana seems a mawkish choice for a young lad with such an appealingly sunny disposition as Danny, it makes sense to him. Lana is his other place. 'She is quite dark and people are usually surprised I love her so much. I'm a really happy person. Everything's great.' With no exceptions? 'It's only things like exams that get in the way, really.' *PF*
IG: @dannyforbess

Christina Vincent Artist

Have you ever been to the Bronx? It's different to Manhattan. 'It's vibrant,' explains singer-songwriter Christina Vincent, sat in a booth in a café that doubles as a film set. Vincent is the quiet type. Of the wide scope that makes up #LOVEME17's stylish youth club, she is the least gregarious. No wallflower, but not a show-off either. She has a look in her eye, something close to steely but with a little more edge. It's hunger. 'I mean, everyone knows Manhattan,' she continues, 'but I bet you don't know the Bronx. It's like a city, it has high buildings and so on but it's more mixed.' Ethnically or economically? 'Both, I guess. It's not as crowded. You can look around. You can take in the world. You can have time to be inspired.'

Vincent lives in this part of the city with her family: 'Two parents, six brothers and five pets.' *Five*? 'Yeah, three cats and two dogs. I have a pitbull who gets on well with one of my cats.' She is currently a senior in high school. She's thinking about going to college but feels that 'it might be a waste of time'. It's hard to argue with that, because her career is already calling. 'I just want to start young: writing music, producing music or making films. I don't feel like I have to take the same road as everyone else. For me it might not be

Jasmine wears vintage cream argyle jumper from ROKIT; *black leather zip-around hot pants by* VETEMENTS X SCHOTT; *platform boots by* MARC JACOBS

JASMINE /
Jasmine has never seen *Keeping Up with the Kardashians* and only knows of Kendall 'from following her on Instagram. I prefer social media to TV'

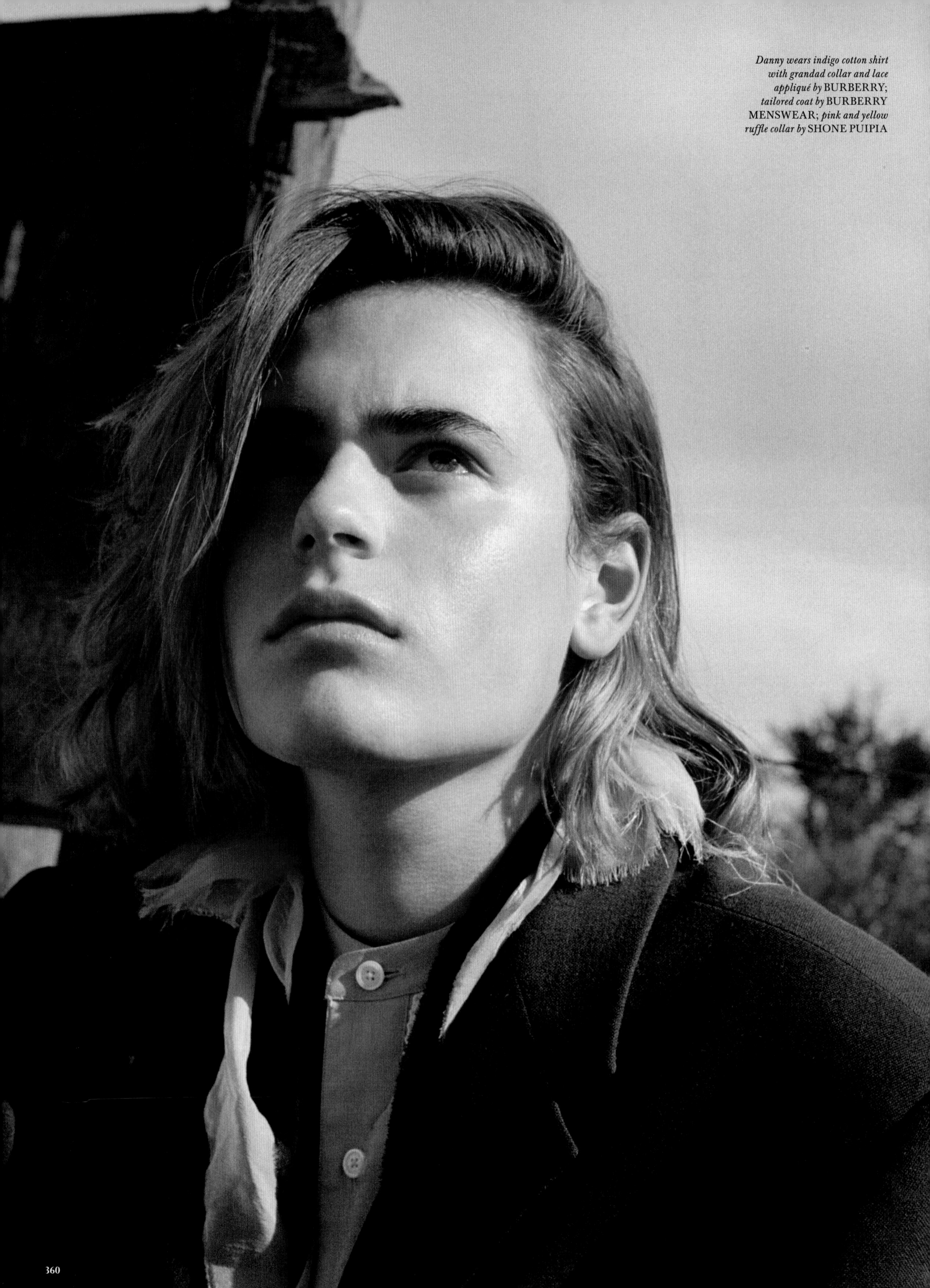

Danny wears indigo cotton shirt with grandad collar and lace appliqué by BURBERRY; *tailored coat by* BURBERRY MENSWEAR; *pink and yellow ruffle collar by* SHONE PUIPIA

DANNY /
'I do have a very particular sense of what I want to look like. I don't go over the top but I try to stand out'

Danny wears indigo cotton shirt with grandad collar and lace appliqué and black leather brogues all by BURBERRY; *tailored jacket by* BURBERRY MENSWEAR; *black trousers by* BALENCIAGA; *pink and yellow ruffle collar by* SHONE PUIPIA; *vintage leather eyelet belt from* PANOS YIAPANIS'S ARCHIVE

Christina wears vintage black pinstripe blazer from CENCI; *cream knit cardigan (worn beneath) by* GUCCI; *white T-shirt by* CALVIN KLEIN; *black trousers by* BALENCIAGA; *socks by* FALKE; *black leather brogues by* BURBERRY; *hat Christina's own*

CHRISTINA /
'I have Instagram but I could go for a week without using it. I don't want to give myself the ability to waste time. I want to change people's lives'

performing so much as writing. I'm part of a film club and we meet every week. We come up with movie ideas, write scripts…' Does she keep notes? 'I like to write ideas down, sure. I usually just sit on the floor of my bedroom with a mic, thinking of melodies and recording.'

So serious is Christina about making a name for herself, she won't let herself be distracted. Not by me, not by friends, and certainly not by her phone. 'I have Instagram but I could go for a week without using it. My friends think I'm something of a mystery. I just don't want to have to rely on it. I don't want to give myself the ability to waste time. I want to change people's lives, not so much physically but emotionally. I want to take them somewhere else.' *JH*
IG: @christina_vincent28

Gwendoline Christie Actor

There's something about Scott's on Mayfair's Mount Street that, rather fittingly for a fish restaurant, warms the cockles of one's heart. Both its price and its food mark it out as memorable. The day before we meet, I suggest this as a destination to my date: Gwendoline Chrisitie, the actor known to millions as Brienne of Tarth from *Game of Thrones*, and to millions more as Captain Phasma from the rebooted Star Wars franchise. Why Scott's? Firstly, I want her to like me (I'm nothing if not a star fucker) and secondly, I hope the infamous razor clams with broad beans and wild garlic will work their steamy, briny voodoo on her notoriously purse lips. Christie is, you see, a very private person, or so I am told endlessly by those I mention our lunch engagement to. Gregarious, sexy, funny, generous, very loud – yes, all these things – but also a staunch defender of her own unshockability, even when sodden with Gavi di Gavi. Well, one can but try.

I arrive early, as I always do to interviews, so I can settle in and do a little light feng shui with the butter dish and cutlery. I did well to be prepared. The first thing to know about Gwendoline is this: she is a bona fide, red-blooded, howl-to-the-moon hoot. Loosen your top button and cling to the tablecloth: Gwendoline Christie is one of the most confrontational people I have ever had the pleasure of interviewing. Her personality doesn't so much appear through polite chit-chat like a spectre knocking on a window as arrive fully in flames like some sort of howling banshee dipped in brandy. There is fun, and then there is Christie.

Other writers have commented on the rugby-tackle that is her laugh, but it's impossible not to mention this feature again. It seems to thwack you about like a cartoon fish, although rather than leaving you cold it leaves you in a state of near-euphoria, blissed out and gurning like a monk who's spent a long weekend at Burning Man with Cara and Suki. It's a drug one could get addicted to, and certainly anyone within 10 metres of our table is fully aware of how much fun we are having. Eventually we order: two hot plates of razor clams, the 16oz cod fillet for her and the John Dory (hold the anchovies) for me. 'We can share the broccoli and the new potatoes,' she barks. 'I don't require exclusivity when it comes to sides.'

Like all good actors, Christie didn't want to be an actor at all. No, first and foremost she wanted to be a rhythmic dancer. If you're wondering what the word 'rhythmic' signifies, as I did, it involves some form of apparatus – a rope, a hoop, a ribbon or some prop through which the dancer must become intertwined. (No doubt such a discipline came in handy while engaging in a far bloodier type of choreography with swords and morning stars years later on the set of *Games of Thrones*.) 'I did ballet and tap, too,' Christie chirps. 'I would train really hard, five or six days a week. I was a child but still the passion for it ran deep. I loved the combination of discipline and expression. I found real freedom in it.' So what happened? 'I grew is what happened.'

Christie's physicality, her glorious female form which is about as close to a Greek goddess as about any human being is able to get, is – for more than most – a significant part of who she is. This isn't objectification on my part, but rather a simple fact. 'I was growing very quickly as a teenager and I was simply told that I couldn't dance any more because of it.' This must have been heart-breaking. 'Well, it was. My physical body was changing so much… Anyway, on hearing this news I was very decisive at the time. I simply thought, "Right if I can't be a dancer I'll become an actor." And that was that. Looking back on it now I'm somewhat taken aback by my own clarity in the matter.'

In taking on a different craft, however, Christie was stonewalled with a comparable prejudice. If we're being honest, even in 2017 professional acting is an industry that only truly wants women to appear in conventionally female roles. 'I went to drama school and – again – I was told that it would be profoundly difficult for me to become an actor. "You have to prepare yourself," they would say, "for the fact that you will not work very much."' Who was the 'they'? 'Everyone! Agents, drama school teachers, casting directors, everyone! Still, I persevered. I loved classical acting work – what I saw as the foundation of all acting, really – and I thought if I could crack that, then this would give me a base. If acting was going to be as hard as they all told me, I wanted to master the hard stuff. Not for me the path well travelled.'

To say Gwendoline Christie likes a challenge is to say Warren Beatty likes women. It is an unequivocal truth. Still, it wasn't only hard work she was drawn to; it was the smashing of glass ceilings and disembowelling of stereotypes that attracted her to a career in acting. 'If I'm being brutally honest,' she says, 'there was part of me that thought, "This isn't fair!" I didn't think it was fair that just because you are a woman and don't look a certain way – conventional, if you want to call it that, although convention is in the eye of the beholder – that neither I nor millions of others should be denied certain opportunities. I went to a drama school that taught students to also be in service of an idea that is bigger than yourself, so your work isn't always so indulgent. And acting can be terribly indulgent. Luckily for me, the character I saw in Brienne of Tarth was the first time I saw the opportunity to do that.'

It's at this point Gwendoline notices something very specific and cackles. 'Jonathan, you know something? We have the same haircut.'

I'm flattered, I tell her. Gwendoline has a very handsome haircut.

There's that laugh again. 'Well, mine has grown out a little, but you have the Brienne of Tarth haircut, Jonathan!'

I've just had it cut, I say.

'Did you take a photograph of Brienne to your barber as preparation for this interview?'

She is now howling. Convulsing like a trustful kid on ayahuasca. The two portly businessmen sat next to us look like they're about to sue for breach of the peace. She can't stop herself. 'Well, this is something else we share other than a side of creamed spinach – a unisex haircut!'

The young, driven rookies as showcased in #LOVEME17 could do worse than use Christie's portrayal of Brienne as something of a case study in how to strive for originality. If anyone starting out on their career path feels that they have never quite fitted in, fear not – even heroines such as Christie start off unsure of their own identities.

'I was in a car with my artist friend Nathaniel Mellors when I heard I'd got the Brienne role,' she says of the part that changed her life. 'It was my agent on the phone and I just burst into tears. I'd worked so hard in trying to get the part. I had totally transformed myself, really. I had made a decision to confront a side of my physicality that was more masculine, the scale of my own body and also perhaps my own vulnerability. It was tough. As I read and prepared for the part I felt I had to step outside my normal self. To look at myself in a different way.'

It worked, of course, as the rest is television history. Had she expected such a reaction to Brienne? 'Well, I knew how I felt about her and how she would affect me personally. But no, not in terms of the global success we've seen. I was determined to do it even if the show was a flop. Why the character seems to resonate with so many people is that essentially everyone faces such issues at some point in their lives. A sense of having to look at oneself clearly in the mirror.'

Does the actor want to change Hollywood? Does Christie have a cause? 'I don't know how Hollywood works, but I can see how people need cinema, need a reflective screen like film. People want empathy, and in this day and age they want diversity. They want something different. We want to see our own lives represented on the screen so we can examine what it means to be human from a distance.'

Up close and personal, it's clear to me that what the myopic world of Hollywood needs more of is Gwendoline Christie. After a coffee, the actor makes her excuses; despite this being a day off she has a meeting with a producer. She pulls on her bespoke Turnbull & Asser grey suit jacket and we promise to see one another very soon. I for one mean it. She leaves. I glance around at the rest of Scott's lunch trade. The restaurant feels quiet and empty all of a sudden. I pay the bill and chuckle all the way back to the office, tying to pretend not to catch my reflection in the posh shop windows as I go. She's right, you know. It is a great haircut. *JH*
T: @lovegwendoline

Gwendoline wears white vintage dress from
PANOS YIAPANIS'S ARCHIVE;
leather thigh-high Texan boots by
VETEMENTS X LUCHESSE

GWENDOLINE /
'If acting was going to be as hard as everyone said, I wanted to master the hard stuff. Not for me the path well travelled'

Destiny wears honey Sandringham long heritage trench coat by BURBERRY

Destiny wears black cotton oversized sweatshirt by VERA WANG; *flax ruffled skirt by* RODARTE; *vintage eyelet belt from* PANOS YIAPANIS'S ARCHIVE; *vintage army boots from* ROKIT

DESTINY /
'I started making weird phone videos. And then I thought I should do it on a camera and do it for real'

JULIAN /
'I got into ballet when I was tiny. I began by dancing on our driveway. My whole family is into it now'

Destiny Anderson Artist

Three months before the #LOVEME17 shoot in the Mojave desert, the wonderful 19-year-old fireball Destiny Anderson took a road trip. She says 'running away' isn't quite the right expression for her and five pals deciding to take a three-day trek across America from their home in the sleepy upstate New York town of Buffalo to their chosen mecca of Los Angeles. 'I wouldn't exactly categorise it as running away from home,' she says, taking the subject seriously. 'It was just that there were so many great opportunities here. So many crazy things have happened since we moved, for all of us.' Perhaps 'adventure' is a more appropriate word. 'Yeah, that sounds right.'

The six friends bundled into a barely functioning Cadillac Escalade SUV, living out of it for their first month in the city. Destiny calls this six-strong friendship group 'my family'. 'They are all that I have here.' Back in Buffalo, long before their exciting road trip, they'd all bonded over music. Destiny made it into a performing-arts school from fifth to 12th grade thanks to her winning rendition of Alicia Keys' 'If I Ain't Got You' before realising music wasn't her thing. 'I don't do music any more because I suck,' she says. 'I had to realise that I can't be good at everything. You have to know what you're bad at to get good at what you're good at.' Her friends range in age from 18 to 23. Destiny says it's handy because when the ones with ID want to go out in the city, there's always some that stay behind, legally bound to keep their whistle dry, at least on the unforgiving LA party circuit. It means they can concentrate on their work, their aspirations, their dreams.

Destiny is a videographer. 'Not to be big-headed, but I'm good, too.' She fell into her chosen field by accident. 'I started doing weird phone videos and then I thought I should start doing this on a camera and do it for real.' She shoots on a Nikon D70-100. She isn't good with regular jobs and back in Buffalo she never held one down for more than six months. 'I was doing catering and working at a grocery store and I had like a billion jobs that I quit because I get bored.' In her first two months in LA she has modelled for magazines and shot a video for local band The Beverly Chills' song 'Big Dog' after returning an open Instagram call for a director. 'I love the song, I love them and they got me over my fear of clowns and heights,' she says of the shoot, which happened over one day in the Hollywood Hills. 'It was their idea to use clowns,' she notes disdainfully. 'They were telling me and I was giving them side-eye.'

Destiny's Sensational Six friends recently found a cheap rental apartment in Altadena, 30 minutes' drive out of the city, in their landlord's back lot. She hasn't had to wait tables yet to make rent. There is something so free-spirited in Destiny that if it came to it, I'm pretty certain she'd jump back in the SUV and make that home until she was able to start again.

It has never struck Destiny before that because she was born the same year Beyoncé and co released their first single 'No, No, No (Part I)', she is quite literally Destiny's child ('What? Seriously? Is that real? That's crazy. I didn't know that. Wow'). She prefers the political Beyoncé of 'Lemonade' to the hen-party model of 'Single Ladies', but saves her special fan worship for Miley Cyrus. 'She's my favourite. She's so free and wild but she's good at what she does. It's not like she's crazy and can't do anything. She has talent. She sings so well.' The only downside of Destiny Anderson's new LA life is the nights she gets caught off guard, missing her six-year-old baby sister. 'She's my little muffin. She reminds me so much of me.'

Destiny was thrilled when the call came through to be part of the #LOVEME17 portfolio. 'I never won nothing,' she says, 'but things have started happening here.' It gives her a chance to talk about her favourite piece of work, a short film she wrote and directed on bipolar disorder called *Mixed States*, starring her friend from back home, Terra Harter. 'She was very good at portraying the character, and we talked a lot about what it involved before we filmed it. She was very good at playing with her emotions. I feel like I tidied it up in four minutes. It shows exactly what happens.'

Bipolar is not a condition Destiny Anderson suffers with. 'But I've had people tell me, "You did a good job at portraying this." I didn't want to misconstrue how it is for someone who really has that. I was really trying to hit it right on the head. I've never been diagnosed with anything but I am a very emotional person.' There is something innately truthful about Destiny, in art as in life. A big future could lie ahead. 'I don't know that I want to shoot a movie because I feel like, I don't know, that would be crazy.'

Never say never! 'Look, you know that I'm going to shoot a movie now, just because you told me I'm too young to do it.' *PF*
IG: @baaabygiraffe

Julian MacKay Dancer

Heard the one about the blue-eyed ballet dancer from Montana who became the first-ever American enrolled in the Bolshoi Ballet Academy in Moscow? Well, if you haven't, you'll soon hear much more from Julian MacKay – think Lucky Blue Smith combined with Rudolf Nureyev – who graduated from both the upper and lower academies of the Bolshoi in 2015. (Clue: if you don't know your arabesque from your plié, this is about as hard as beating Stephen Fry in a pub quiz.)

Scouts from the notoriously tough Russian school spotted Julian back when he was 11 in New York where he had just had roses thrown at his bandaged, crumpled feet after winning a Youth Grand Prix medal. 'They asked me to train in Moscow on a trial run. At first it was very tough, but they soon accepted me – it helped that I learned Russian within a year.' Since then, life has been one long grand ronde de jambe.

'I got into ballet when I was tiny,' explains Julian, whose achievements thus far include wins in over a half a dozen prestigious international competitions, a year-long apprenticeship at the Royal Ballet in London and, more recently, a modelling and talent contract with IMG. 'I began by dancing on our driveway. My whole family is into it now – my older sister started the trend and then Nadia, a younger sister, took it on. Then I danced and my younger brother Nicholas followed me.' Is there a link between ballet and Montana? 'Not at all. There are lots of bison but not much ballet. It's actually very beautiful, but fairly starved of culture.'

So why the Bolshoi? What makes this the Parsons School of Art for going 'en pointe'? 'It's so prestigious. Russians like to say that they can take anyone and with the Russian method they can make them a dancer. The teachers there are unbelievable. It's like ballet boot camp. They work you incredibly hard but you have to commit to it if you are serious. For me it was always the challenge that drove me on. The harder it was, the more I wanted to succeed. The more someone tells me I can't do something, the more I push back. Resistance only makes me want to prove people wrong.'

What interests Julian now is finding a way to fuse contemporary, modern culture with an art form as old as ballet. 'These dance moves are sometimes hundreds of years old. Suddenly you have a choreographer like Wayne McGregor who's putting radical twists on such a traditional

Julian wears grey melange cotton-blend jersey sweatshirt with lace insert by BURBERRY

JULIAN /
'The Bolshoi is like ballet boot camp.
And the harder it was,
the more I wanted to succeed'

Julian wears vintage black petticoat from PANOS YIAPANIS'S ARCHIVE; *tights by* WOLFORD

Julian wears grey melange cotton-blend jersey sweatshirt with lace insert by BURBERRY; *vintage black petticoat from* PANOS YIAPANIS'S ARCHIVE; *tights by* WOLFORD

Hailee wears natural cashmere cotton and wool cable-knit sweater by BURBERRY

HAILEE /
'It's complete madness before a show. I guess once you've found a routine it's different. But I'm a brand new artist'

HAILEE /
Since her pop smash 'Love Myself', Hailee's music sideline has taken a more central position in her life

dance form; he asks people like Mark Ronson to produce the music and so on. This inspires me. In fact, I want to become a choreographer myself. I'm going to the Russian Art Institute in Moscow to learn to be a ballet master.'

When Julian isn't scissor-kicking his way into the history books, you can find him bombing around Moscow on his skateboard, as seen in his #LOVEME17 application video. 'Skateboarding is great for balance, actually. And also for strengthening the calves.'

And what about girls? Surely Julian has a long line of white swans lined up outside the theatre each night, all desperate for their Prince Charming? 'Well, it's difficult to date in the ballet world, especially someone in your own company.' How so? 'Well, what if you fall out? Then you have to do a love story with them the next season on stage. It would be… awkward.' *JH*
IG: @julianmackay

Hailee Steinfeld Actor and pop star

Hailee Steinfeld isn't quite sure whether we should be referring to her as a movie star, pop star or some brand-new 21st-century hybrid of both at the moment. 'I mean, you tell me?' she says, hunching her shoulders. Hailee, you will recall, opened her career seven years ago with a stunning performance in the Coen Brothers' *True Grit* at 13 years of age. Her last cinematic coup was as Nadine, the brilliant, troubled teen star of *The Edge of Seventeen*, whose hot best friend and super-popular brother get together, only highlighting her social nervousness. Nadine gets major guidance from the high-school tutelage of her benevolent teacher, played by Woody Harrelson. Hailee says yes, the film was in part titled in homage to the Stevie Nicks song. As to whether the Fleetwood Mac vet has seen it yet, she isn't sure. 'Can we make that happen?'

The six busy years between *True Grit* and *The Edge of Seventeen* have seen Hailee's pop sideline, one that began with her irresistible, sophisticated smash 'Love Myself', take a more central position in her life. When we meet in the desert, Hailee has just finished an opening slot for Meghan 'All About That Bass' Trainor's arena tour.

Life on the road, she says, was not quite what she anticipated. If Hailee is at a premium pop gig – she did Drake, Bieber and Kanye, the big three of summer 2016 – she says she'll spend her time watching the floor fill with audience prior to the artist's arrival and wonder what's going on backstage. 'What is the artist doing right now? Are they sleeping? Are they doing vocal warm-ups? Are they freaking out? Now, having been on tour and been on the other side of that, it's crazy to go to a show and really see how they're going to lay it out. How they're going to come out, what the energy is going to be like.' For the artist herself, her own pre-show experience has become all too familiar. 'Me, Hailee, personally? Always freaking out. It's complete madness going up to a show. I never really realised that before. I guess once you've found a routine it's different. But for me, I'm starting from the ground up with music. I'm a brand-new artist.'

Hailee says the demands on her time from both the pop camp and movie pressures can mount up. 'They conflict, sure. It's not easy, and I'm learning that now. People are like, "So, which one are you going to choose?" and I'm like, "Look, I'm not." I am going to do both and I am fully aware that that may be near impossible. But there is always a way to work that out.'

What's next for Hailee is, as luck would have it, a perfect amalgam of the two strands of her talent, a reprisal of her role in the super-duper all-singing, all-acting girl-group franchise, *Pitch Perfect*. When we meet, she's still waiting on a script. But she has songs in mind already that she'd like to see on the soundtrack, including her major artist crush Drake's 'One Dance'. Haven't we heard that a bit too much in the last 12 months? 'Yes, but not by 12 women and an a cappella group,' she corrects. 'We've never heard it like that before. I feel like a Drake song needs to be in *Pitch Perfect*. I feel like that could up the level of cool for all of us.' *PF*
IG: @haileesteinfeld

Marti Ragan Model, musician and art director

What can I call you? Martika? Misfit? Marti? 'It don't really matter,' laughs the early-morning face in front of me, blowing cool breath over a mug of something that is too hot. Whatever her moniker, she is certainly striking: her hair is blown out to the size of freshly spun candy floss, while her eyes are narrow and suspicious. She reminds me a little of Linda Evangelista: sparrow-like features, yet wily. She's street-smart rather than Ivy League-educated. 'How about we try *Marti*?' she tuts. 'Need me to spell that for you? M-A-R-T-I. Now, what else do you want to know?'

Sitting down Marti, a 24-year-old model, musician and art director from Washington DC, you'd think I was a parent about to issue a final warning about late homework. Or a careers adviser asking dumb questions about a generation I'll never understand. The young can do this, of course, open and shut the doors to their worlds as nonchalantly as a cat pawing balls of wool. All at once they can make you feel included in their plans for the day, the future, while at the same time making you feel about as cool as Piers Morgan's tie rack.

How did you get involved in #LOVEME17, Marti? 'Through my feed. Someone DMed me the link to enter, I think. I'd seen it a few weeks back and thought it looked like a cool project. I was down.' Marti's Instagram is a pretty good place to start building a picture of why this woman is so unique: her 'thing' seems to be a revelling in a lack of conformity. 'I don't want to look like anyone else,' she states with vigour. 'Hell, we all look different anyhow. I want to be the anti-role model. A role model who doesn't expect obedience but instead demands diversity. This is real life, motherfucker.'

Although Marti's interests are fairly free range, it's currently music that she is back working on with the most diligence. 'It's sort of Go-go music,' she explains patiently. I feel like an octogenarian being told how to turn on an iPhone. 'It grew out of DC in the Sixties and Seventies – basically it's like drum and bass, but more punk. Dirtier. Sexier. The whole scene knows one another in DC; it's tight. I started off in a band but I've always suffered from social anxiety, maybe from being bullied at school.' And how does the modelling fit in? 'Being a muse is cool, but you're always the focus of someone else's creativity.'

A wily, wild Go-go punk from DC who gets 'tunrt' at the weekend and resembles an intergalactic villain from *The Fifth Element*, Marti knows where she's heading. And right now that is being shot by Kendall Jenner on a dune edge somewhere in the desert. Does this muse have any preconceptions about the famous model-turned-photographer about to shoot her? 'Well, we've never crossed paths, put it that way. Our worlds are pretty different, I think it's fair to say. But I hope we want the same thing for the future of the planet: more love, more education and more art.' Proof that not all millennials are made equal. *JH*
IG: @amerykahsmisfit

Hailee wears natural cashmere cotton and wool cable-knit sweater (just seen) by BURBERRY

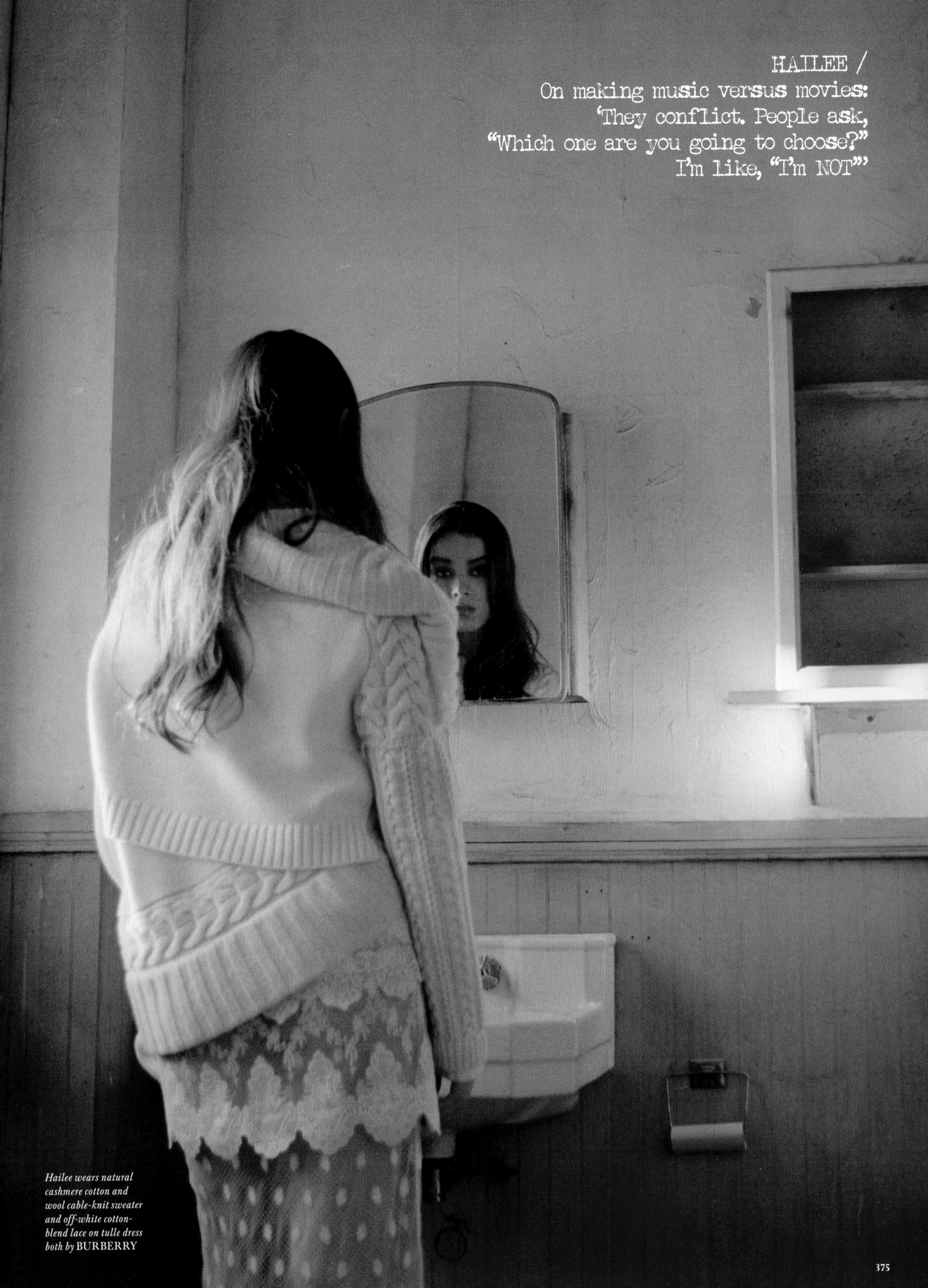

HAILEE /
On making music versus movies:
'They conflict. People ask,
"Which one are you going to choose?"
I'm like, "I'm NOT"'

Hailee wears natural cashmere cotton and wool cable-knit sweater and off-white cotton-blend lace on tulle dress both by BURBERRY

Marti wears white herringbone cotton shirt-dress with lace inserts by BURBERRY

MARTI /
'I don't want to look like anyone else. I want to be the anti-role model. This is real life, motherfucker'

MO'NE /
'Meeting Kevin Hart and
President Obama was a highlight.
But that stuff is all just extra.
I just want to play'

Mo'ne wears vintage blue pinstripe shirt by POLO RALPH LAUREN; *red feather-trimmed bralette by* PRADA

ABBY /
Drama school was 'the most intense two years of my entire life. Have you seen *Whiplash*? It's like that'

Mo'ne Davis
Sports star

'Show Me the Mo'ne!' Two years ago, this was a slogan that would regularly follow Mo'ne Davis, 15, around on placards. Two months after her 13th birthday, Mo'ne, a baseball player from Philadelphia, Pennsylvania, became one of the most promising athletes in the United States: she was the 18th girl to have ever played in the 68 years of the Little League World Series and the first ever female pitcher to have thrown a 'shutout' – that is, she completed a game without the opposing team scoring a single run. You don't need to know anything about baseball to know that this is pretty awesome.

Like Lionel Messi on a football pitch, Michael Phelps in an Olympic pool or British boxing champion Anthony Joshua in the ring, Davis proves that soaring talent sometimes isn't just down to the scientifically proven 10,000 hours of practice, the right coach and a monastic diet: sometimes it's simply a gift and one that, if nurtured properly, can transform a life, a family, a whole dynasty. 'I managed to meet a lot of people doing what I do,' states Mo'ne fairly dispassionately. Give her a ball or a bat and she's explosive; give her a call time and a few styling cues and she's a little less, well, let's say gregarious. 'Getting so much fame overnight was a shock back then. I met the likes of Kevin Hart, and also President Obama – that was a highlight. But that stuff is all just extra. I just want to stay focused. I want to play.'

Icon status for Mo'ne isn't so much about if but when. She appeared aged 13 on the front cover of *Sports Illustrated* with the cover line 'Mo'ne Davis: Remember Her Name. (As If We Could Ever Forget)' – although since then she has switched her attention from the baseball diamond to the basketball net. Like so many gifted athletes, Mo'ne isn't just good at one sport: she can jump, shoot and hustle quite like no other. 'Although I'm pretty slight physically, I can handle myself on the court. I haven't completely decided, but I think this is what I want to focus on now.'

For someone so young, Mo'ne is also sensitive to the fact that women have a far tougher time in sports than men. They attract smaller competition prizes and smaller salaries and ad deals. None of this impresses her, as you can imagine: 'No matter what level it is, everything a man or a women does should be treated as equal. Look at the likes of [US gold medallist] Simone Biles and what she achieved in the Olympics last summer, aged only 19. Give girls a chance and we'll show you why we should have more TV coverage.' From a half-time hero to feminist crusader? Frankly, you wouldn't put anything past Mo'ne Davis at this point. *JH*
IG: @monee_011

Abby Wilson
Actor

How did you get involved in #LOVEME17?
'Someone told me to apply. I thought I might as well. My friend was, like, "Babe, submit. Do it!"'

Where do you live?
'London. I'm from Croydon originally but now I'm in Shepherd's Bush.'

What do you do?
'I'm an actress. I just graduated from [Kings Cross drama college] The Poor School last June.'

Does acting run in the family?
'My dad used to work in the meat industry and now he's got into the vaping market. He has a brand called Snake Oil. He started that by mixing his first batch at home.'

What was drama school like?
'The most intense two years of my entire life. I did fashion for a bit beforehand, then I did some modelling – I'm with Anti-Agency. With The Poor School you're able to juggle a few things, modelling being one of them. The guys that run the school are a bit off the wall.'

What was the process like at drama school?
'They wanted to break you. Have you seen *Whiplash*? Well, it's a little like that. They make you lose all your inhibitions and sense of self; they want to reveal your raw, untapped emotions. Sometimes we went on field trips to London Zoo, animal studies – it was that sort of a place. I think I picked an ostrich.'

An ostrich?
'Yeah. It's all about physicality.'

Are you getting much work?
'Fits and starts. I also have to waitress to make the rent. I work at a Japanese restaurant on the King's Road.'

What's been you favourite acting job so far?
'I did a short film for Topman with the guy from *Game of Thrones*, Jacob Anderson – that was fun. Also I did an ad for Manix condoms. I was the drummer. It was cooler than it sounds.'

Are you an extrovert?
'Sure! I love showing off. I hope it's not too annoying.'

Who's your acting crush at the moment?
'Cate Blanchett blows my mind. Although I really wanted to see Billie Piper in *Yerma*.'

Is it hard to be a working actor in 2017?
'God, yes. I am a big believer, however, that if you keep your head down and keep working you'll get to where you deserve to be.' *JH*
IG: @abbyow

Kaia Gerber
Model

'I think this might be the place where my mom did that Pepsi commercial. She mentioned it to me before I rode out here. We should find the exact same spot. And the fridge!' Kaia Gerber is, if you didn't know, the 15-year-old daughter of Cindy Crawford and Randy Gerber, the businessman who turned drinking tequila with BFF George Clooney into a 40 per cent proof superbrand. Liquor baron daddy. Supermodel mommy. Kaia Gerber: so far, so SoCal.

The advert that Kaia is so fizzed up about this morning is one of the most famous ever to be shown on American television. When a red Lamborghini pulled up outside the Halfway Café in 1991 and Cindy stepped out from under one of its gull-wing doors, dressed in a tight white vest and a pair of butt-cheek-skimming denim cut-offs to Doris Troy's 'Just One Look', history was made. Not only did it make Cindy a star beyond style's glossiest pages, it fused the worlds of high fashion and big commerce in a way that had rarely been so successful before.

Kaia and her mum are right, however: this morning, Saddleback Butte State Park, about two hours north of LA, looks very familiar. Did she see James Corden's recent parody of her mum's Pepsi ad for a *Late Late Show* skit? 'Yeah I did, and it was hilarious,' laughs Kaia. 'I mean, I don't usually stay up that late for talk shows, but I saw that clip on YouTube. James is so talented and funny; a lot of my friends are close

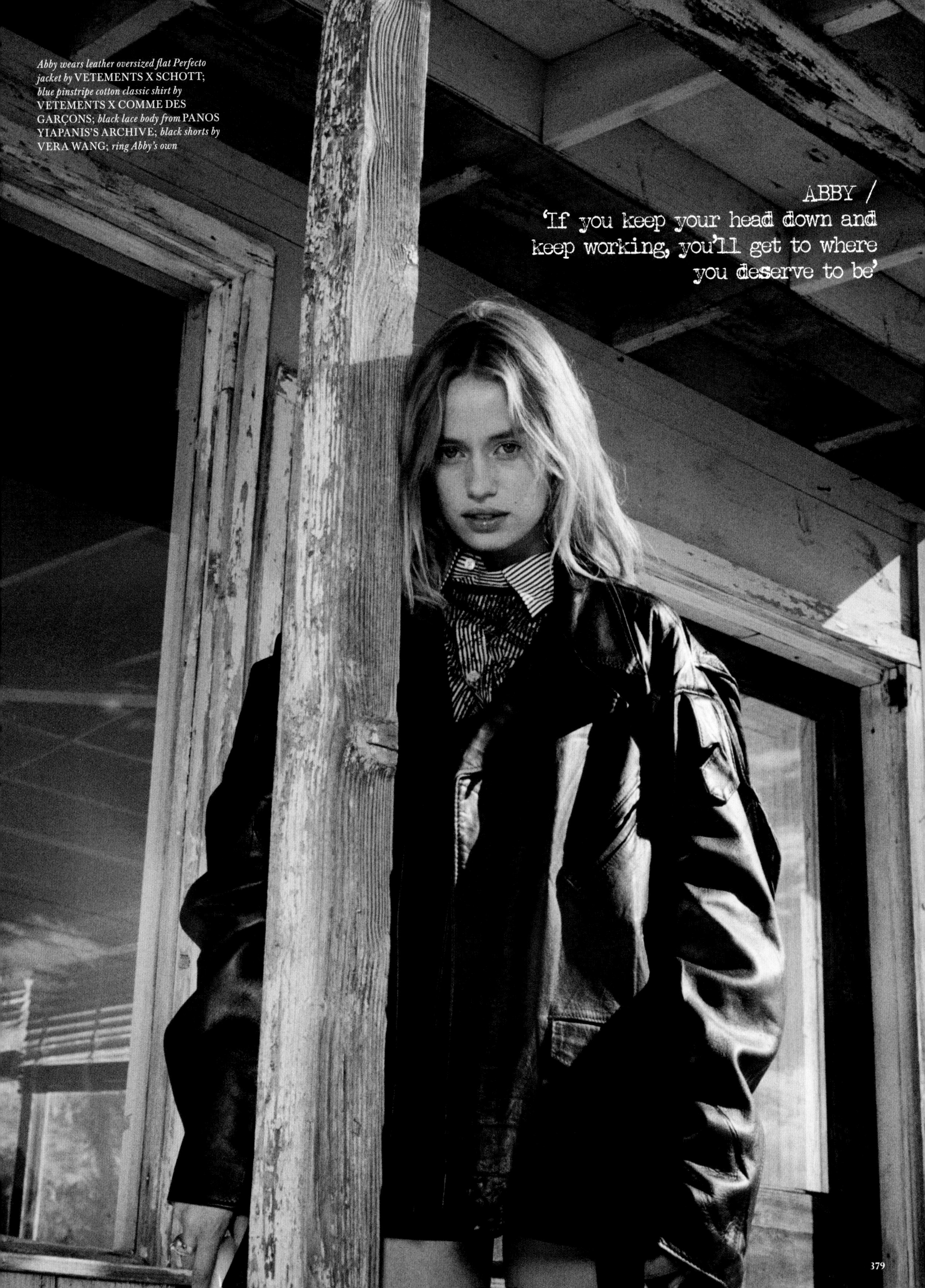

Abby wears leather oversized flat Perfecto jacket by VETEMENTS X SCHOTT; *blue pinstripe cotton classic shirt by* VETEMENTS X COMME DES GARÇONS; *black lace body from* PANOS YIAPANIS'S ARCHIVE; *black shorts by* VERA WANG; *ring Abby's own*

ABBY /
'If you keep your head down and keep working, you'll get to where you deserve to be'

KAIA /
'Although my mom knows the industry well, this is something I personally want to pursue rather than her forcing it upon me'

Kaia wears ruffle-embellished blouse by RODARTE; *vintage black bustier corset from* CENCI; *vintage denim jeans from* BLITZ; *ruffled wool trousers by* PANOS YIAPANIS'S STUDIO; *vintage belt from* PANOS YIAPANIS'S ARCHIVE; *jewellery Kaia's own*

KAIA / 'For me, modelling comes down to one thing: it's about trying really hard to not pose'

to him in LA. He does Carpool Karaoke and you think he's going to be a terrible singer but he's got an incredible voice. He's killing it right now.'

Kaia talks about The Biz like a solid industry vet. Let's face it, she's already been exposed to more Hollywood machinery than half of LA. 'I got my first modelling job when I was 10,' Kaia explains without so much as a flinch as to how wild this sounds. 'It was the first thing I ever did out in Borrego Springs – also out in the middle of nowhere – for Young Versace. I then took a break, as I wasn't sure it was right for me. But about a year and a half ago I started exploring modelling again. I got signed by IMG and now, I guess, it's what I do.'

As far as industry tutors go, Kaia is in the Ivy League. Let's just say that when it comes to throwing shapes and pouting, Kaia is fully home-schooled. Has her mum taught her how to flounce – a requirement of all top models – when she doesn't get her own way on set? 'Well, something like that! First off she tells me modelling is all about having fun. Or at least it should be. If you stop having fun, quit. Although my mom knows the industry well, this is something I personally want to pursue rather than her forcing it upon me. And secondly she told me one of her secrets was to always to have a thought behind the pose. Use emotion to push your body into different places. If *you* don't believe it, how will the viewer?'

If this comes across as precocious, then Kaia's cute tones aren't translating properly: her professionalism and amiability go way beyond her years. Also she's got every reason to be somewhat surefooted: becoming The Next Big Thing isn't so much a cert for Kaia as her destiny. Is she ready for fashion's fame lens to train its crosshairs on her? 'I mean, so far as being in front of the camera goes, I'm used to it. Even if I'm not shooting professionally, my dad has always been walking around taking snaps. I've never felt out of my comfort zone on set. It's about being natural, at the end of the day. For me, modelling comes down to one thing: it's about trying really hard to not pose.'

It's hard to remember that despite the jet-set life, dad's movie-star pals, a world-famous mom and a routine wherein opportunity comes easy, Kaia Gerber is also, quite simply, a schoolgirl weighing up her options. Does she have a favourite subject at school? 'French! And dance. Oh, and self-defence – I know how to get myself out of bad situations. I can knock someone's nose out of joint if I have to. You can thank my brother for teaching me that.' And what if she suddenly woke up ugly? Kaia laughs. 'I hope that doesn't happen! I do want to go to college, Ivy League if possible. I've always wanted to minor in criminal psychology.' Is she a young Sherlock at heart? 'Well, it's less about solving crimes and more about getting into the minds of the people that do it. Finding out why.'

Kaia first got involved with #LOVEME17 by sending in a video offering her heartfelt support to all the young entrants. She considers herself something of a cheerleader for the millions of voiceless creatives online. 'I go through Instagram all the time and see such beautiful girls; I'm gobsmacked that some of these people just don't get the chances they deserve.' Not that she isn't a little worried about how much screen time we all seem to be clocking up. 'I had my childhood. Sure, I had a phone but I wasn't on it all the time. We wouldn't be on our iPhones round the dinner table, no way.'

Does her own rapid rise and fashion's social-media-supercharged new pace worry Kaia? 'Yeah, it's a lot of pressure for young girls. I think we need to learn from a young age how to deal with stuff. My mom was famous and there were paparazzi, but they would only be around if there was news or if she had a cover coming out. We're a different generation. It's harder in some ways. During my mom's time people had to wait to see her; now your entire life is being documented. There was more mystery. I'm worried that people are going to get sick of me already! I'm only 15. What's going to happen when I'm, like, 20?'

Astute, down to earth and already well on the scene – so where does a young, beautiful Californian Sure Thing go to get away from it all nowadays? 'I have my places where me and my friends can stay hidden. We live in Malibu which is quieter than Hollywood and we go to my dad's restaurant Café Habana a lot.' I guess her father likes to keep an eye on her? 'Of course! I went to a hip hop gig recently and my parents were worried about me. I love rap music, which my parents do not love. There was a mosh pit. We were careful.' And dating? 'Well, between my dad and my brother guys have no chance – between the two of them I'm off the market.'

Oh, to be a teenager again. Kaia Gerber needn't worry of course; for this sun-kissed LA ingénue, the world will wait, albeit impatiently. *JH*

IG: @kaiagerber

Kaia wears white cotton-blend lace T-shirt by BURBERRY; *vintage Aran-knit jumper from* BEYOND RETRO; *ruffled wool trousers by* PANOS YIAPANOS'S STUDIO; *vintage belt from* PANOS YIAPANIS'S ARCHIVE; *vintage army boots from* ROKIT

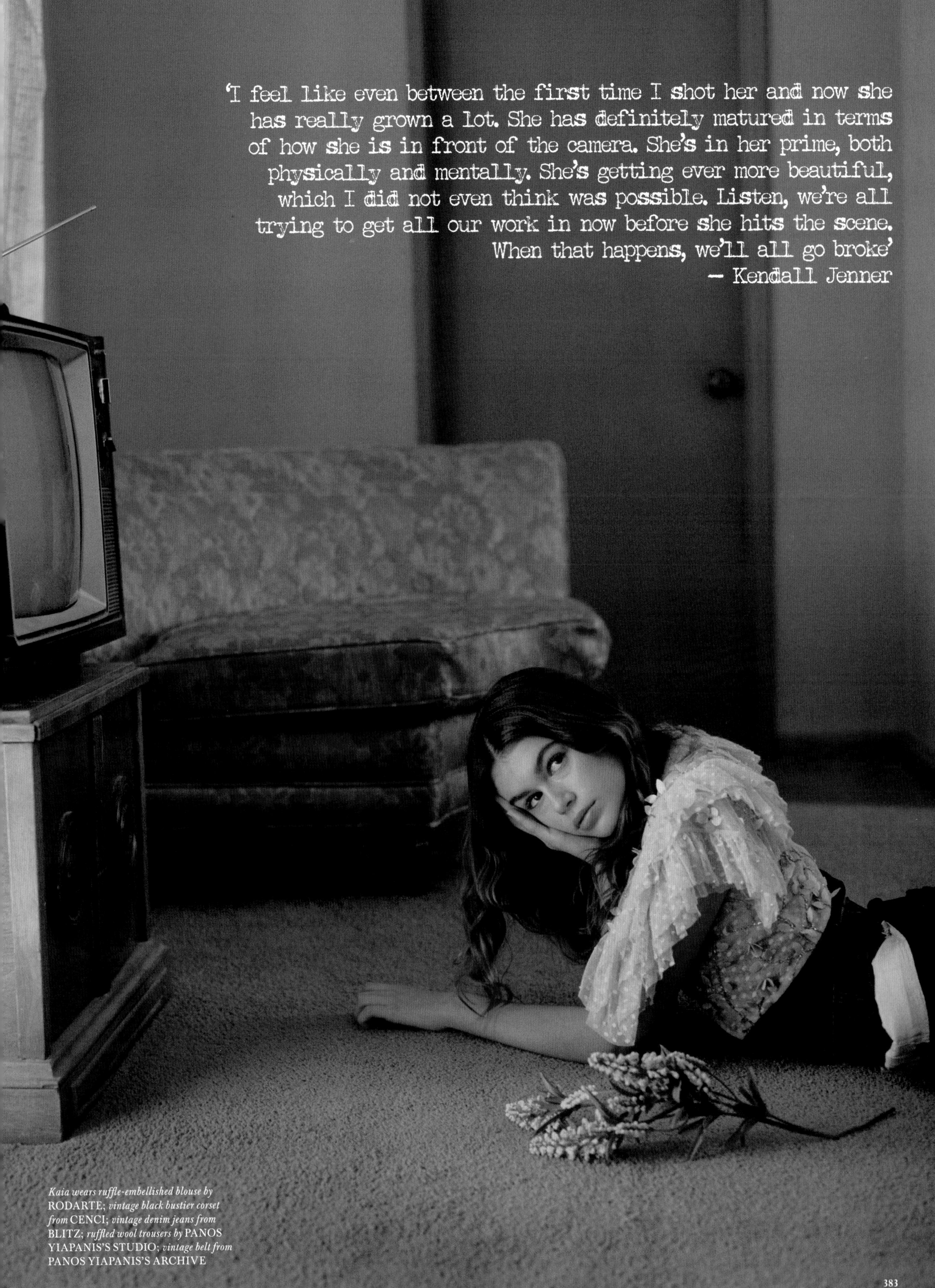

'I feel like even between the first time I shot her and now she has really grown a lot. She has definitely matured in terms of how she is in front of the camera. She's in her prime, both physically and mentally. She's getting ever more beautiful, which I did not even think was possible. Listen, we're all trying to get all our work in now before she hits the scene. When that happens, we'll all go broke'
— Kendall Jenner

Kaia wears ruffle-embellished blouse by RODARTE; *vintage black bustier corset from* CENCI; *vintage denim jeans from* BLITZ; *ruffled wool trousers by* PANOS YIAPANIS'S STUDIO; *vintage belt from* PANOS YIAPANIS'S ARCHIVE

Kaia wears charcoal blazer by BURBERRY; *vintage eyelet belts and black vintage Bodymap leggings all from* PANOS YIAPANIS'S ARCHIVE; *vintage army boots from* ROKIT

Kaia wears ruffle embellished blouse by RODARTE; *vintage black bustier corset from* CENCI; *vintage denim jeans from* BLITZ; *ruffled wool trousers by* PANOS YIAPANIS'S STUDIO; *vintage belt from* PANOS YIAPANIS'S ARCHIVE; *vintage army boots from* ROKIT

KAIA /
'These days your entire life is documented. I worry that people are going to get sick of seeing me already!'

Elizabeth wears navy embroidered bandeau by MIU MIU

ELIZABETH /
'If someone remembers me for my hair, then great. But my voice also tends to pique people's interests'

Elizabeth wears white cotton-blend lace T-shirt by BURBERRY

ARIANNA /
'I might take a gap year
and really give the singing and acting a go.
Maybe a bit of modelling'

Elizabeth Wheeland
Actor

Remember the time – before she was full of fillers and regret – Lindsay Lohan had that flammable mix of talent, sassiness and something extra – let's call it sheer ambition? Elizabeth Wheeland, 16 from Chicago, has something not too dissimilar. There's an innocence, a rawness, as there should be with someone so young. But there's also an inner will that you can sense when you meet her. A drive to get to where she wants to be that defies her years.

If this makes her sound like a brat then you've got her wrong; she couldn't be any sweeter. She's just that exceptional thing: a strong young woman with her inner compass already set. Not that she's precocious – far from it. 'I think most of what happens to me I can blame on my hair,' she laughs, pushing her painted fingers through her tangled trestles. Her hair is indeed spectacular: big, swooping and the sort of 'do Kim Basinger would have taken a pay cut for in *9½ Weeks*.

'I mean, I guess it makes me stand out a little bit, which I think can be important in this industry. If someone remembers me for my hair, then great. My voice also tends to pique people's interests...' Low and husky, Elizabeth's voice doesn't fit her face: it's the voice of a Paris madam, carved from a diet of Gauloise and calvados. She has the Aston Martin of voices. With such assets it seems little wonder that Elizabeth already has over 200,000 followers on Instagram.

Elizabeth wants to do that thing that all models want to do if they could chose to: act. 'I spend a huge amount of time in and around the Second City. I'm only happy when I'm seeing a show, whether that be a little jazz show or some improv theatre happening. I mean, coffee and baby back ribs make me pretty happy too, but acting is something that just feels right. I would write my own skits and make home videos; I've also done a little community theatre. I think eventually I'm going to move out to Los Angeles and just see where it takes me. I'm a city girl at heart and it feels that LA is where the action is still. I'll get out here, get a job and start auditioning...'

Whether it be Jack White or Mark Rylance, there are some members of the creative classes who seem to have been born with something else. A bonus gene that gives them, if you can excuse the hippie drippiness of how this sounds, an aura, a Ready Brek glow, an advantage in the audition room than no amount of work can begin to match. You can't quite put your finger on it but it's there. Elizabeth Wheeland is just such a thing: a bona fide star. *JH*

IG: @elizabethwheeland

Arianna Singh-Hicks
Singer

'I'm really sorry – I'm losing my voice so I have to talk really quietly...' Arianna Singh-Hicks has fallen to Earth fully formed. Well, apart from the horrid cold, although it's nothing a little hot water and lemon can't control. 'I'm sorry I'm ill but I'm so glad to be here. I've come from Toronto.' Ah, the land of Bieber and Ryan Gosling. 'Funnily enough I don't know either of them.' The girl's got wit. 'My mum is originally from Guyana in the West Indies, and my dad is Jamaican, German, French. I'm at school. I go to college next year although I'm undecided as to what to major in. I might take a gap year and really give the singing and acting a go. Maybe a bit of modelling.'

She sounds nonchalant, but Arianna Singh-Hicks could try her hand at any one of these professions and have a career most could only ever dream of. Give her the right teacher and time to develop, and who knows how good she could get. Still, if the arts don't work out she has an interesting fall back: 'Track and field. I've been hurdling since I was in fourth grade and I'm also a pole-vaulter.'

I don't know how many pole-vaulters you've met, but Arianna Singh-Hicks isn't what I had imagined. Isn't she a little... 'Short!' she parries with a rusty chuckle. 'I've only been training a year but I've done pretty well.' How well is 'pretty well'? 'City's champion.' I understand how the next question makes me sound but I need to ask it anyway: does she ever worry about the pole breaking? 'Sometimes, sure. And falling backwards. But it's all mental strength; telling yourself you'll be fine. Run tall, plant the pole and *whoosh*!'

When she's not launching herself over high bars, she's doing homework and hoping for that big break. 'We do loads of projects at school; I've been getting into kinesiology – bones, muscles, how the body works. I made a foot joint out of wood.' And when she's not sculpting an anatomically correct piece of bone? 'Watching TV. I love *The Vampire Diaries* and *Say Yes to the Dress*. I also totally watch *Keeping Up with the Kardashians...*' How does she feel about Kendall shooting her? 'I'm trying to be all cool. But inside I'm a mess.'

In a week's time Kendall will be on the Victoria's Secret catwalk, something Arianna is desperate to ask her about. 'I mean, I would *love* to do that. I like that the women have to train like athletes for that catwalk rather than just starve themselves. Adriana Lima is just a goddess.' Arianna has a hero complex for strong, beautiful, sometimes murderous women, it seems. 'I love comics, too. To me, Margot Robbie as Harley Quinn is just perfect.'

A producer calls her over: it's time for her to get into wardrobe. 'Oh, now I'm nervous.' Don't worry, it's a cinch: walk tall, plant the pose and *whoosh*. *JH*

IG: @ariannahicks

ARIANNA /
'I've been hurdling since I was in fourth grade and I'm also a pole-vaulter'

Arianna wears white cotton poplin and lace dress with broderie anglaise trim by BURBERRY; *camouflage shorts by* MARC JACOBS

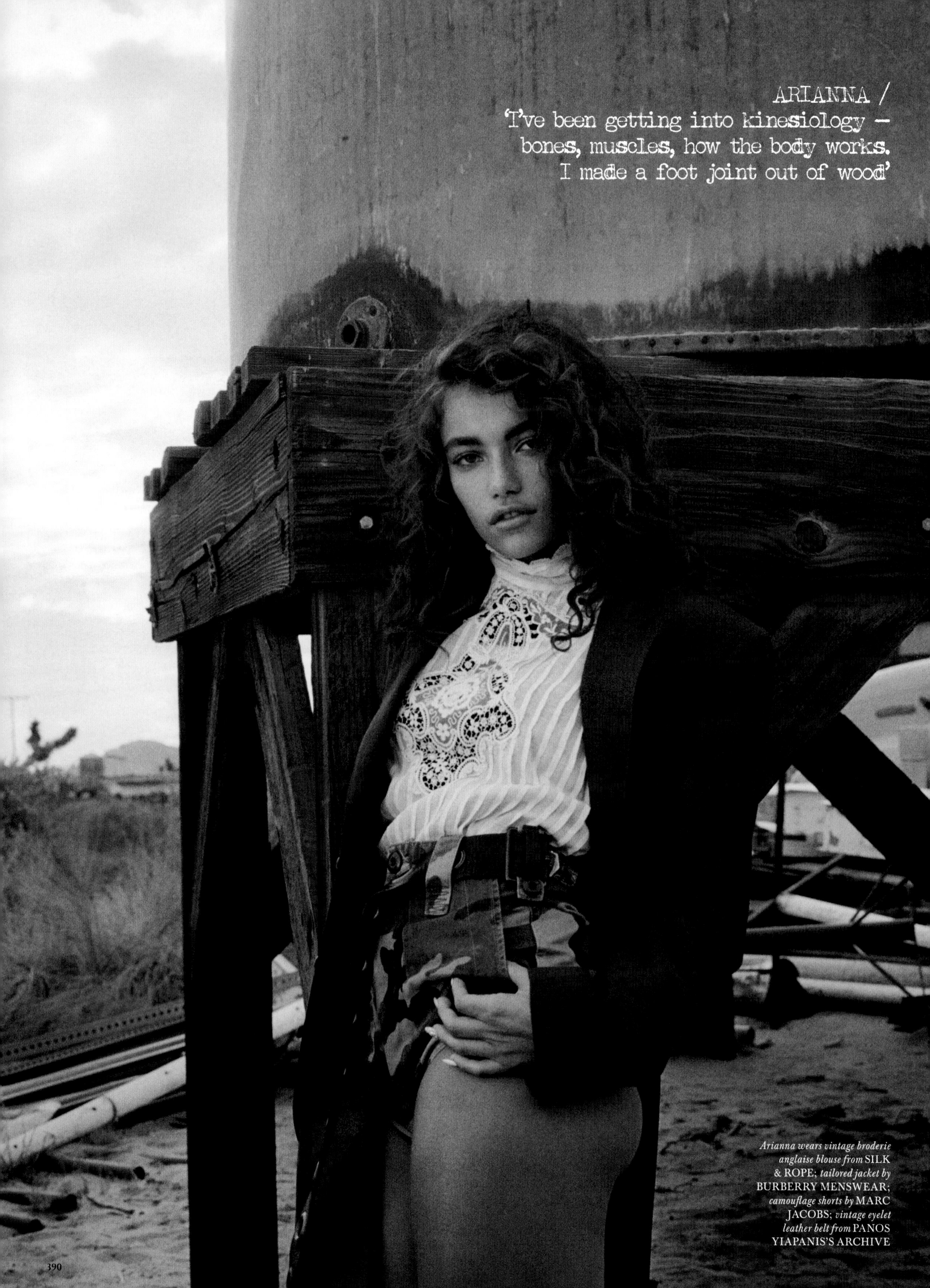

ARIANNA /
'I've been getting into kinesiology – bones, muscles, how the body works. I made a foot joint out of wood'

Arianna wears vintage broderie anglaise blouse from SILK & ROPE; *tailored jacket by* BURBERRY MENSWEAR; *camouflage shorts by* MARC JACOBS; *vintage eyelet leather belt from* PANOS YIAPANIS'S ARCHIVE

Arianna wears white cotton poplin and lace dress with broderie anglaise trim by BURBERRY; *camouflage shorts and platform boots all by* MARC JACOBS

Hair ASHLEY JAVIER Make-up CIARA O'SHEA Executive producer OLIVER HICKS FOR NORTH SIX Producers MARCUS WARD AND CYNTHIA BECHET FOR NORTH SIX Repro ICON LA Retouching JUSTINE FOORD FOR SILHOUETTE STUDIO NYC Production equipment SIREN STUDIOS Photographic equipment QUIXOTE STUDIO Digital capture MILK STUDIOS Photographic assistance ANTHONY IGNACIO, MARK NAKAGAWA Digital technician CLAY RASMUSSEN FOR MILK Fashion assistance SUSAN WALSH, ISABELLA KAVANAGH, TAYLOR ERICKSON, JACQUELINE ARKO Hair assistance KIMBERLEY GARDUNO, ALEXANDRA ADAMS, JOSHUA LIU Make-up assistance VERITY CUMMING, NICOLE WHITTMAN Fashion work experience HAYLEY FRANCISE, QUINTON JACKSON, ANISA RAYAN, ABAN SONIA. A million, million thanks to ASHLEAH GONZALES, JOEY JALLEO, THE STANDARD HOTEL DOWNTOWN LA Thanks to CHRIS ALTY, HARRIET VERNEY, OLIVER VOLQUARDSEN, PRINCIPAL YIP

BALENCIAGA

HEAD BOYS

What happened when LOVE took Charles Jeffrey and Matty Bovan to Paris and let them loose in the studio with John Galliano to reinterpret his Maison Margiela collection for spring

Photographer TIM WALKER
Creative Director JOHN GALLIANO
Fashion Editors ALEXIS ROCHE, CHARLES JEFFREY, KATIE GRAND, MATTY BOVAN

It came as no surprise when those brightly coloured Wunderkinder of the London scene Matty Bovan and Charles Jeffrey revealed to LOVE that they are big fans of John Galliano. After all, the whole archetype of the British designer as a hedonistic, idiosyncratic, discipline-transcending visionary which the boys fit so perfectly was forged in John's image. So LOVE decided to bring them together in Paris to shoot John's spring collection for Maison Margiela, as well as items from the current Margiela couture collection.

The process of setting up the shoot began with a conversation between John and the photographer Tim Walker, in which the designer explained the ideas that had driven his new collections. The atmosphere of unrest, radicalism and political conflict that had been evident on the streets of Paris in 2016 had prompted John to take another look at his famous Saint Martins graduate collection from 1984, inspired as it was by the French Revolution: it's why several elements from that collection turn up in his latest work. 'John showed me images of street gangs from the time of the French Revolution,' says Tim. 'There was this picture of a woman in an empire-line dress and a big bonnet: the brim was turned up, so it stood about three feet high. John said it looked like a baseball cap – which is why there's one with a massive peak in the collection.' The liberal use of neoprene came from the windsurfers John had been looking at, those athletes whose bodies keep moving to adjust to the changing profile of their environment. 'Because of this political unrest, John feels we are all living very much in the moment right now.'

Then Matty and Charles jumped on the Eurostar to meet John. They met over lunch at Margiela HQ where John threw caution to the wind, abandoning his usually strictly observed macrobiotic diet for pot pie. Unfortunately there was a mix-up in the kitchen and everyone except John ended up getting the macrobiotic option. In the studio the next day he was seen tucking into a bag of salt and vinegar crisps – which is about as wild as John's intake gets these days.

'It was quite daunting,' admits Matty of working with John, 'but the whole experience had been set up so quickly we didn't really have time to get nervous. And he's very personable and funny.' 'I was more giddy than nervous,' says Charles. 'I just kept thinking, fucking hell, I'm actually working with one of my heroes.' The general sense of fandom extended to the models, too. When Jean Campbell turned up on set she phoned her mum to confide: 'I can't believe it – all my heroes are here in one room.' Charles had brought a bag full of inflatable neck pillows, bits of sleeping bag and various other devices to pad out the clothes and distort the bodies of the models. 'I thought it might be like a life-drawing project at St Martins,' he says, 'where they'd get us to dress a model and then sketch the result.'

John's intention was to keep everything as spontaneous as possible. 'He sketched with the camera,' says Tim. They'd set up a shot, Polaroid it, look at the image and then go back to the models to 'exaggerate the look, shove on a hat, make the hair bigger'. John had brought a book of Egon Schiele's paintings and sketches with him as a reference and walked around saying, 'The illustrative line, my dears, the illustrative line,' as a directive on the overall aesthetic. Also on set was John's partner Alexis, with whom he'd cast the story, Katie Grand and her dog, Red.

No one knew till the day itself whether John would agree to be photographed: he usually likes to prepare for a portrait and it was clear he would already be preoccupied with overseeing the shoot. As it turned out he was more than happy to oblige. However as he stepped in front of the camera to pose with Alexis and the boys, just out of shot to his right, Red, who had been fed a sausage that evidently didn't agree with her, launched an avalanche of diarrhoea onto the studio floor. It was immediately apparent to the noses of everyone on set that something had happened. 'John turned to me,' recalls Charles, 'and said, "I know you're excited, but really..." Then we saw Red creeping away with her tail between her legs. It fucking stank.'

Reflecting on how John interacted with Charles and Matty, Tim observes, 'It was like watching an experienced chef with two new chefs. They were really appreciative of each other. And they're all very pretty people. Matty in particular photographs in a very refined way. Charles is like an exclamation mark, standing up very straight and always very busy. John was very charming, very bon viveur, with this calm, quiet voice and a loud, booming laugh. He's an animator, he charges up the room. We all picked up on his energy. The moment he left the studio, we felt his absence.' *Murray Healy*

The Master at Margiela

In conversation with John Galliano

Writer ALEX FURY

At the lunch before the LOVE shoot, with Matty Bovan and Charles Jeffrey, John Galliano and his partner Alexis Roche all clustered around a table groaning with food and candles and creative detritus, I notice a giant illuminated star hanging in Galliano's office at Maison Margiela. It's the kind you get at fairgrounds, or at Blackpool's world-famous illuminations: about four feet wide, and the same in height, suspended before a floor-to-ceiling mirror. Galliano says it is a hangover from an impromptu karaoke party with the Margiela design team a week or so before we meet. Intentionally or not, that star is emblematic of John Galliano's entire career. Because Galliano has always seemed to be under a lucky star: the blessed one, a golden child of fashion. The fanaticism his talent has elicited, ever since his Saint Martins graduation, has carried him through penury, bankruptcy and controversy. His is both a cautionary tale and an inspiration to younger talents, an ode to the exuberance of full-throttle creativity, the magic it can make, and the dangers it can hold.

To many – including me – 56-year-old Galliano is a living legend. As Matty Bovan says, he's daunting to meet. Everyone has someone that makes them go weak at the knees and catch their breath. Galliano is precisely that for an entire generation. In fact, make that two – I'm a good decade older than Matty and Charles. We grew up in different times, looking at different fashion shows. They saw Galliano in his fly-by-the-seat-of-your-pants early-Noughties incarnation, all neon catwalks, towering platforms and mountains of fabric carving shapes to summon the lost ghosts of Empress Sisi, The Last Emperor, or maybe Liz Taylor in *Cleopatra* crossed with RuPaul. Mine was the romance of his Nineties output, quivering chiffons and crinolines and Shalom Harlow camping it up as Mata Hari.

Matty, John, Charles and Alexis all wear their own clothing and accessories

All clothing throughout by MAISON MARGIELA *unless otherwise stated*

Theo wears cotton knit sweater, green short-sleeved skinny-rib polo shirt (worn beneath), metallic blue leather belt, turquoise latex stockings and lace-up shoes; black ballet skirt by BLOCH; *white cotton suspender belt by* GILES DEACON COUTURE; *vintage polka-dot swimsuit (just seen) from* CENCI VINTAGE LONDON

Regardless of the time or place, it was all extraordinary. It all made you dream.

There's the same sensibility in his art direction for the LOVE shoot, conjuring a world of characters, a new story. In the Nineties, Galliano was renowned for whispering stories into his models' ears: who she is, where she lives, how she lives. Charles and Matty say it's the way they still teach at Central Saint Martins – making young designers think like Galliano, to get the best out of them. His Margiela shows, all stark white backdrops, may be different to the cast-of-thousands spectaculars of his past, but he still whispers those stories in models' ears. 'The ones I know will pick up on it and will get it,' Galliano says. 'Or Alexis is like, "Please, turn on the story – she's never had the story."' Galliano grins, wide. 'The little ones love it!' They're fans, too.

I suspect Galliano inspires a very distinct breed of rampant fandom – the kind that can only come from being a kid obsessed. That's because Galliano's 33-year career encompasses most of the lifetime of many industry figures, and the entirety of the life of his younger fans. Despite all that adoration, however, in person there is nothing to be daunted by about him: he is amusing, acerbic, open, hilariously funny, breathtakingly down-to-earth and, frequently, brutally honest.

The honesty comes when discussing the well-known details of his dismissal from the house of Christian Dior and his eponymous label in 2011, unpicked with breathless incredulity and in absolute minutiae by tabloids across the globe. 'There is something between being famous and then infamous,' says Galliano, ruefully, of the attention he received – and still does – upon his return from the Meadows rehabilitation facility in Arizona. We're talking before lunch, just the two of us, holed up in the corner of his office, under his star. Opera plays at a volume rather too grandiose, and it takes us about 10 minutes of mutual scrambling to find the remote. There is no phalanx of PRs, no observers to record and question questions. Just Galliano himself.

He's still tanned from a summer break in Los Angeles, and his accent still reeks of South London, where he grew up, rather than Paris, where he's lived for the last 25 years. Perhaps that's why Galliano has so easily given up on his role as the star, on the flashy catwalk bows and on the incandescent public visibility that was as much his leitmotif as a bias-cut dress. 'I don't miss it at all. Was it easy? Yeah!' Galliano laughs, loudly. 'I just love the idea of fitting all night, then I don't have to deal with what I used to have to deal with backstage. The 25 filmed interviews when you haven't slept for three nights. I don't miss that at all, I'm so grateful.' I ask if he has ever seen one of the infamous pictures of Miuccia Prada backstage, crowded by jostling journalists thrusting iPhones into her face. 'Not mics any more, John,' he deadpans. 'See how long it is since I've done it!'

Margiela's maison is in the 11th arrondissement, a down-at-heel area of Paris that's the equivalent of London's East End. The headquarters are next to a store that sells plastic floor coverings. It's all very similar to where Galliano's career began. He grew up in Dulwich alongside two sisters; his dad was a plumber, his mother a flamenco teacher. But he started his true career as a fashion designer in a Dickensian warehouse in Earl Street, even then partially demolished and now fully gone. When he first moved to Paris in the early Nineties, he slept on friends' floors and ate at McDonald's – via cash advances doled out to friends such as André Leon Talley by figures including Anna Wintour – while working from a ramshackle studio in the Passage du Cheval Blanc, further down in the 11th near Bastille. Galliano's star, however, was on the rise. Later, of course, came Givenchy and Dior, the lure of couture on the other side of the city, in the eighth arrondissement, where the posh houses (and clients) graciously reside.

The full-circle thing feels apt. After two decades producing clothes whose layers of technique and history made them feel painstakingly precious, Galliano's Margiela feels like something of a creative renewal: rarefied, but raw. There's a direct link to the work he created in London, from that East End studio, at the start of the Eighties, collections fuelled by the capital's club culture and Galliano's youthful exuberance and immersion in its world. Through the Nineties, his forays into London nightlife continued to inspire collections: even when the clothes were couture, the attitude was club. At lunch, when Charles mentioned his own club night – the cultish East London-based Loverboy, also a subtitle to his clothing line which, like Galliano's work, is intrinsically linked to nightlife – Galliano immediately wants to come. 'I can pull out some looks,' he cries out. 'I don't do queues, though,' he adds, arching an eyebrow.

There's a distinct flavour of Eighties clubland about the aesthetic he has going on at Margiela, something very London – he showed his first Margiela Artisanal collection there in January 2015, rather than as part of Paris haute couture week (Margiela was temporarily booted off the official schedule for the infraction). 'I was transported back to the Eighties,' Galliano says, of his approach to Margiela. 'The experimentation. The Thatcher years. Your back up against a wall – and when it is, you strike out and create. Then it just came, little by little.' Ask him about Donald Trump, in that context, and his face twists a little. In a previous incarnation at Dior, Galliano created Melania Trump's wedding gown, a pile-up of ivory duchesse satin with a price tag in the region of $200,000.

There are various reminders of Galliano's past scattered through our discussion: it isn't explicitly off-limits, although it is somewhat veiled. Our talk is punctuated with frequent cigarettes, wreathed in their smoke. That is his one remaining vice: he drinks herbal tea, eats a mostly-macrobiotic diet, and of course doesn't consume alcohol. He occasionally falls into a confessional conversational style that hints at the therapy he's still undergoing; he continues to attend Alcoholics Anonymous meetings. 'There are moments when the creative process is all-consuming,' he allows. 'It's something I have to check, to keep in check. Trying to go away to the country with Alexis, when we can... I have to make sure that I'm out of here. People help me. They try not to make appointments after 7pm. That's good for me.'

The conversation is fast-paced, spectacularly sharp, outrageously funny – elements that have always been there, in all of Galliano's collections, but which suddenly seem so much clearer at Margiela. The humour of what he does there, for instance, is difficult to overlook: he knows exactly what he's doing with the kooky crazy-lady make-up, the wigs of nubbly deflated balloons, their knotted ends dangling like suckered nipples, or the goofball combinations of clogs, inside-out coats and cable-knit socks. It's supposed to look off-kilter and amusing. The back-packing, yoga-mat-clutching crusty travellers of Margiela's spring/summer 2017 collection were based, in part, on the Dalai Lama. 'He's looking right,' says Galliano. He describes a few of the powdery Barbara Cartland colours of his autumn/winter 2016 Artisanal collection – such as the bubbly pale blue organza coat in the LOVE shoot – as 'menopausal', with a screech of laughter.

Just as Matty, Charles and I are passionate admirers of Galliano, so Galliano was of Martin Margiela, long before he arrived here. 'Ardent fan, faithful loyal client,' emphasises Galliano. 'I bought this stuff, all this stuff.' Which is why people buy what Galliano is creating for the label now, both commercially (revenues rose 30 per cent in his first year at the house) and – perhaps more importantly – ideologically. Hence the absolute relevance of Galliano right now. There's a whole new breed of flashy, dressed-up club kids emerging in London, mainly, and New York too, whose swaggering ensembles tie perfectly with Galliano's limitless ideas. Why not wear your jacket as a skirt, or your coat upside-down, or tug out your lining and wear it as a dress?

Those kids are probably not buying Margiela's luxurious wares, but they are doing it themselves, in the same spirit. It is also, oddly, being picked up by other designers: referencing Margiela's past overtly and, more covertly, Galliano's present. I couldn't count the number of chopped-up shirts-cum-dresses I saw through the spring/summer 2017 season, or trench coats with their fabric bunched and oddly wrapped about the body. For me it all led back to Galliano and the twisted wardrobe he's fashioning at Margiela. Perhaps I just see that because I'm a fan; or maybe those other designers are, too. Which, for Galliano, proves that what he's creating right now is perfect for the moment. 'I had a conversation with Anna [Wintour] before I came here,' he says. 'It's totally relevant. Martin with recycling, sustainability, all those "Margielaisms"... I think for the world and where we are today, it's just really right, isn't it? It's what's going on in the world.' Galliano also insists that Margiela is right not just for now, but for him. 'Nothing feels forced or contrived. I feel good,' he states, simply. 'It's not a torturous experience. It's quite organic. The energy is... I don't know how to put it into words. It's a very nice state to be in, where I am in my life now, and this place. The people I've chosen to surround myself with. It's really nice.'

He extinguishes a cigarette. The overriding impression you get out of all this is that he is the biggest fan of fashion itself. He loves it, he lives it, he breathes it into his clothes. They vibrate with his energy, and his passion, and in turn they pull new fans in. 'Fashion is fun,' states Galliano, emphatically. 'It should be fun, shouldn't it?'

From left: Maarten wears navy nylon windcheater, blue mohair knit tube skirt with neoprene panels, scuba tabi ankle boots, knitted harness belt, red and white printed scarf (tied around belt) and blue felt hat. Cameron wears beige bodysuit, grey checked wool skirt, pink felt hat, black lace-up shoes, gold yellow metallic leather belt (just seen) and blue latex stocking (draped over belt); purple rib cotton and silk socks by NEW & LINGWOOD

Irina wears nylon windcheater, pink silk satin bra, yellow latex band (worn beneath), yellow lace and aqua embroidery nylon skirt with PVC lining, flat leather sandals, beige felt hat and leather belt; green rubber gloves by SAINSBURY'S; *geometric socks by* PANTHERELLA

Tom wears yellow waxed cotton empire-line trench dress, neon-panelled knit cotton sweater, beige cotton trench coat, green short-sleeved skinny-rib polo shirt, blue and white striped poplin cotton shirt (worn beneath, just seen), leather belt (just seen), turquoise and orange latex stockings and leather lace-up shoes; beige stocking (just seen) by WOLFORD

Hoyeon wears black and orange nylon zip-up top, white and yellow jersey skirt, flax cotton flared tank dress with misshapen rubber hemline (worn beneath, just seen), knitted mesh Watteau-backed drawstring dress (worn beneath, just seen), blue and turquoise knitted climbing rope harness (worn as belt) and perforated leather clogs; socks by BURLINGTON

Adwoa wears grey checked taffeta nylon caban, grey green flax cotton flared tank dress with misshapen rubber hemline, yellow latex stockings and leather platform boots; suspender belt by GILES DEACON COUTURE; *black tulle ruffle skirt by* BLOCH

Jules wears scuba bodysuit; Tricorn hat by STEPHEN JONES *for* MAISON MARGIELA ARTISANAL *designed by* JOHN GALLIANO

From left: Maarten wears navy windcheater, scuba tabi ankle boots, embroidered leather gloves and blue felt hat; blue feather from NEW TRIMMINGS. *Jean wears black cotton popeline skirt (worn as top), green neoprene band, red lace skirt, green workwear jacket (tied around waist), leather clogs with plexiglass sole and white felt hat; socks by* HAPPY SOCKS. *Irina wears navy windcheater, yellow latex band, pink silk satin bra, yellow lace and aqua embroidery nylon skirt, leather sandals, beige felt hat, red metallic belt and floral printed scarf (held in hand); rubber gloves by* SAINSBURY'S; *socks by* PANTHERELLA

Lily wears yellow waxed cotton hunting jacket, navy-blue crystal-embellished skirt, green short-sleeved skinny-rib polo shirt, tartan check belt and leather sandals; printed tights by PANTHERELLA

Irina (left) wears emerald-green silk organza blouse, powder-blue wool gauze trench coat (worn as skirt), white nylon fastener belt, orange latex stockings, perforated leather clogs, light blue felt hat and silver crystal earring; orange gloves from LEYLAND SDM. *Estella wears satin organza dress printed with 'British Birds' (2008) by* NICK KNIGHT; *blue knitted cycling top, clogs and turquoise latex gloves all by* MAISON MARGIELA ARTISANAL *designed by* JOHN GALLIANO; *grey synthetic gloves (worn beneath latex gloves) from* LEYLAND SDM

Jean wears grey tweed upside-down jacket, brushed silk intarsia sweater, lavender silk frock coat (tied around waist) and hand-painted clogs all by MAISON MARGIELA ARTISANAL *designed by* JOHN GALLIANO; *white tights by* WOLFORD

Kyona wears blue wool and cloqué silk coat, marabou-trimmed baby-doll dress, sandals and knitted socks all by MAISON MARGIELA ARTISANAL *designed by* JOHN GALLIANO; *pink rubber gloves by* SPONTEX

Maarten (left) wears printed cotton shirt, poplin cotton boxer shorts, yellow latex stockings, sandal-shoes, handbag, earrings with brass details and crystal ear-attaching necklace with brass details; black tulle skirt (just seen at waist) by BLOCH. *Adwoa wears silk jacquard dress printed with 'British Birds' (2008) by* NICK KNIGHT *and black tabi boots all by* MAISON MARGIELA ARTISANAL *designed by* JOHN GALLIANO; *crystal and silver earrings by* MAISON MARGIELA; *rubberised glove (on floor) from* LEYLAND SDM

Tom (left) wears pink bouclé wool bathing suit with black satin sash, pink bouclé wool cardigan and lace-up shoes; grey socks by BURLINGTON; *white tutu by* BLOCH. *Cameron wears taupe cotton trench coat, check cotton shorts, harness belt and leather loafers; engraved wooden cuffs by* MAISON MARGIELA ARTISANAL *designed by* JOHN GALLIANO; *printed leather fabric (tied to belt) by* CHARLES JEFFREY; *rubber gloves by* SAINSBURY'S; *socks by* NEW & LINGWOOD; *pink feather from* NEW TRIMMINGS

Lily wears orange upside-down caban, waxed cotton shift dress (worn beneath), black leather belt, black thigh-high tabi boots and navy cotton baseball cap with oversized visor all by MAISON MARGIELA ARTISANAL *designed by* JOHN GALLIANO

Hair SYD HAYES Make-up (women) HIROMI UEDA Make-up (men) LUCY BRIDGE Set design GARY CARD Lighting director PAUL BURNS Production JEFF DELICH Printed by GRAEME BULCRAIG AT TOUCH DIGITAL Models ADWOA ABOAH, CAMERON N'JIE, ESTELLA BOERSMA, HOYEON JUNG, IRINA LISS, JEAN CAMPBELL, JULES MAS, KYONA VAN SANTEN, LILY NOVA, MAARTEN CONVENS, TOM FOOL, THEO BIANCONI Photographic assistance SARAH LLOYD, TONY IVANOV, HARRIET MACSWEEN Fashion assistance OGUN GORTAN, LAURA NEWRZELLA Hair assistance PAULA McCASH, RYAN WOOD, JASON LAWRENCE Make-up assistance (women) CLAIRE URQUHART, ANASTASIA HESS, PORSCHE POON, EMMA BROOM Make-up assistance (men) MATTIE WHITE, RACHEL SHRAM Set design assistance AIDAN ZAMIRI, DANIEL TAYLOR Production assistance LESLIE BORG, EDDIE BLAGBROUGH, LAUREN SAKIOKA Thanks to CLM/GREAT BOWERY for set sponsorship, DIRECT PHOTOGRAPHIC, RIDA STUDIOS

The Suburbs

Brokenhearted teddy girls sip cans on the lawn with silent tears while sun-lounger mom smokes cigarettes. White picket fences, lace and red cups optional

Photographer ALASDAIR McLELLAN
Fashion Editor KATIE GRAND

Langley wears blue crepe shirt by ROCHAS; *black classic trousers by* NEIL BARRETT; *studded black leather belt by* RODARTE; *earrings Langley's own*

BOYS
LIE

Kendall wears floral embroidered white tulle triangle bra by LA PERLA; *red satin Penelope briefs by* L'AGENT

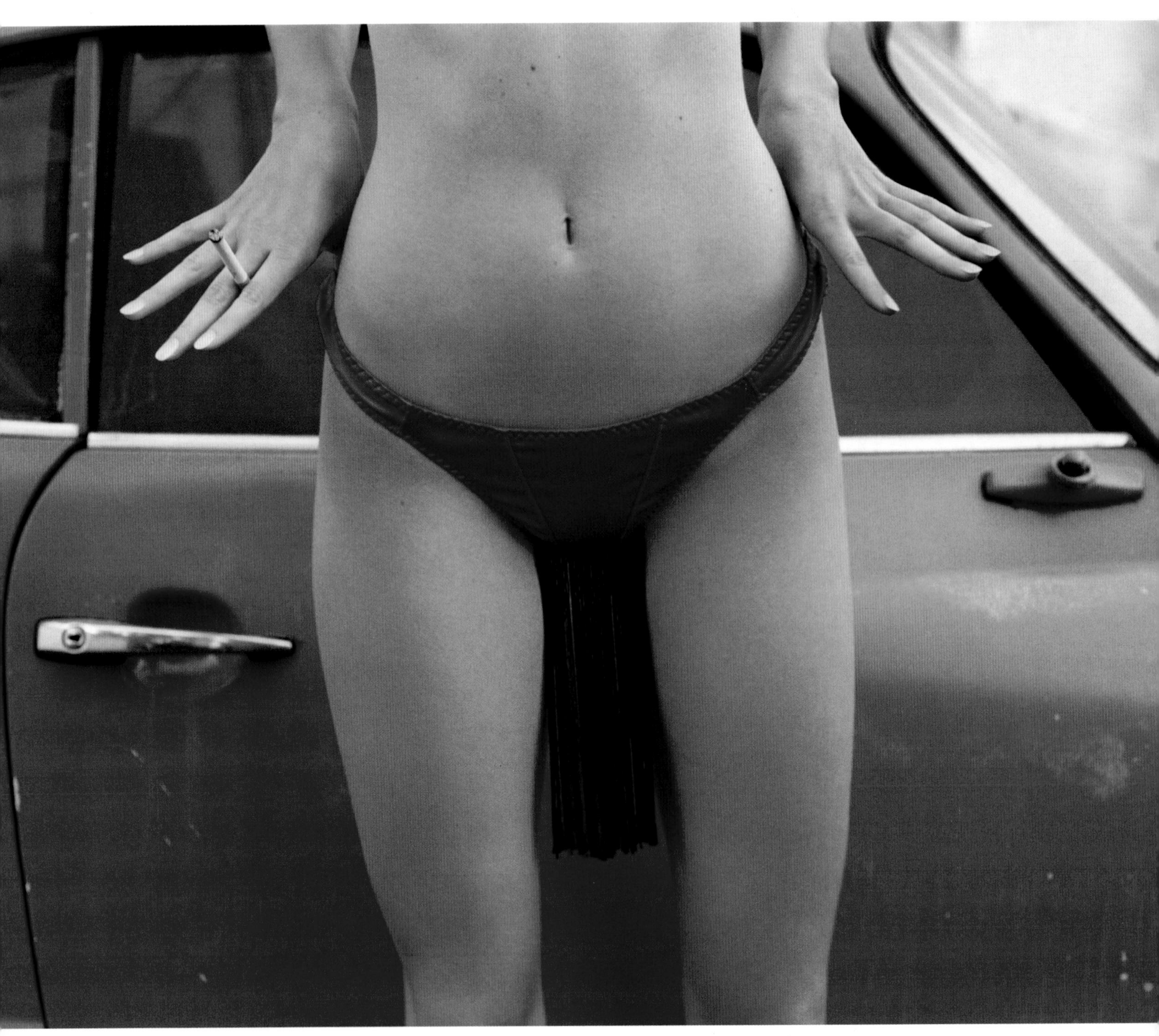

Kendall wears red satin Penelope briefs by L'AGENT, *customised with black fringe by Katie Grand*

Kendall wears floral embroidered white tulle triangle bra by LA PERLA; *red satin Penelope briefs by* L'AGENT; *customised with black fringe by Katie Grand*

Ellen wears graffiti hearts sweatshirt by MATTY BOVAN FOR HOGAN; *simple ivory tulle veil by* VIKTOR & ROLF MARRIAGE COLLECTION; *Kiki platform buckle boots by* MARC JACOBS; *black fishnet tights by* WOLFORD

Lulu and Grace both wear white cotton dresses by DIESEL BLACK GOLD

Grace (left) wears off-white Etamine woven dress by CÉLINE. *Lulu wears white compact cotton dress by* STELLA McCARTNEY

Lulu wears long white chiffon dress by ALBERTA FERRETTI; *amber yellow suede Victoria shoes embroidered with nickel coins and beads by* SANTONI

Langley wears vintage white cotton shirt from ALFIE'S ANTIQUE MARKET; *Tellna viscose shorts by* BOSS; *white calfskin Odette sling-back shoes by* HERMÈS; *red socks by* COMME DES GARÇONS; *necklace Langley's own*

Ellen wears cream blush minidress by ERMANNO SCERVINO; *vintage white silk knickers (just seen) from* MODES AND MORE

Lulu wears Erin denim skirt by AG JEANS; *yellow cotton ID triangle bra by* CALVIN KLEIN UNDERWEAR; *Dawn brown wedge sandals by* MARC JACOBS

Lulu wears yellow cotton ID triangle bra by CALVIN KLEIN UNDERWEAR; *fish earring by* HILLIER BARTLEY

Ellen wears white cotton viscose poplin short-sleeved tunic by BALLY

Grace wears black and cream cotton Dobby Western shirt and black and cream floral Shayla pinstriped wool trousers both by RALPH LAUREN COLLECTION; *black and rainbow creepers by* UNDERGROUND LONDON FOR MANISH ARORA; *green ankle socks (just seen) by* FALKE

Langley wears stretch viscose knit vest by GIORGIO ARMANI; *blue silk loose fitted trousers with drawstring pocket by* EMPORIO ARMANI; *studded black leather belt by* RODARTE; *necklaces and earrings Langley's own*

Langley wears blue crepe shirt by ROCHAS; *black classic trousers by* NEIL BARRETT; *studded black leather belt by* RODARTE; *white calfskin Odette sling-back shoes by* HERMÈS; *red socks by* COMME DES GARÇONS; *earrings and rings Langley's own*

James (left) wears striped long-sleeved nylon T-shirt with 3D effect stripes by BYBLOS; *vintage checked trousers from* CENCI VINTAGE LONDON

Irina wears midnight blue embroidered heavy viscose Jemina dress by MULBERRY

James wears rabbit-fur coat and plexi ankle-strap heeled shoes all by MIU MIU

Olesya (left) wears bright blue silk shantung one-shoulder flounce dress with sequin patch on sleeve by GUCCI. *Irina wears jet-black embroidered Shipwreck dress by* ALEXANDER McQUEEN; *black lace knickers (just seen) by* MIMI HOLLIDAY

Irina wears jet black embroidered Shipwreck dress by ALEXANDER McQUEEN

James wears black romantic lace dress by SONIA RYKIEL; *vintage Pirates Hammer Head boots (autumn/ winter 1981) and Clint Eastwood black and grey socks (autumn/winter 1984) all by* WESTWOOD McLAREN *from* RELLIK

Kendall wears grey wool suiting Lady coat by CHARLES JEFFREY LOVERBOY

Langley wears black leather jacket with brown inserts and black pleated trousers both by NEIL BARRETT; *vintage green and white top from* ROKIT LONDON; *necklaces and earrings all Langley's own*

Langley wears cotton drill workwear minidress by HERMÈS; *vintage pink point d'espirit gloves from* MODES AND MORE; *vintage leopard-print beret from* CENCI VINTAGE LONDON; *earrings Langley's own*

Grace wears white patent leather Lisina pumps by BALLY; *dark green ribbed ankle socks by* FALKE

Irina wears leather minidress with stucco and leather flowers by FENDI

Olesya wears long-sleeved silk organza Daisy dress with satin flowers by CHRISTOPHER KANE; *metal and resin earrings by* CHANEL

Cara wears arabesque printed tulle woven dress by CÉLINE; *white knickers (worn beneath, just seen) by* CALVIN KLEIN UNDERWEAR

Lauren wears patterned rubber coat and blue ribbed viscose bikini top both by MIU MIU

Lauren wears grey Witches suit (autumn/winter 1983) and Pirates hat, white shirt and lace-up shoes (autumn/winter 1981) all by WESTWOOD McLAREN *from* RELLIK; *white ankle socks by* FALKE

Lauren (left) wears Buffalo hat (autumn/winter 1982) and Pirates brocade suit, waistcoat, boots and sash (autumn/winter 1981) all by WESTWOOD McLAREN *from* RELLIK. *James wears Pirates hat and shirt (autumn/winter 1981), Savage socks (spring/summer 1982) and Witches three-tongue trainers (autumn/winter 1983) all by* WESTWOOD McLAREN *from* RELLIK

Lauren (left) wears Buffalo hat (autumn/winter 1982) and Pirates brocade suit jacket, waistcoat and sash (autumn/winter 1982) all by WESTWOOD McLAREN *from* RELLIK. *James wears Pirates hat and shirt (autumn/winter 1982) both by* WESTWOOD McLAREN *from* RELLIK

Lauren wears printed T-shirt, silk dress and wool coat all by SACAI; *vintage lace-up brogues from* WESTERN COSTUME; *ankle socks by* FALKE

Lauren wears hooded cotton coat and military tech Milano logo bra top (worn beneath, just seen) both by DKNY

Lara wears rabbit-fur coat and pink patent leather bathing cap both by MIU MIU; *black knickers by* WOLFORD

Langley wears floral printed white cotton dress by MSGM; *vintage brown and white lace-up brogues from* WESTERN COSTUME; *white ankle socks by* FALKE; *earrings and rings all Langley's own*

Olesya wears chiffon dress with ostrich feather trim by PRADA

Cara wears linen and patent calf shirt by BOTTEGA VENETA

Langley (left) wears stretch viscose knit vest by GIORGIO ARMANI; *blue silk loose fitted trousers with drawstring pocket by* EMPORIO ARMANI; *studded black leather belt by* RODARTE; *vintage brown and white lace-up brogues from* WESTERN COSTUME; *striped socks by* HAPPY SOCKS; *necklaces, earrings and rings all Langley's own. Dree wears Mousseline Fleurs au Trait Babyloo play suit by* FIFI CHACHNIL; *white calf-leather shoes with black grosgrain ribbon by* AGL; *white ankle socks by* FALKE

Dree wears men's recycled knit jumper by STELLA McCARTNEY; *fish earring by* HILLIER BARTLEY; *other earrings Dree's own*

Langley wears harlequin patchwork jacket in leather and various couture fabrics by RONALD VAN DER KEMP; *black, white and rust coloured space-dye bikini by* MISSONI; *bright nickel flat leaf wrap bracelet (worn as a necklace) by* RODARTE; *necklace, earrings and rings all Langley's own*

Langley wears platform boots by JULIE VERHOEVEN FOR MARC JACOBS

Hair ANTHONY TURNER Make-up MARK CARRASQUILLO Manicure ASHLIE JOHNSON Prop design COLIN DONAHUE Production NINA QAYYUM at ART PARTNER On-set production NORTH SIX Models CARA TAYLOR, DREE HEMINGWAY, ELLEN ROSA, GRACE CHEN, IRINA SHAYK, JAMES KING, KENDALL JENNER, LANGLEY FOX, LAUREN HUTTON, LULU LEIKA, OLESYA IVANISHCHEVA Photographic assistance LEX KEMBERY, MATTHEW HEALY, SIMON MACKINLAY, DOUGAL MacARTHUR, ANGEL RAMOS Fashion assistance OLIVER VOLQUARDSEN, OGUN GORTAN, ANISA RAYAN, TAYLOR ERICKSON, NICO X ORTEGA, QUINTON JACKSON, SONIA ABAN, HAYLEY FRANCISE Hair assistance CLAIRE GRECH, RACHEL LEE BRADLEY, JOSHUA LIU Make-up assistance AI YOKOMIZO, NATHAN HEJI Prop assistance MATTHEW RAY

Sonia wears red Maharani briefs by LA PERLA; *point d'esprit tights by* GERBE

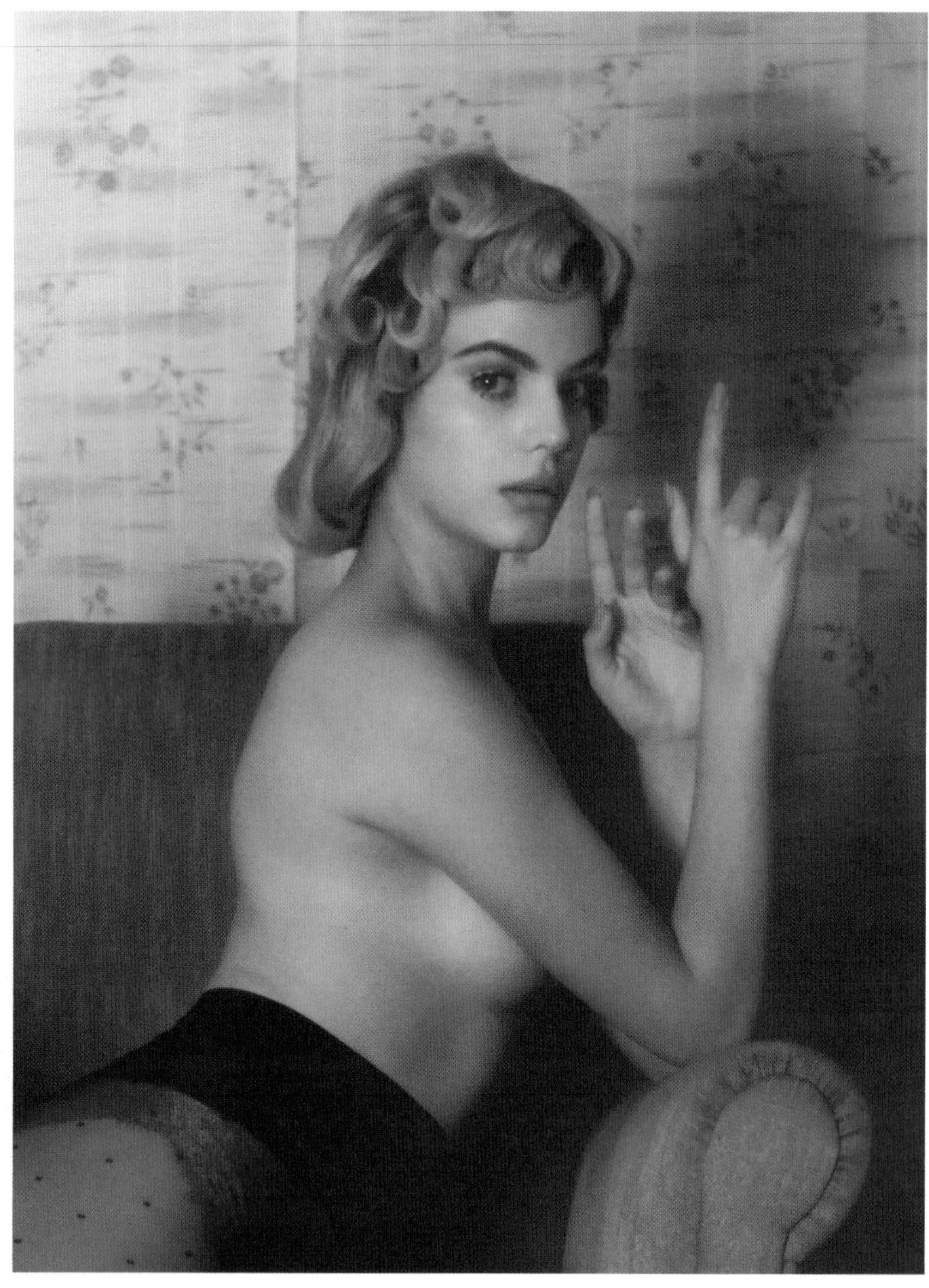

Nudes, a Study

Photographer DAVID SIMS
Fashion editor KATIE GRAND

Tweak the nipple and call this number now for red nails, eyeliner and lingerie

Elsa wears pink silk shorts by MIMI HOLLIDAY; *seamed hold-up tights by* AGENT PROVOCATEUR

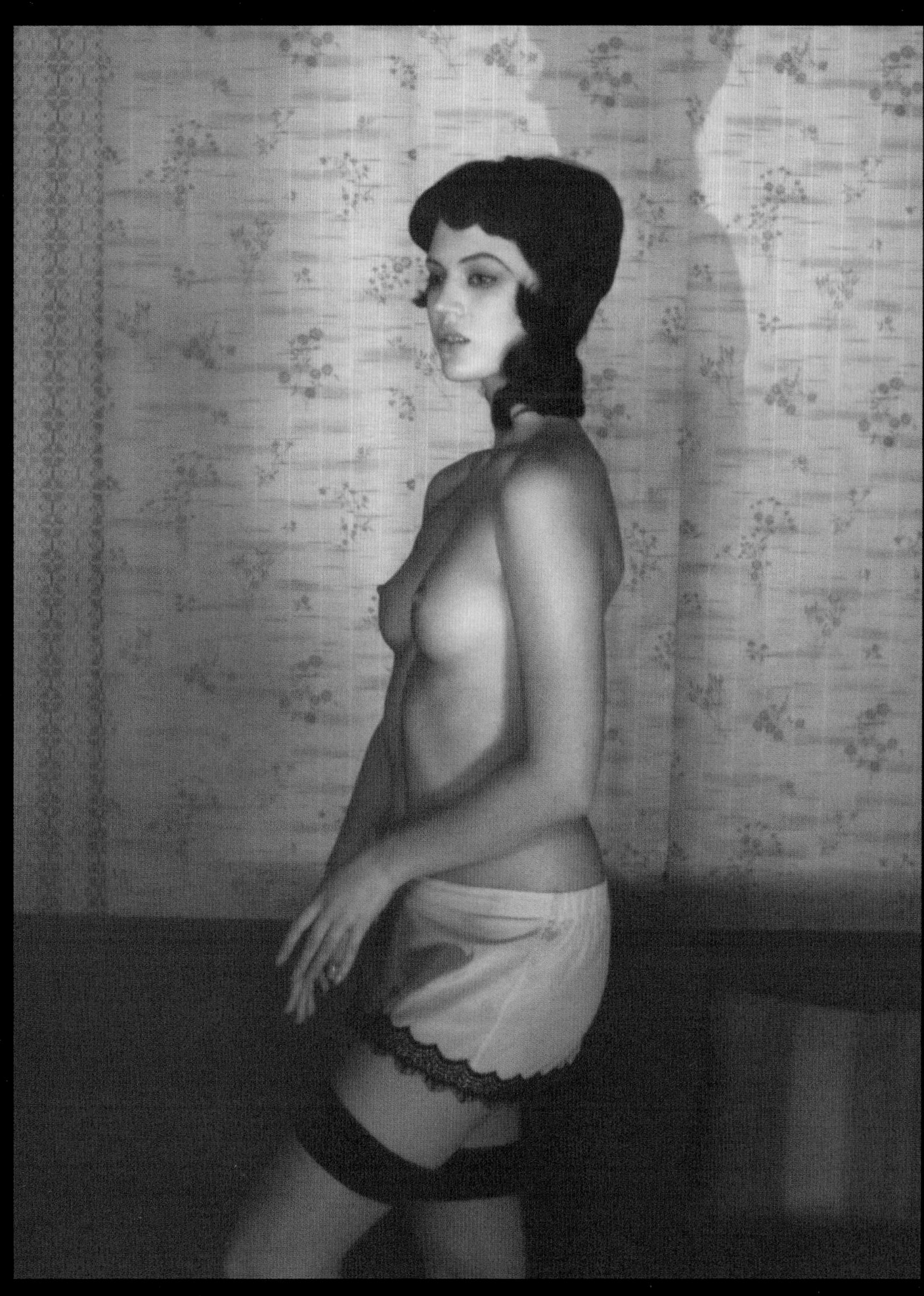

Sara wears blue poplin dress by MIU MIU; *G-string by* INTIMISSIMI

Birgit wears garter fishnet tights by LEG AVENUE; *thong by* INTIMISSIMI; *black suede Ethel heeled loafers by* TABITHA SIMMONS

FICTION

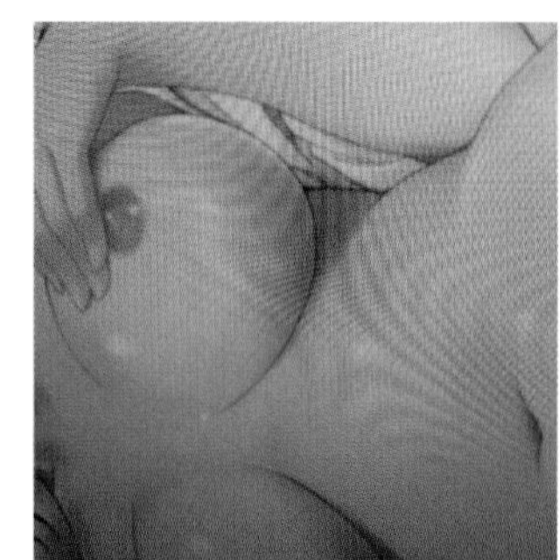

Raquel wears seamless thong by INTIMISSIMI; *fishnet hold-ups by* WHAT KATIE DID; *plexi ankle-strap heels (on floor) by* MIU MIU; *pink silk robe (draped over chair) by* ID SARRIERI

Raquel wears seamless thong by INTIMISSIMI; *fishnet hold-ups by* WHAT KATIE DID; *plexi ankle-strap heels (on floor) by* MIU MIU; *pink silk robe (draped over chair) by* ID SARRIERI

Goodbye t
the CREEPS
Self Defence
Six Page
Special
Los Angeles
Women's Clinics
in actio
Acting For
agitprop thea
More Army than
in Leeds

Raquel wears seamless thong by INTIMISSIMI; *fishnet hold-ups by* WHAT KATIE DID; *plexi ankle-strap heels by* MIU MIU; *pink silk robe (draped over chair) by* ID SARRIERI

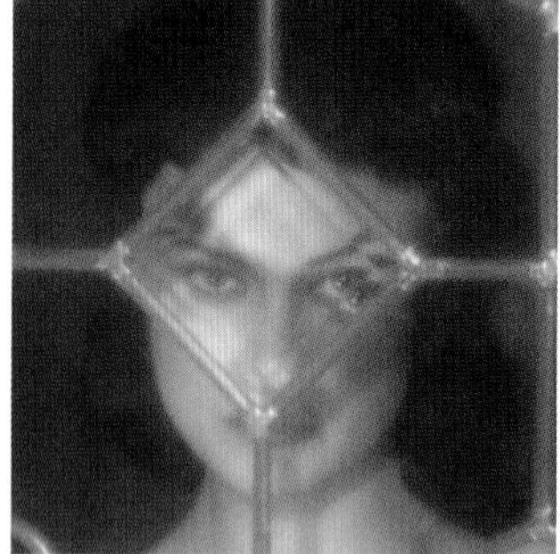

ars
hong by
SSIMI;
d-ups
T
ID;
e-strap
loor) by
U; *pink*
draped
by ID
RI

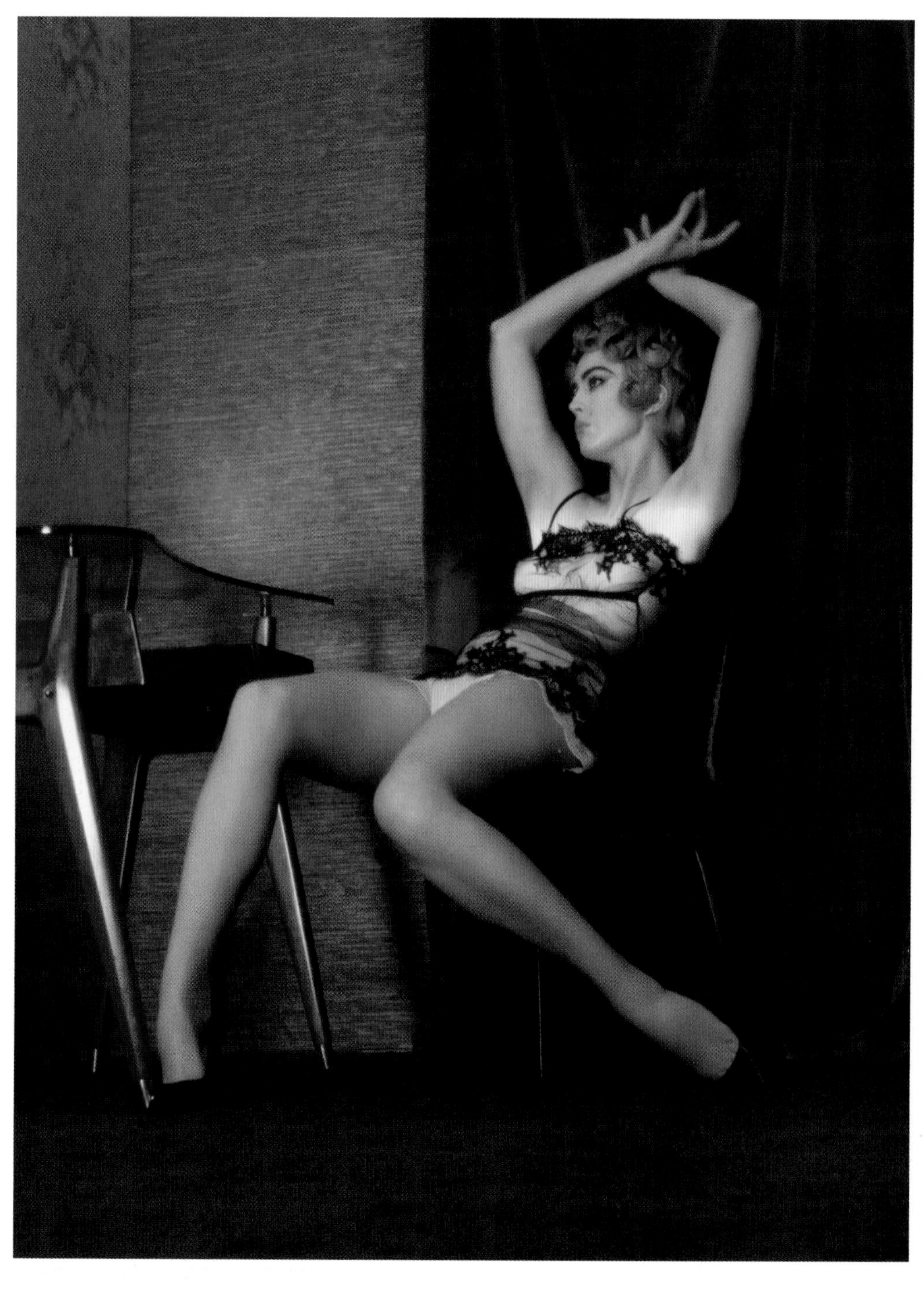

Raquel wears Jamais le Premier Soir tulle mini chemise with lace inserts by ID SARRIERI; *Lily Blushing shorts (worn beneath) by* STELLA McCARTNEY; *black satin Anouk high-heeled shoes by* JIMMY CHOO

Hair GUIDO Make-up DIANE KENDAL Manicure MEGUMI YAMAMOTO Set design STEFAN BECKMAN Production LAURA HOLMES PRODUCTION Post production SKN Models BIRGIT KOS, ELSA BRISINGER, SARA SAMPAIO, SONIA BEN AMMAR, RAQUEL ZIMMERMANN Fashion assistance OLIVER VOLQUARDSEN, OGUN GORTAN, DAVID CASSAVANT, JULIA VIRKLER, MEGAN SORIA, AMANDA DAY, LUCA GALASSO

Kendall Jenner

Happy 21st Kendall

The celebrities and the celebrations at Kendall Jenner's landmark West Hollywood birthday party

Photographer THEO WENNER

Caitlyn Jenner
Paris Hilton
Kendall

Jaden Smith

Hrush Achemyan

Romee Strijd,
Taylor Hill and Shanina Shaik

Riccardo Tisci

Romee Strijd
and Hailey Baldwin

Vic Mensa

Kendall and
Hailey Baldwin

Kendall

Paris

Kylie Jenner

Cara Delevingne and Kendall

Kris Jenner

Kendall and guest

Kris Jenner

Cara Delevingne

Photographic assistance BENEDIKT FRANK
Retouching OCTOBER

Fabio Piras

Continued from page 194

took over the MA course. 'That was fabulous!' When she returned two years later as Professor Louise Wilson, he stepped away from the school, focusing instead on brand consultancy.

It was only once he'd come back in 2009 that he finally asked Louise why she had invited him to teach on the MA in the first place. 'It took me years before I even dared ask her, because I was terrified of the answer. She liked the fact that I'd initiated [Commune] and she thought it would be an interesting experience for her students to hear about. She always tried to have tutors that were very close to the students in terms of age or experience. Which is something I continue to implement – it's important to have that.'

Why did Fabio agree to teach on the MA, given his own frustrating experience of it? 'I did it because it was a way to do the MA over and over again in my head. It's like an unresolved scenario. You haven't achieved what you want, so you keep redoing it till you do it.'

Now, after two years as MA course director, Fabio has come to an understanding of the myth of Louise Wilson and why it had to exist. 'The persona was so beyond enormous, and that's what you remember: the drama, the vocabulary. But this desk makes you become that.' He's speaking figuratively, of course: the desk is simply a totem of power. 'Which you can't abuse, but that's where you are. This is a teaching room, so you have students coming in with their collections, with two or three models, dressing, undressing. And all of that makes you somebody who has to perform. You can't be you. You can't have any insecurity or shyness or whatever. I'm someone who normally doesn't raise his voice. But you become an actor, and your voice becomes bigger. Because everything relies on the interaction between you and the student, who needs to feed off you and bounce back. That requires adrenaline, and it's exhausting. But at the same time that's what makes it fantastic. So you become an über-you. That's what you are.'

Is Fabio ever surprised by what comes out of his mouth when he's in teaching performance mode? 'Always. It surprises you how completely involved you are. You become dramatic: people *disappoint* you *immensely*, because you're so involved in it.' But it's never about the teacher. 'You're simply part of the process, and your voice in that process has an importance to the creative entity that is the student in front of you.'

He has by now exorcised his own bad experience of the MA and reached a satisfying conclusion as to what the course is for. 'It's a moment that you take to focus on yourself, to understand ideally "what should I be, who am I?" It works brilliantly for students that really have the bravery to follow their own project – that's when it's at its best. And in terms of others, who go on to join the industry as designers, it's about making them focus and find a clearer language around their creativity and their aesthetics or their background. *Focus* – that's what it is. It's a moment of luxury, in a way.'

Just having that time is a luxury.

'It is. There was a time when the MA was also for people [in fashion] to take some time off work. That period is long gone, because we are now in an era that is all about "one shot, one chance", which is terrible. Somebody in their late thirties would be considered too old to start a career now, which is not necessarily a good thing; I hope one day we'll backtrack on that, and I think we will very soon. Today it's a luxury also in terms of money, which is why there's maybe less freedom. Not freedom in terms of creativity, but there's more angst.'

Because of the financial pressures placed on students?

'I think so, a lot. It's really difficult for students. And it's more than the fact they don't have money. We live in a world that makes you feel like you can't do it if you don't have money. you would like to see, I don't know, BodyMap coming back, Vivienne Westwood – that energy, the Belgian Six, all that. You would like to see those clubs… But that's nostalgia. What you have to see is what's happening today and whether that has an equivalence, and you have to celebrate that, you have to celebrate today. And I do see it happening. I'm very proud that the people doing it are our alumni. Because I really respect somebody like Charles Jeffrey: he has made all those rules explode, in a way. He is the fashion statement, his life is the fashion statement. And that maybe also is where fashion is going. It's like, what is it you're actually producing? Your product might be your activity as an entity, as a person. One day you do some styling, one day you do a collection, one day you can run a club.

'Rottingdean Bazaar, Matty Bovan, Charles Jeffrey – it's creativity galore'

When I was a student, even though the political and social context was pretty scary, there was still that feeling that, yeah, it's a shit world, but you could still have that ambition to do your own label on a credit card. Which is what I did, and others did too.'

Do you think having that ambition is less realistic now?

'No, I think it's more realistic. They have this dream, but with all this [awareness of the] reality. That's why it's very stressful to them – they get it, they understand. They have access to information that we didn't have access to, they know so much about everything. So they know what to expect. I mean, I have students that are stocked in Dover Street Market. They have experiences sometimes that make me go like, "Wow, incredible!"'

You gave an interview recently in which you mentioned 'the energy of the Eighties'. There's been some discussion about politics while putting together this issue of LOVE because the political landscape now is more obviously polarised than at any time since the Eighties.

'I agree with that completely. I mean, it's a terrible moment – for the world, really. Like, God, how low can you get? That corresponds to the Eighties: it was a really cynical era. That's when suddenly all this hyperconsumerism and not caring about people who might need a little bit more help suddenly became really cruel. There was a middle class that was getting richer and richer – and that's it, everybody else can eat cake. Because that's what the Eighties were, really: the glorification of the enrichment of the middle class. But at the same time, it was a really creative moment because of the horror, socially and politically. It had a real underground, with people who were really angry and needed to express something. And I really hope we are at that moment [again]. You have glimpses of it. I've been thinking a lot about this, because obviously But they have to be able to sustain that, and he is. [Likewise] Matty Bovan. It only takes MAC cosmetics to meet Matty Bovan to understand that they can have a great visionary working for them. Rottingdean Bazaar, too – it's creativity galore, isn't it? It is a new generation. I think they have an incredible validity because they are universal: they can communicate with the art world, they can communicate with the fashion world and they can communicate with people who might even be laughing at them.'

And that corresponds with the Eighties, when there were personalities in London who might turn their hand to anything, making clothes or set design or running a club. It feels like we've finally reached the end – well, for this generation, anyway – of that post-Tom Ford model of designer as brand manager, designer as careerist.

'Er… *(Long pause)* Correctly or incorrectly, I hope we are at that moment. I hope the future is going to be more about that [ie Matty and Charles] and less about a fashion system that has killed creativity completely and then complains about it. I mean, they all talk about the business and sales, but if you merchandise to such an extent or dilute the product to such an extent of having countless collections per season, then what makes it desirable? *Nothing.* It's just stuff! Stuff at a very high price. With some [creativity] – well of course, you would expect it to have some sort of idea creatively, but it's not desirable because there's so much of it. I think we need to have much less of it. If we call it luxury, it needs to have the content of luxury, the quality of luxury. And luxury can be many things. It can have an intellectual content, it can have a fantastic craft content, it can have a fun content, it can have a social content – it can have anything. I think that's where [fashion] is going to go anyway, because it has not been working out.'

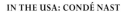

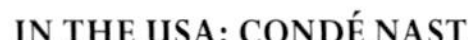

IN THE USA: CONDÉ NAST
Chairman Emeritus: S.I. Newhouse, Jr.
Chairman: Charles H. Townsend
President & Chief Executive Officer: Robert A. Sauerberg, Jr.
Artistic Director: Anna Wintour

IN OTHER COUNTRIES: CONDÉ NAST INTERNATIONAL
Chairman and Chief Executive: Jonathan Newhouse
President: Nicholas Coleridge
Vice Presidents: Giampaolo Grandi, James Woolhouse, Moritz von Laffert, Elizabeth Schimel
Chief Digital Officer: Wolfgang Blau
President, Asia-Pacific: James Woolhouse
President, New Markets and Editorial Director, Brand Development: Karina Dobrotvorskaya
Director of Planning: Jason Miles
Director of Acquisitions and Investments: Moritz von Laffert

GLOBAL
President, Condé Nast E-commerce: Franck Zayan
Executive Director, Condé Nast Global Development: Jamie Bill

THE CONDÉ NAST GROUP OF BRANDS INCLUDES:
US
Vogue, Vanity Fair, Glamour, Brides, Self, GQ, GQ Style, The New Yorker, Condé Nast Traveler, Allure, Architectural Digest, Bon Appétit, Epicurious, Wired, W, Golf Digest, Teen Vogue, Ars Technica, Condé Nast Entertainment, The Scene, Pitchfork

UK
Vogue, House & Garden, Brides, Tatler, The World of Interiors, GQ, Vanity Fair, Condé Nast Traveller, Glamour, Condé Nast Johansens, GQ Style, Love, Wired, Condé Nast College of Fashion & Design, Ars Technica

FRANCE
Vogue, Vogue Hommes International, AD, Glamour, Vogue Collections, GQ, AD Collector, Vanity Fair, Vogue Travel in France, GQ Le Manuel du Style, Glamour Style

ITALY
Vogue, L'Uomo Vogue, Vogue Bambini, Glamour, Vogue Sposa, AD, Condé Nast Traveller, GQ, Vanity Fair, Wired, Vogue Accessory, La Cucina Italiana, CNLive

GERMANY
Vogue, GQ, AD, Glamour, GQ Style, Myself, Wired

SPAIN
Vogue, GQ, Vogue Novias, Vogue Niños, Condé Nast Traveler, Vogue Colecciones, Vogue Belleza, Glamour, AD, Vanity Fair

JAPAN
Vogue, GQ, Vogue Girl, Wired, Vogue Wedding

TAIWAN
Vogue, GQ

MEXICO AND LATIN AMERICA
Vogue Mexico and Latin America, Glamour Mexico and Latin America, AD Mexico, GQ Mexico and Latin America, Vanity Fair Mexico

INDIA
Vogue, GQ, Condé Nast Traveller, AD

PUBLISHED UNDER JOINT VENTURE:
Brazil: Vogue, Casa Vogue, GQ, Glamour, GQ Style
Russia: Vogue, GQ, AD, Glamour, GQ Style, Tatler, Condé Nast Traveller, Allure

PUBLISHED UNDER LICENSE OR COPYRIGHT COOPERATION:
Australia: Vogue, Vogue Living, GQ
Bulgaria: Glamour
China: Vogue, Vogue Collections, Self, AD, Condé Nast Traveler, GQ, GQ Style, Brides, Condé Nast Center of Fashion & Design
Czech Republic and Slovakia: La Cucina Italiana
Hungary: Glamour
Iceland: Glamour
Korea: Vogue, GQ, Allure, W, GQ Style
Middle East: Condé Nast Traveller, AD, Vogue Café at The Dubai Mall, GQ Bar Dubai
Poland: Glamour
Portugal: Vogue, GQ
Romania: Glamour
Russia: Vogue Café Moscow, Tatler Club Moscow
South Africa: House & Garden, GQ, Glamour, House & Garden Gourmet, GQ Style
The Netherlands: Glamour, Vogue
Thailand: Vogue, GQ, Vogue Lounge Bangkok
Turkey: Vogue, GQ, Condé Nast Traveller, La Cucina Italiana, GQ Style, Glamour
Ukraine: Vogue, Vogue Café Kiev

Baaaa

Baaaa

L'Etoile
DIOR.COM - 020 7172 0172